STAR WARS
THE FORCE AWAKENS

CHUCK WENDIG
Writer

LUKE ROSS (#1-2 & #4-6)
& MARC LAMING (#3)
Artists

FRANK MARTIN
with **GURU-eFX** (#6)
Colorists

VC's CLAYTON COWLES
Letterer

ESAD RIBIĆ; MIKE MAYHEW; MIKE DEODATO JR. & FRANK MARTIN;
MIKE DEL MUNDO; RAFAEL ALBUQUERQUE; PAOLO RIVERA
Cover Artists

HEATHER ANTOS
Editor

JORDAN D. WHITE
Supervising Editor

C.B. CEBULSKI
Executive Editor

Based on the screenplay by
LAWRENCE KASDAN & J.J. ABRAMS and MICHAEL ARNDT

For Lucasfilm:

MICHAEL SIGLAIN
Creative Director

FRANK PARISI
Senior Editor

RAYNE ROBERTS, PABLO HIDALGO, LELAND CHEE, MATT MARTIN
Lucasfilm Story Group

COLLECTION EDITOR: **JENNIFER GRÜNWALD**
ASSISTANT EDITOR: **CAITLIN O'CONNELL**
ASSOCIATE MANAGING EDITOR: **KATERI WOODY**
EDITOR, SPECIAL PROJECTS: **MARK D. BEAZLEY**
VP PRODUCTION & SPECIAL PROJECTS: **JEFF YOUNGQUIST**

SVP PRINT, SALES & MARKETING: **DAVID GABRIEL**
EDITOR-IN-CHIEF: **AXEL ALONSO**
CHIEF CREATIVE OFFICER: **JOE QUESADA**
PRESIDENT: **DAN BUCKLEY**
EXECUTIVE PRODUCER: **ALAN FINE**

FRONT COVER ART: **PHIL NOTO**
BACK COVER ART: **ESAD RIBIĆ**

STAR WARS: THE FORCE AWAKENS ADAPTATION. Contains material originally published in magazine form as STAR WARS: THE FORCE AWAKENS ADAPTATION #1-6. First printing 2017. ISBN# 978-1-302-90203-2. Published by MARVEL WORLDWIDE, INC., a subsidiary of MARVEL ENTERTAINMENT, LLC. OFFICE OF PUBLICATION: 135 West 50th Street, New York, NY 10020. STAR WARS and related text and illustrations are trademarks and/or copyrights, in the United States and other countries, of Lucasfilm Ltd. and/or its affiliates. © & TM Lucasfilm Ltd. No similarity between any of the names, characters, persons, and/or institutions in this magazine with those of any living or dead person or institution is intended, and any such similarity which may exist is purely coincidental. Marvel and its logos are TM Marvel Characters, Inc. **Printed in the U.S.A.** DAN BUCKLEY, President, Marvel Entertainment; JOE QUESADA, Chief Creative Officer; TOM BREVOORT, SVP of Publishing; DAVID BOGART, SVP of Business Affairs & Operations, Publishing & Partnership; C.B. CEBULSKI, VP of Brand Management & Development, Asia; DAVID GABRIEL, SVP of Sales & Marketing, Publishing; JEFF YOUNGQUIST, VP of Production & Special Projects; DAN CARR, Executive Director of Publishing Technology; ALEX MORALES, Director of Publishing Operations; SUSAN CRESPI, Production Manager; STAN LEE, Chairman Emeritus. For information regarding advertising in Marvel Comics or on Marvel.com, please contact Vit DeBellis, Integrated Sales Manager, at vdebellis@marvel.com. For Marvel subscription inquiries, please call 888-511-5480. **Manufactured between 9/1/2017 and 10/2/2017 by QUAD/GRAPHICS WASECA, WASECA, MN, USA.**

10 9 8 7 6 5 4 3 2 1

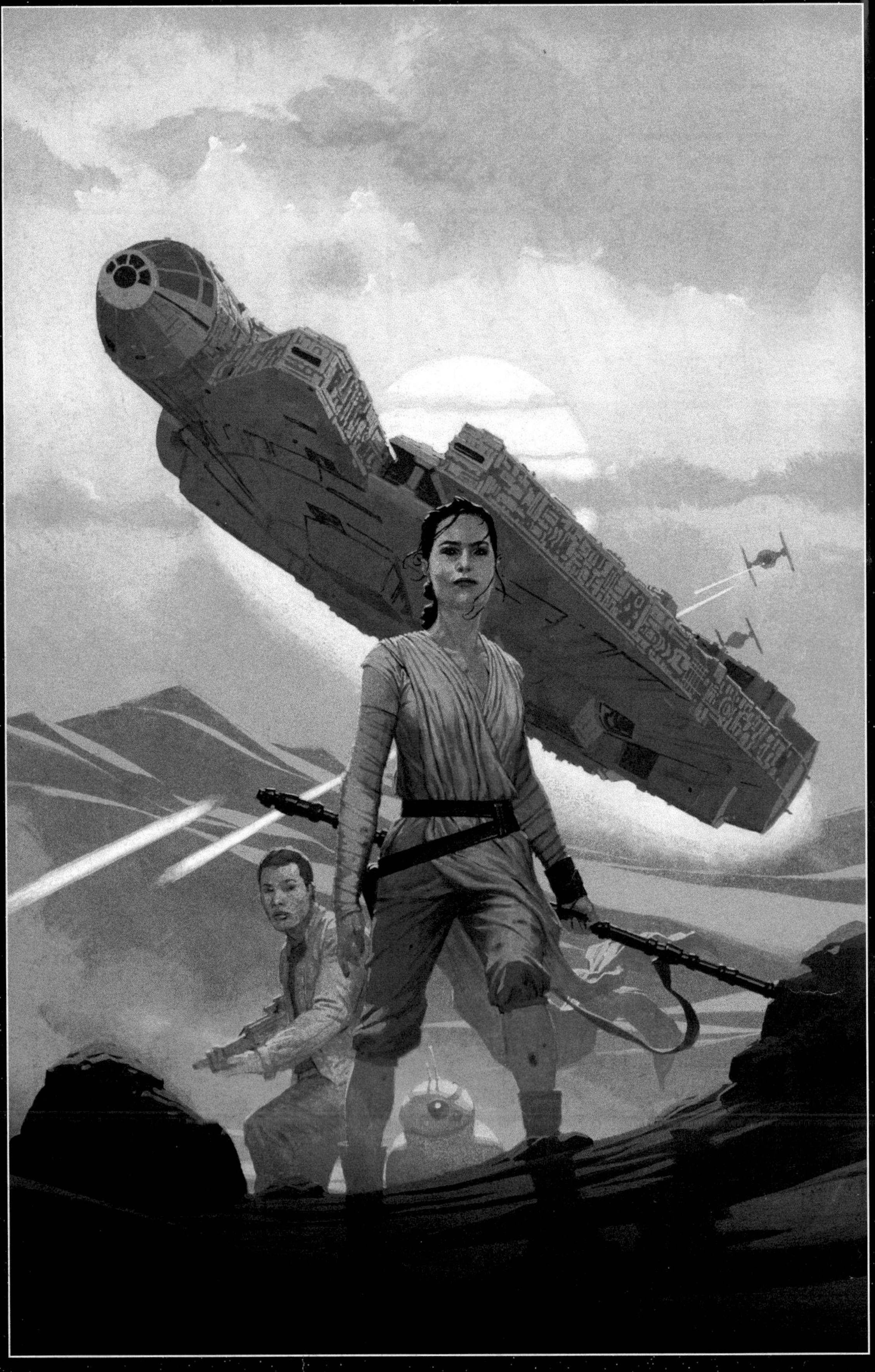

THE FORCE AWAKENS #1

A long time ago in a galaxy far, far away....

ST

WA

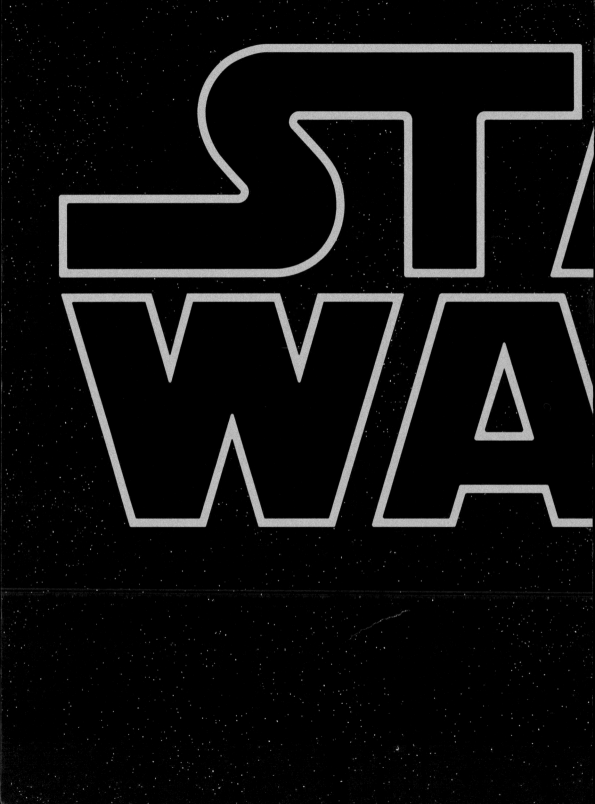

AR

RS

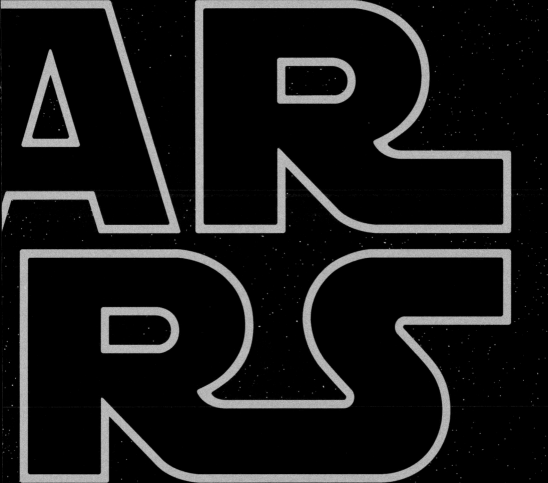

Episode VII
THE FORCE AWAKENS

Luke Skywalker has vanished. In his absence, the sinister FIRST ORDER has risen from the ashes of the Empire and will not rest until Skywalker, the last Jedi, has been destroyed.

With the support of the REPUBLIC, General Leia Organa leads a brave RESISTANCE. She is desperate to find her brother Luke and gain his help in restoring peace and justice to the galaxy.

Leia has sent her most daring pilot on a secret mission to Jakku, where an old ally has discovered a clue to Luke's whereabouts....

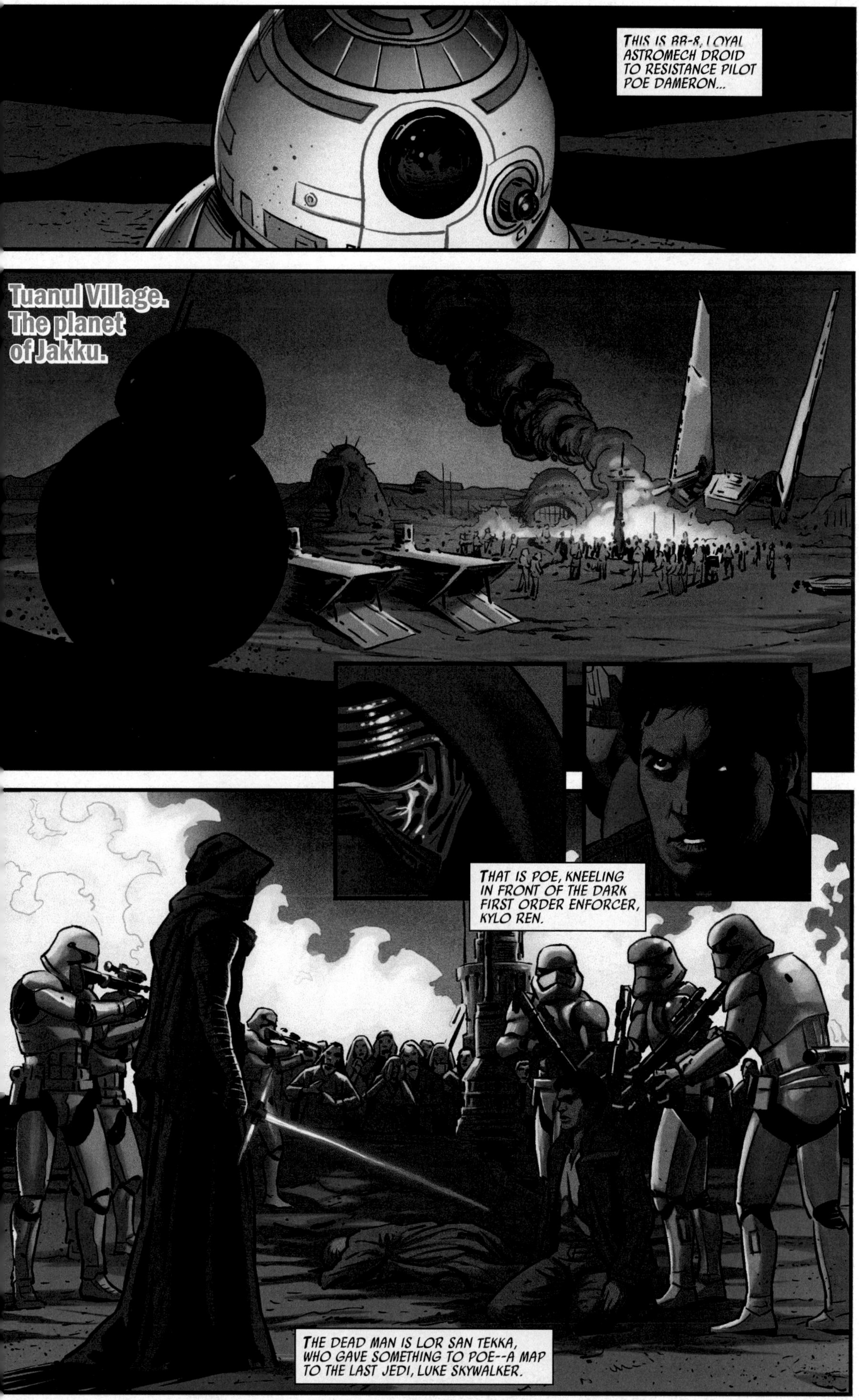
THIS IS BB-8, LOYAL ASTROMECH DROID TO RESISTANCE PILOT POE DAMERON...
Tuanul Village. The planet of Jakku.
THAT IS POE, KNEELING IN FRONT OF THE DARK FIRST ORDER ENFORCER, KYLO REN.
THE DEAD MAN IS LOR SAN TEKKA, WHO GAVE SOMETHING TO POE--A MAP TO THE LAST JEDI, LUKE SKYWALKER.

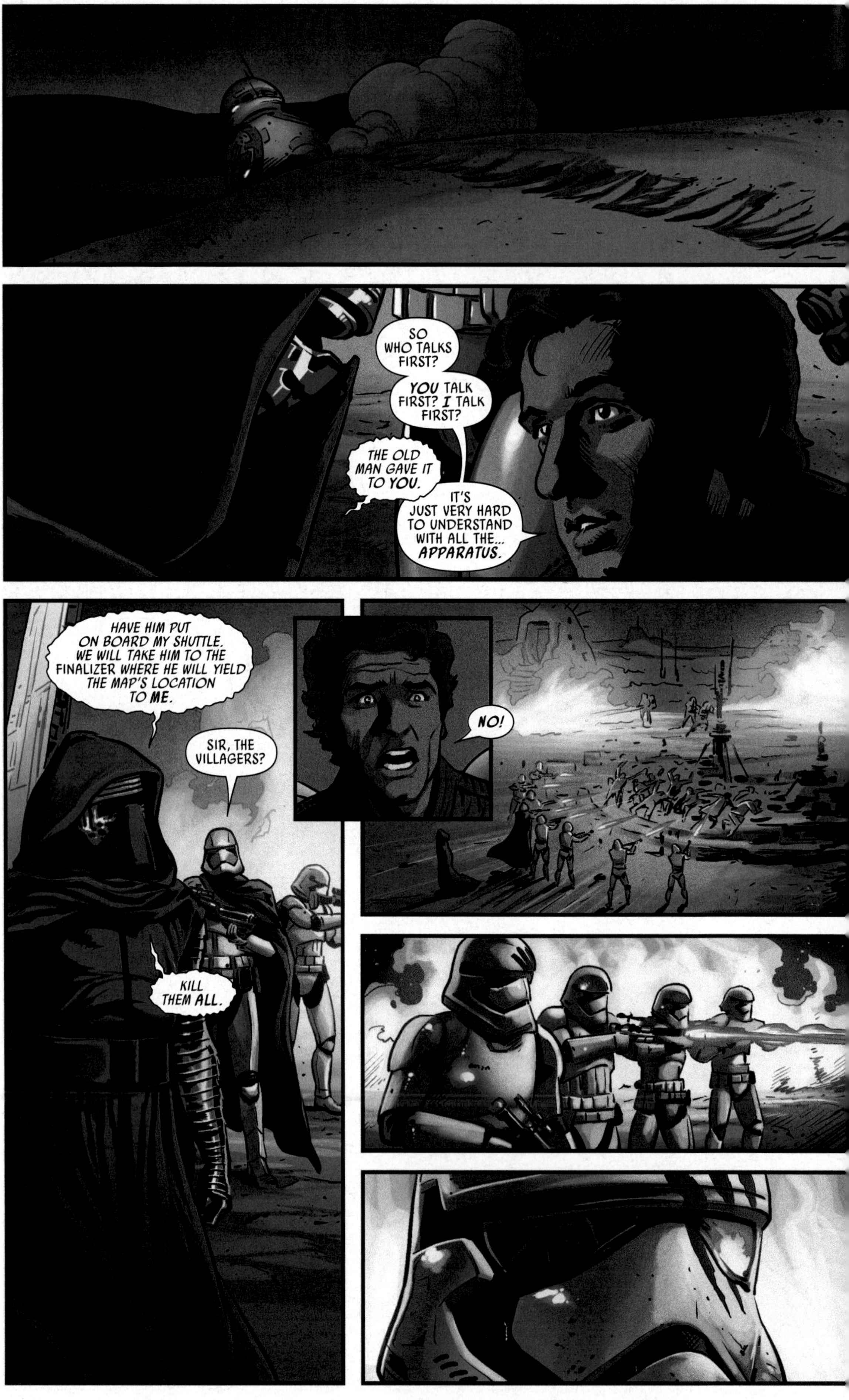
SO WHO TALKS FIRST?
YOU TALK FIRST? I TALK FIRST?
THE OLD MAN GAVE IT TO YOU.
IT'S JUST VERY HARD TO UNDERSTAND WITH ALL THE... APPARATUS.
HAVE HIM PUT ON BOARD MY SHUTTLE. WE WILL TAKE HIM TO THE FINALIZER WHERE HE WILL YIELD THE MAP'S LOCATION TO ME.
SIR, THE VILLAGERS?
KILL THEM ALL.
NO!

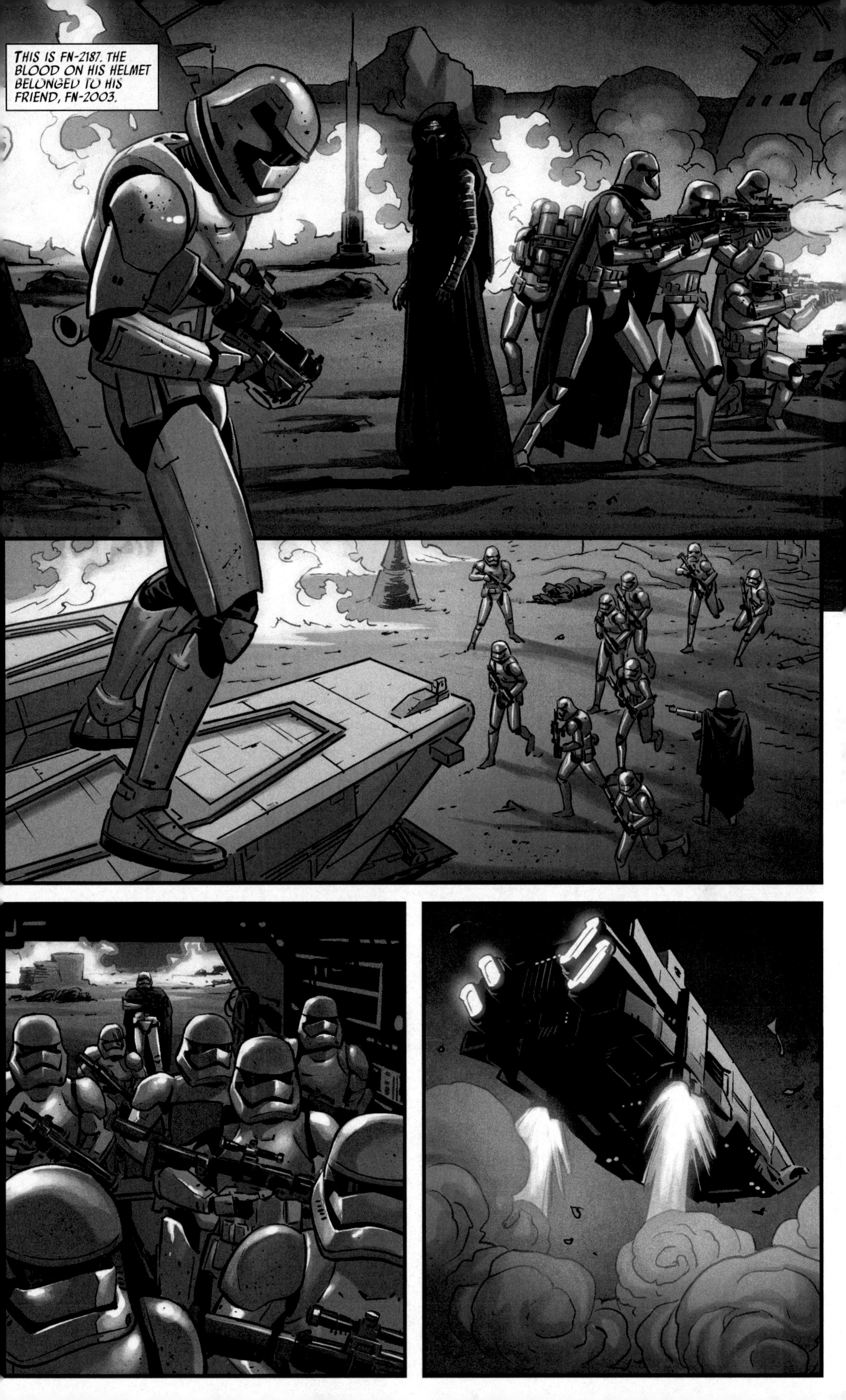
THIS IS FN-2187. THE BLOOD ON HIS HELMET BELONGED TO HIS FRIEND, FN-2003.

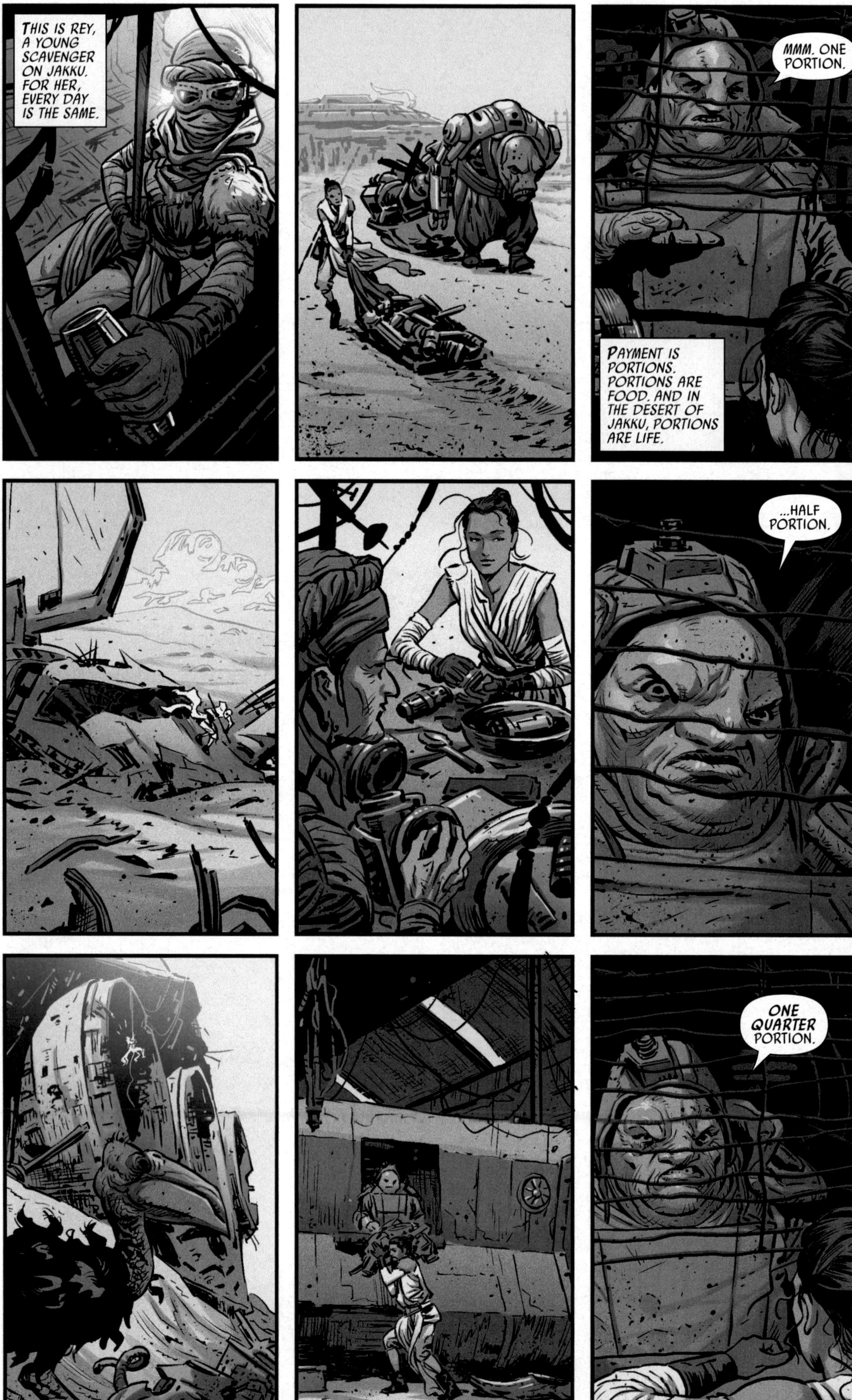
THIS IS REY, A YOUNG SCAVENGER ON JAKKU. FOR HER, EVERY DAY IS THE SAME.
MMM. ONE PORTION.
PAYMENT IS PORTIONS. PORTIONS ARE FOOD. AND IN THE DESERT OF JAKKU, PORTIONS ARE LIFE.
...HALF PORTION.
ONE QUARTER PORTION.

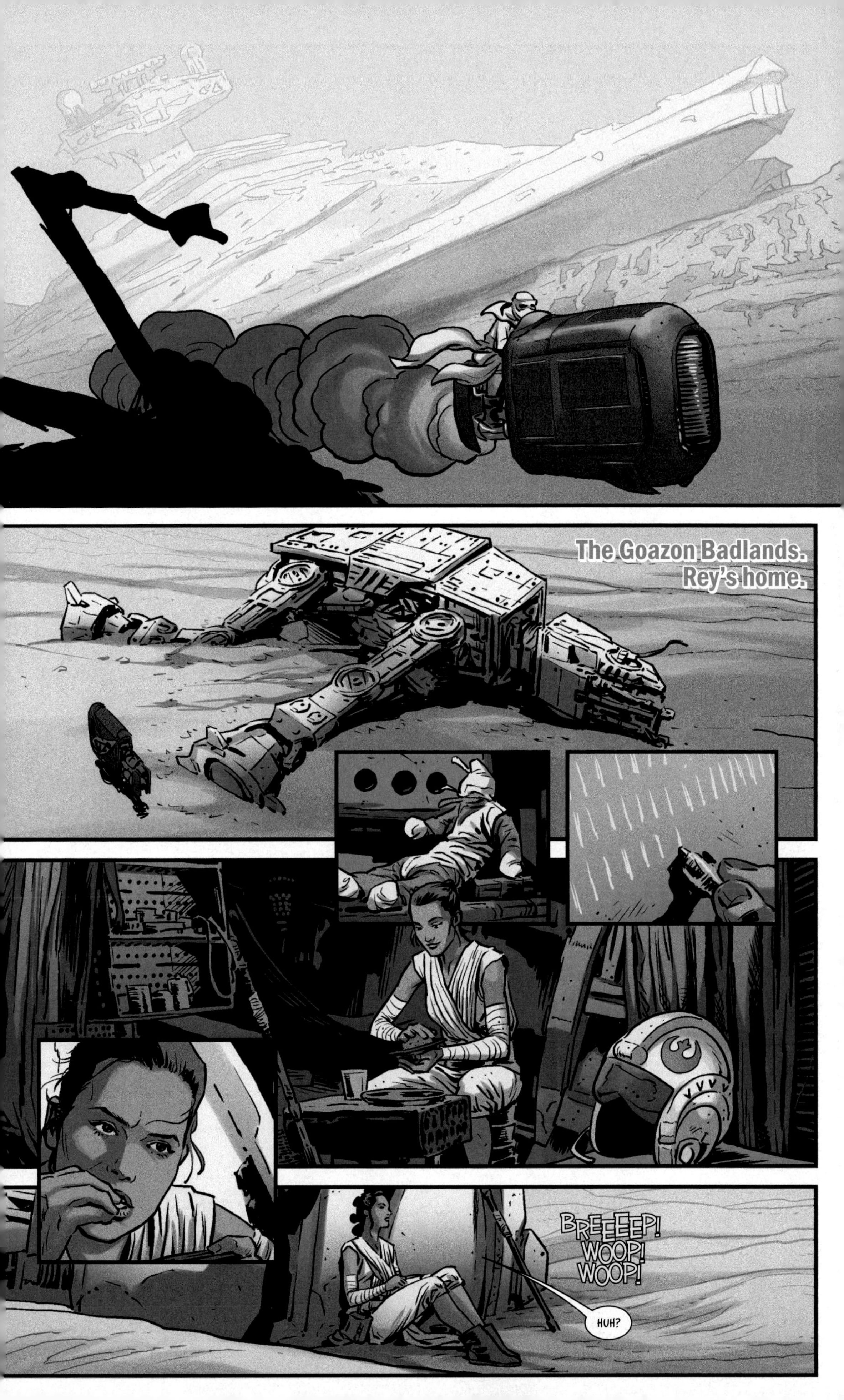
The Goazon Badlands.
Rey's home.
BREEEEP!
WOOP!
WOOP!
HUH?

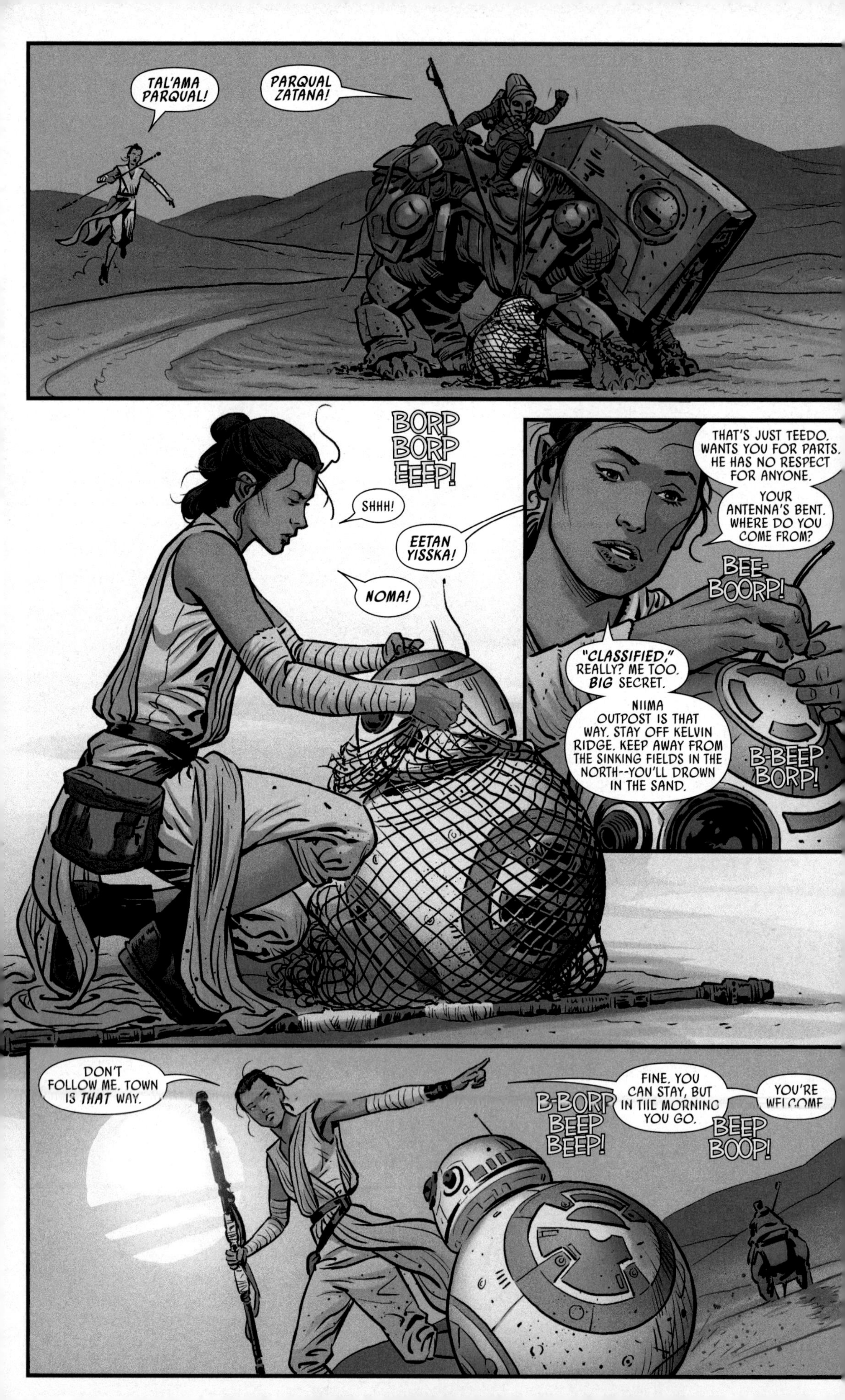
TAL'AMA PARQUAL!
PARQUAL ZATANA!
BORP BORP EEEP!
SHHH!
EETAN YISSKA!
NOMA!
THAT'S JUST TEEDO. WANTS YOU FOR PARTS. HE HAS NO RESPECT FOR ANYONE.
YOUR ANTENNA'S BENT. WHERE DO YOU COME FROM?
BEE-BOORP!
"CLASSIFIED," REALLY? ME TOO. BIG SECRET.
NIIMA OUTPOST IS THAT WAY. STAY OFF KELVIN RIDGE. KEEP AWAY FROM THE SINKING FIELDS IN THE NORTH--YOU'LL DROWN IN THE SAND.
B-BEEP BORP!
DON'T FOLLOW ME. TOWN IS THAT WAY.
B-BORP BEEP BEEP!
FINE. YOU CAN STAY, BUT IN THE MORNING YOU GO.
YOU'RE WELCOME.
BEEP BOOP!

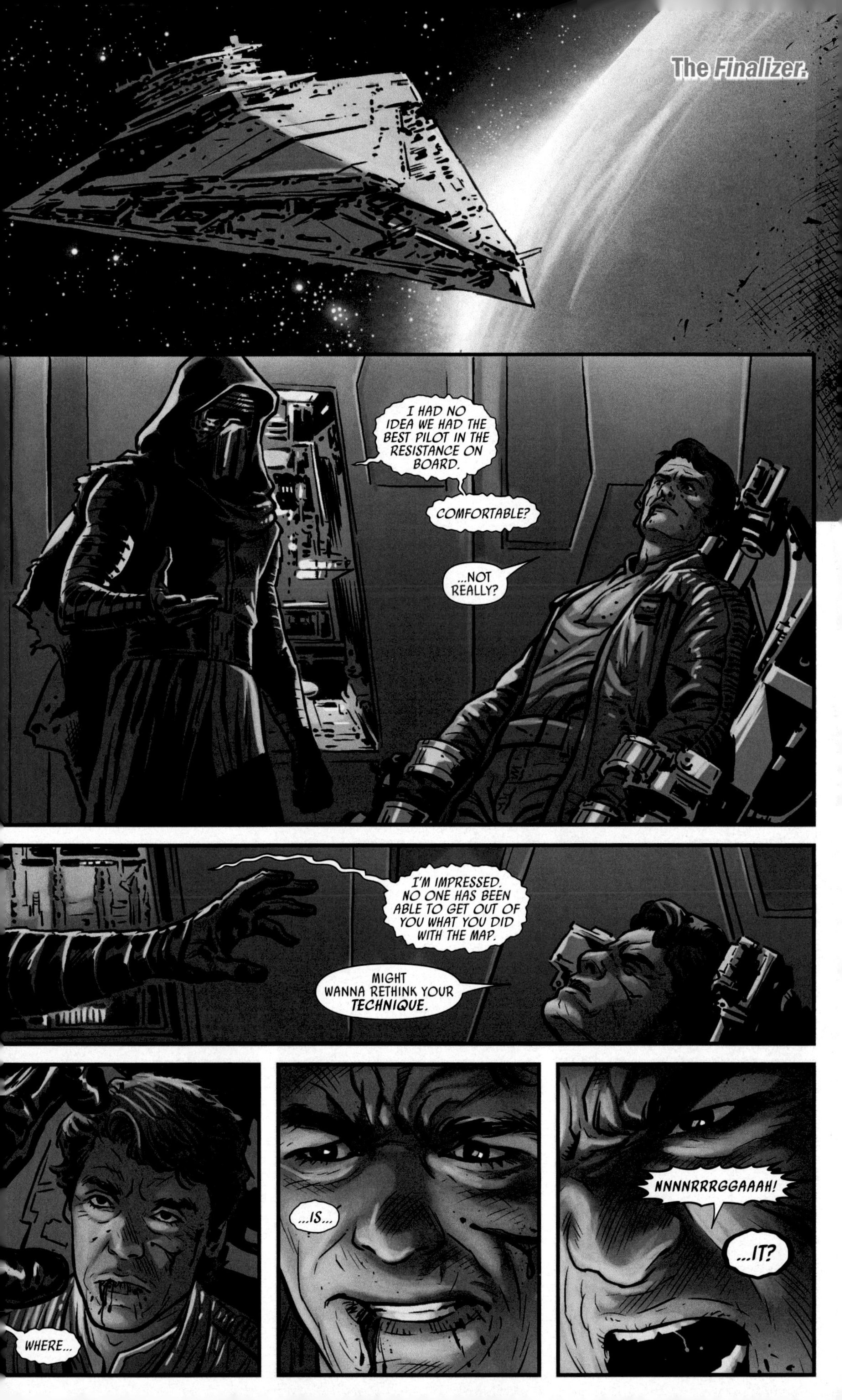

The Finalizer.
I HAD NO IDEA WE HAD THE BEST PILOT IN THE RESISTANCE ON BOARD.
COMFORTABLE?
...NOT REALLY?
I'M IMPRESSED. NO ONE HAS BEEN ABLE TO GET OUT OF YOU WHAT YOU DID WITH THE MAP.
MIGHT WANNA RETHINK YOUR TECHNIQUE.
WHERE...
...IS...
NNNNRRRGGAAAH!
...IT?

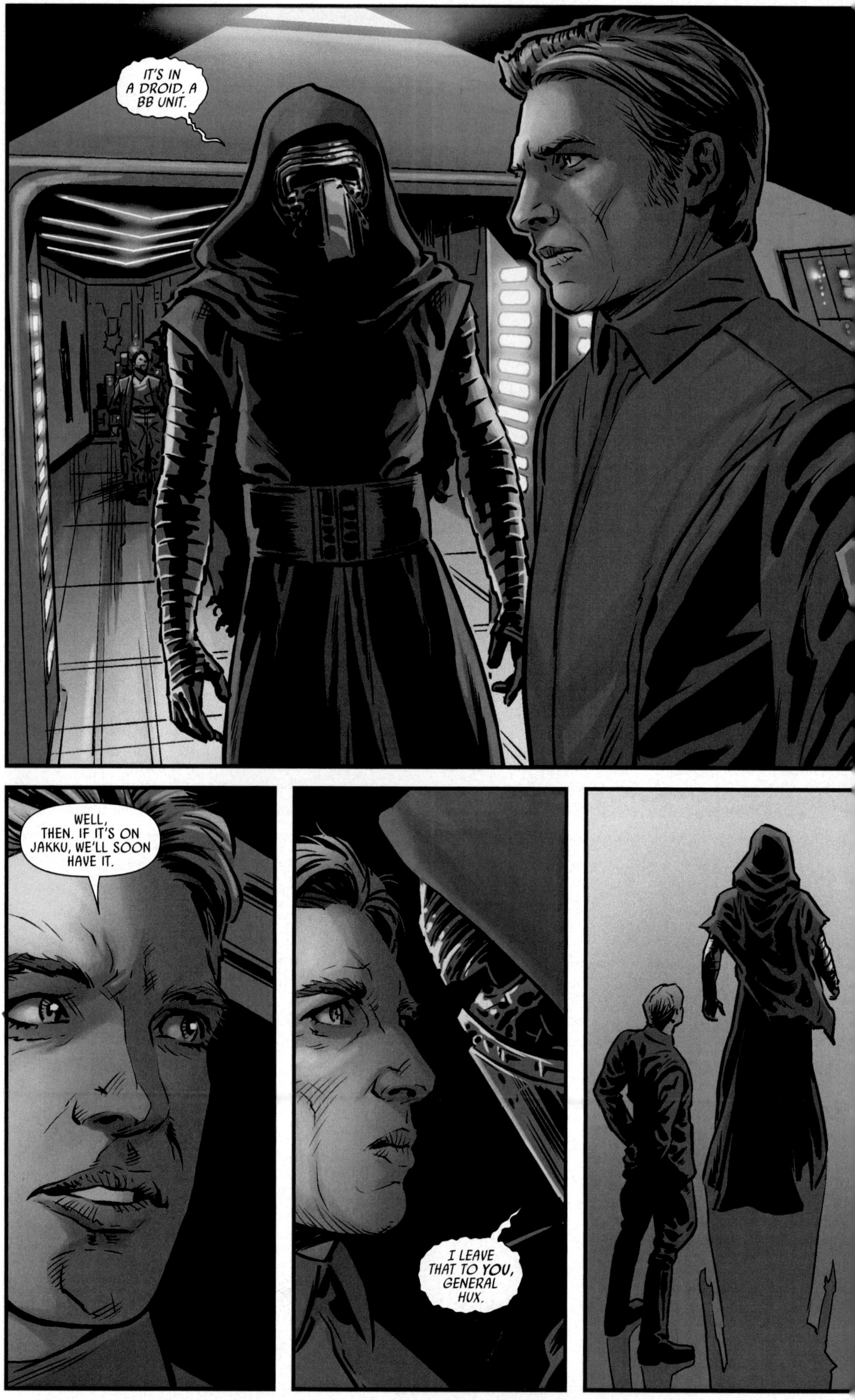
IT'S IN A DROID. A BB UNIT.
WELL, THEN. IF IT'S ON JAKKU, WE'LL SOON HAVE IT.
I LEAVE THAT TO YOU, GENERAL HUX.

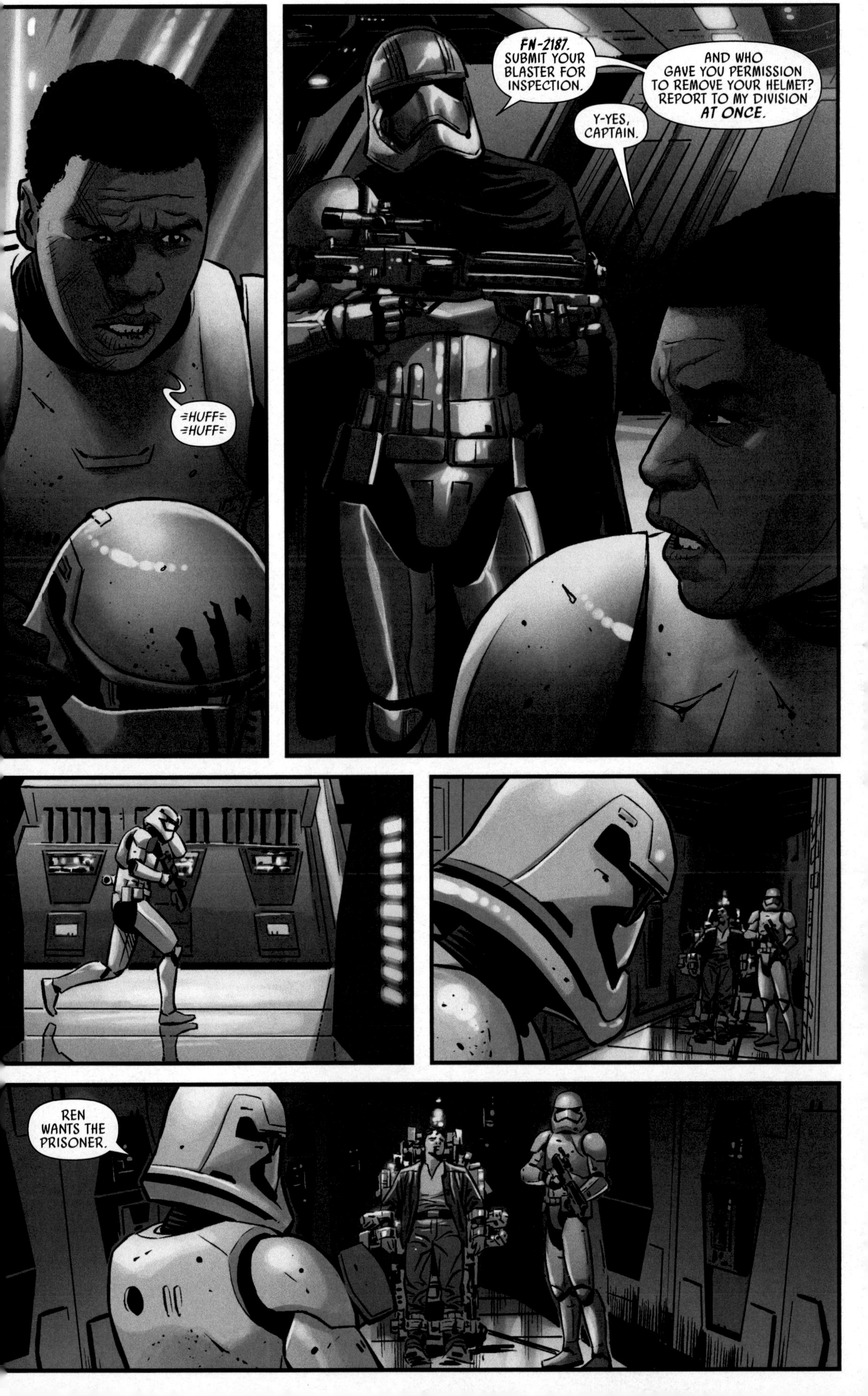
HUFF HUFF
FN-2187. SUBMIT YOUR BLASTER FOR INSPECTION.
AND WHO GAVE YOU PERMISSION TO REMOVE YOUR HELMET? REPORT TO MY DIVISION AT ONCE.
Y-YES, CAPTAIN.
REN WANTS THE PRISONER.

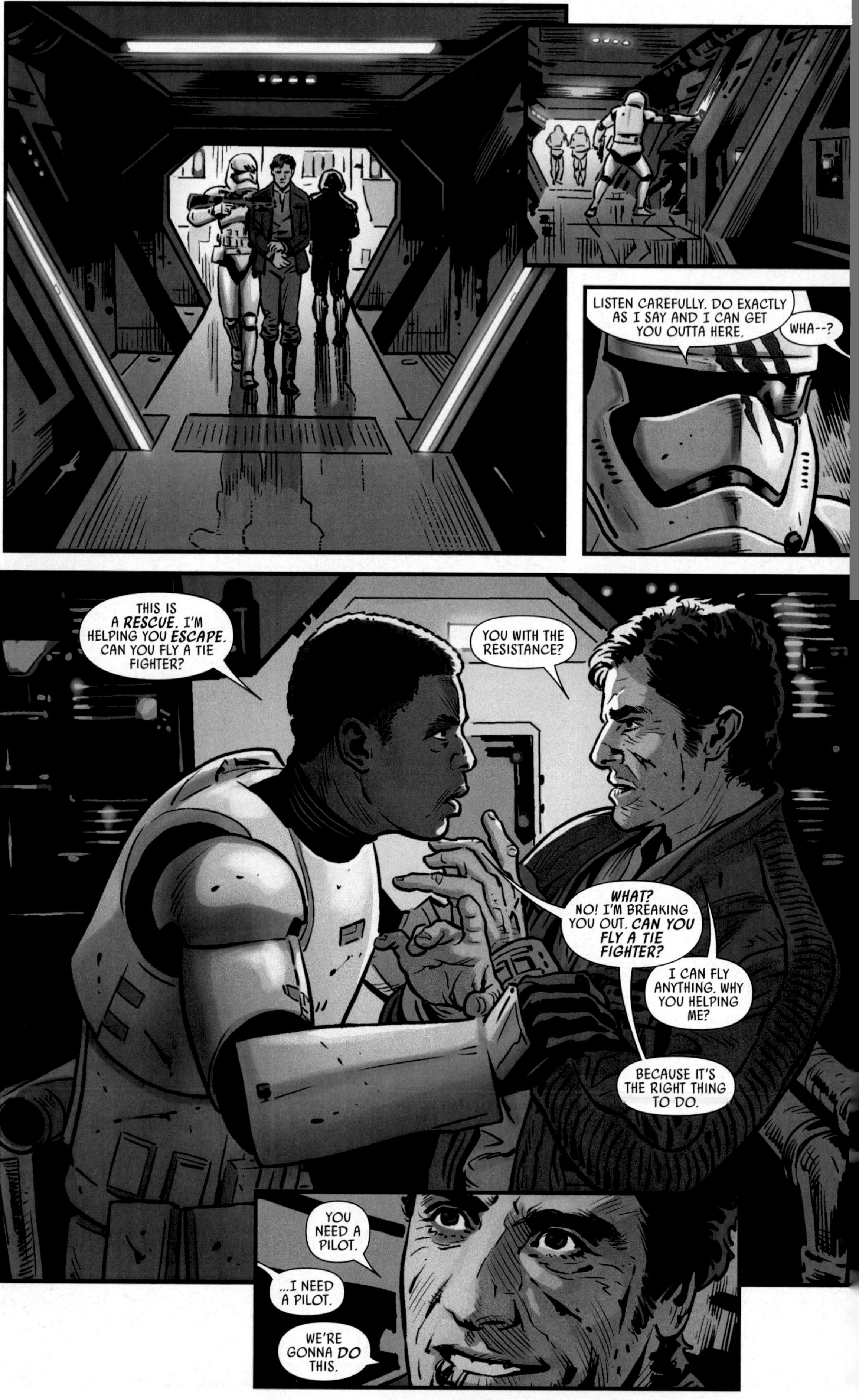

LISTEN CAREFULLY. DO EXACTLY AS I SAY AND I CAN GET YOU OUTTA HERE.
WHA--?
THIS IS A ***RESCUE.*** I'M HELPING YOU ***ESCAPE.*** CAN YOU FLY A TIE FIGHTER?
YOU WITH THE RESISTANCE?
WHAT? NO! I'M BREAKING YOU OUT. ***CAN YOU FLY A TIE FIGHTER?***
I CAN FLY ANYTHING. WHY YOU HELPING ME?
BECAUSE IT'S THE RIGHT THING TO DO.
YOU NEED A PILOT.
...I NEED A PILOT.
WE'RE GONNA ***DO*** THIS.

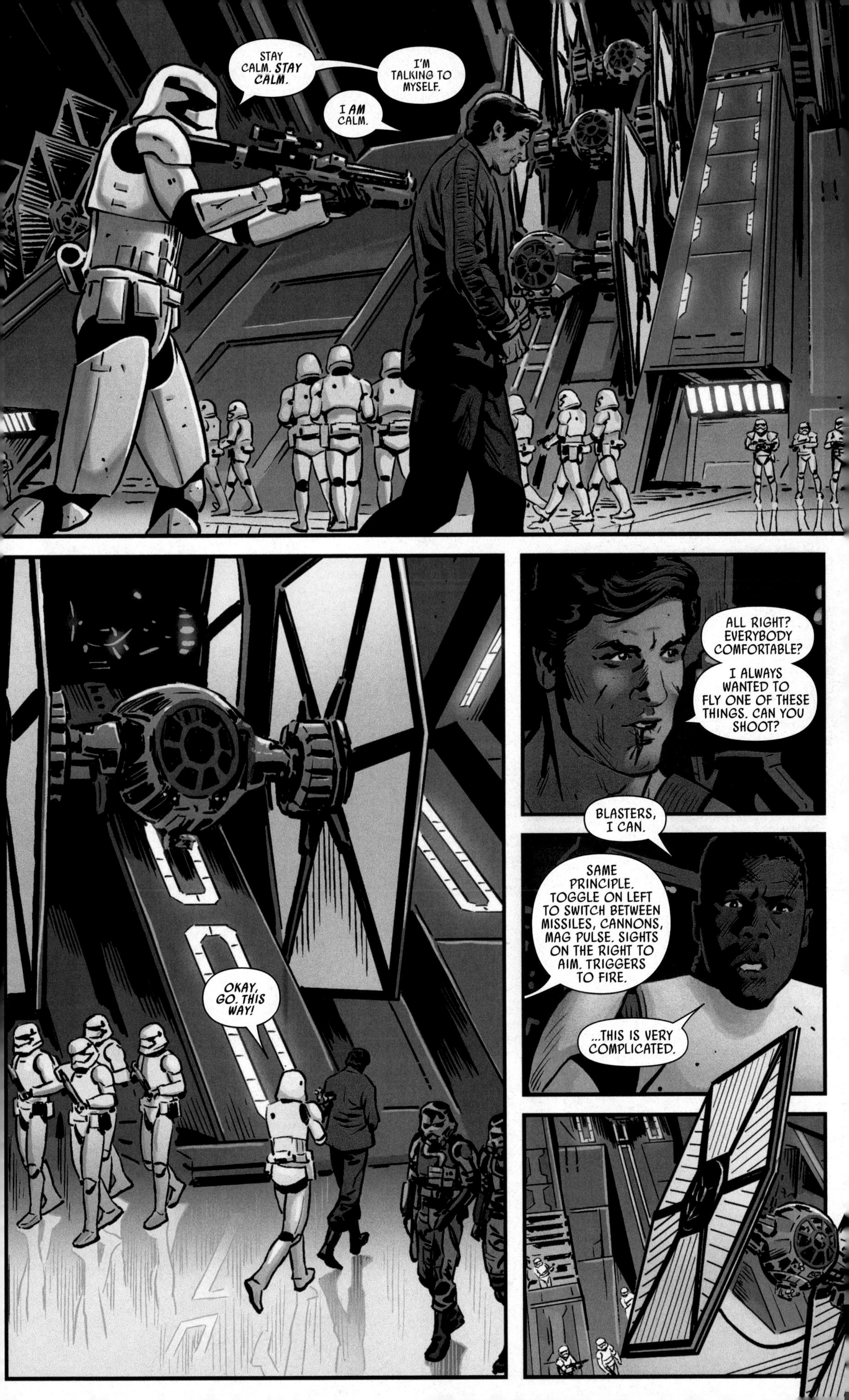
STAY CALM. STAY CALM.
I'M TALKING TO MYSELF.
I AM CALM.
ALL RIGHT? EVERYBODY COMFORTABLE?
I ALWAYS WANTED TO FLY ONE OF THESE THINGS. CAN YOU SHOOT?
BLASTERS, I CAN.
SAME PRINCIPLE. TOGGLE ON LEFT TO SWITCH BETWEEN MISSILES, CANNONS, MAG PULSE. SIGHTS ON THE RIGHT TO AIM. TRIGGERS TO FIRE.
...THIS IS VERY COMPLICATED.
OKAY, GO. THIS WAY!

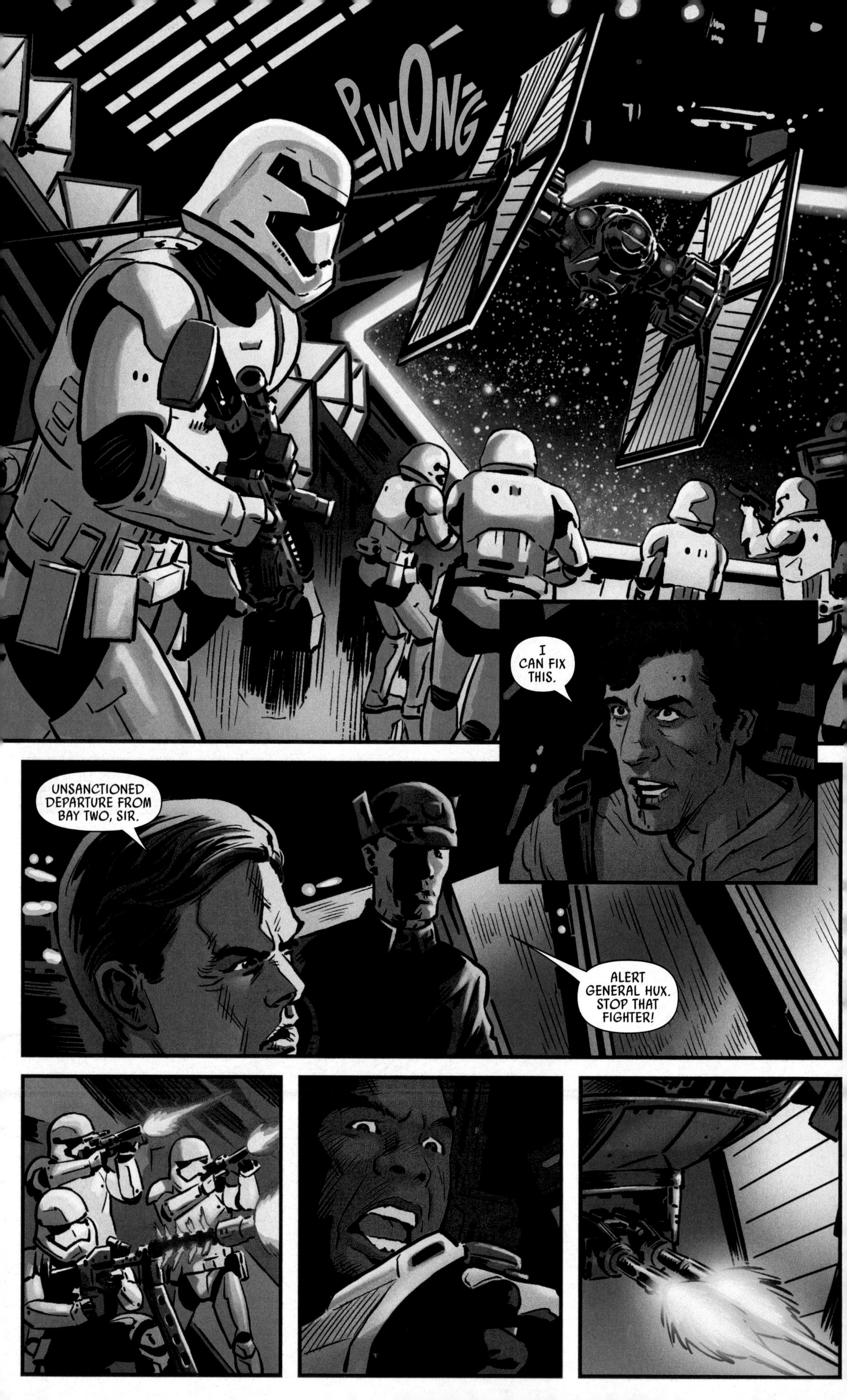
PWONG
I CAN FIX THIS.
UNSANCTIONED DEPARTURE FROM BAY TWO, SIR.
ALERT GENERAL HUX. STOP THAT FIGHTER!

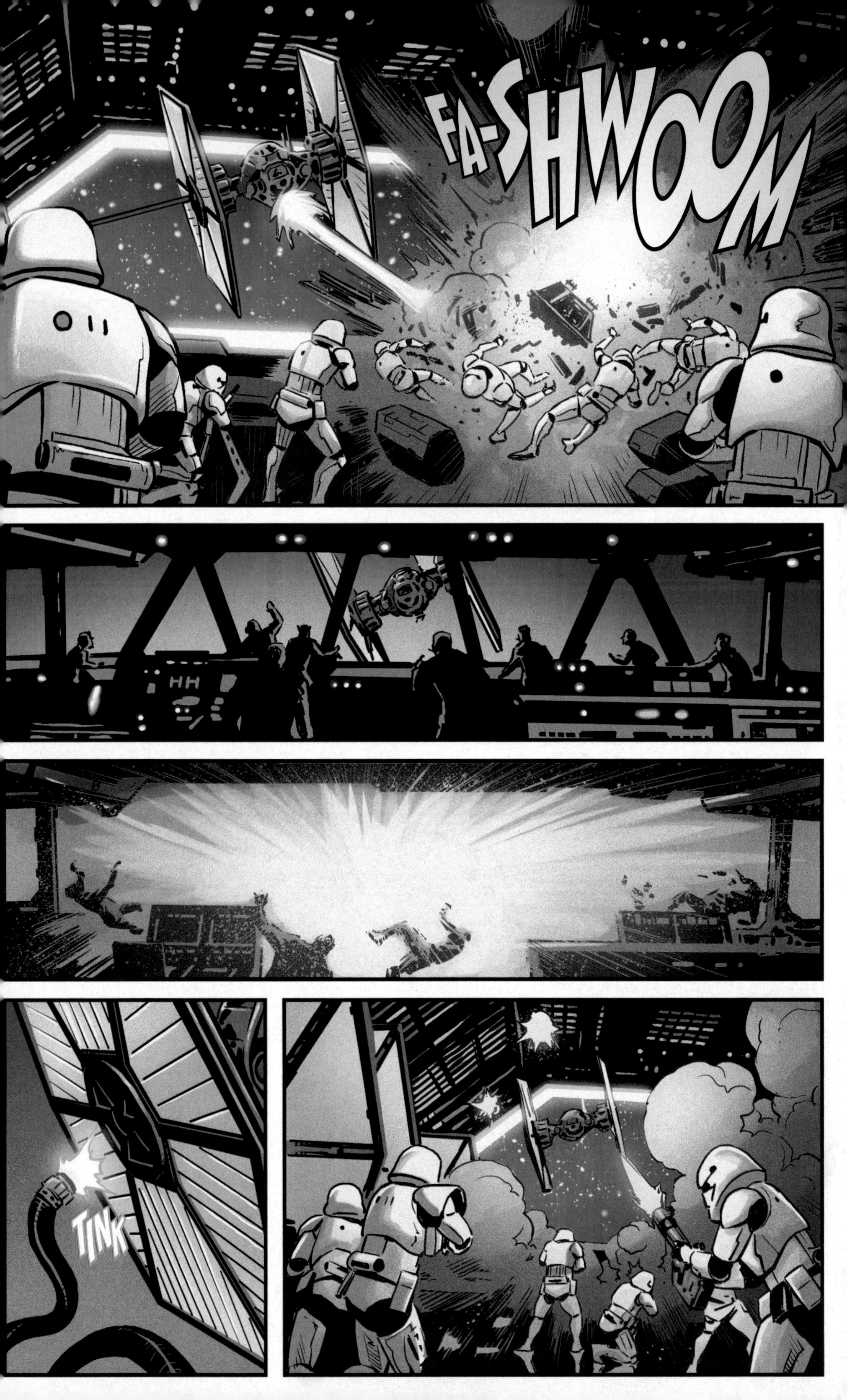
FA-SHWOOM
TINK

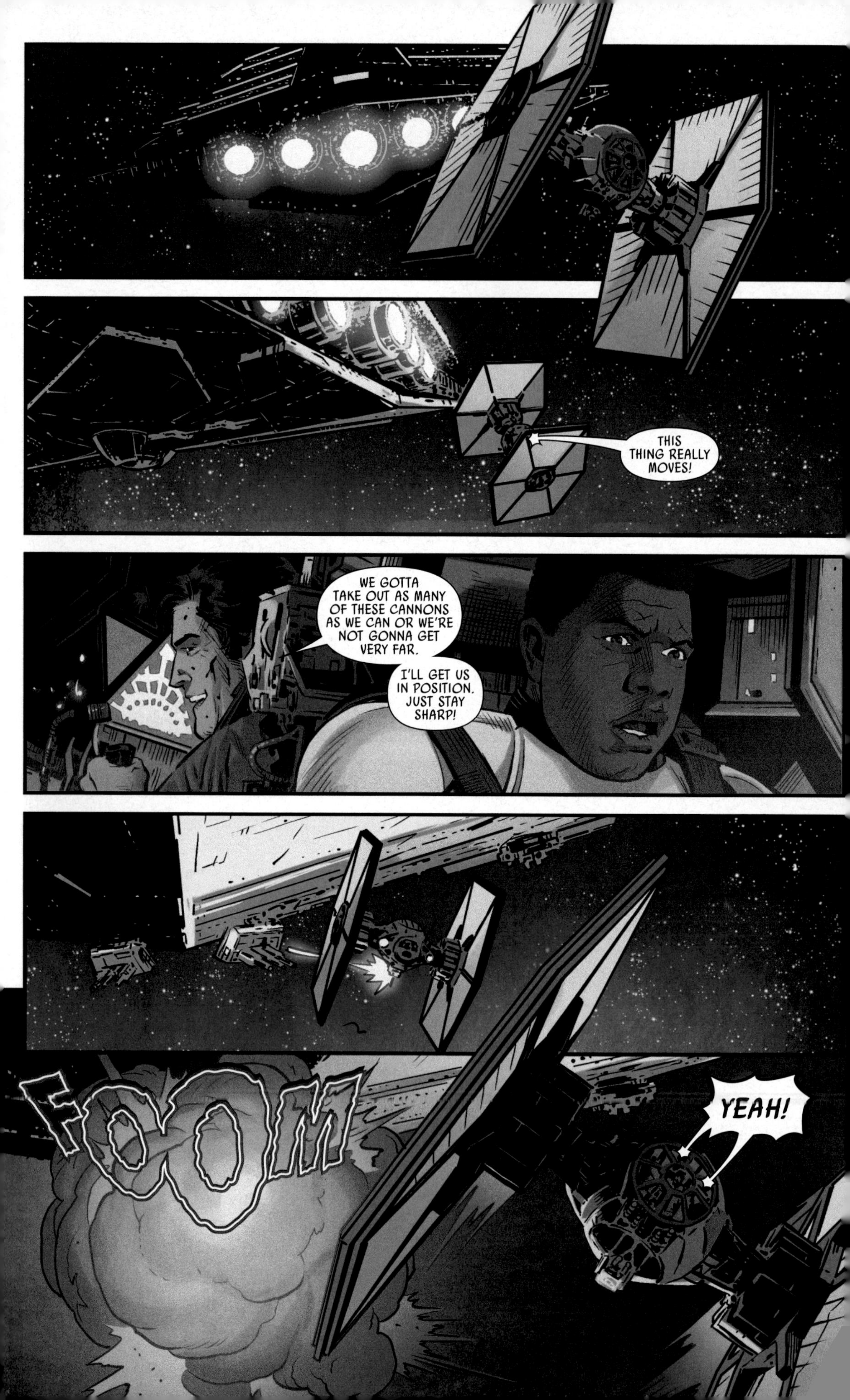
THIS THING REALLY MOVES!
WE GOTTA TAKE OUT AS MANY OF THESE CANNONS AS WE CAN OR WE'RE NOT GONNA GET VERY FAR.
I'LL GET US IN POSITION. JUST STAY SHARP!
FOOM
YEAH!

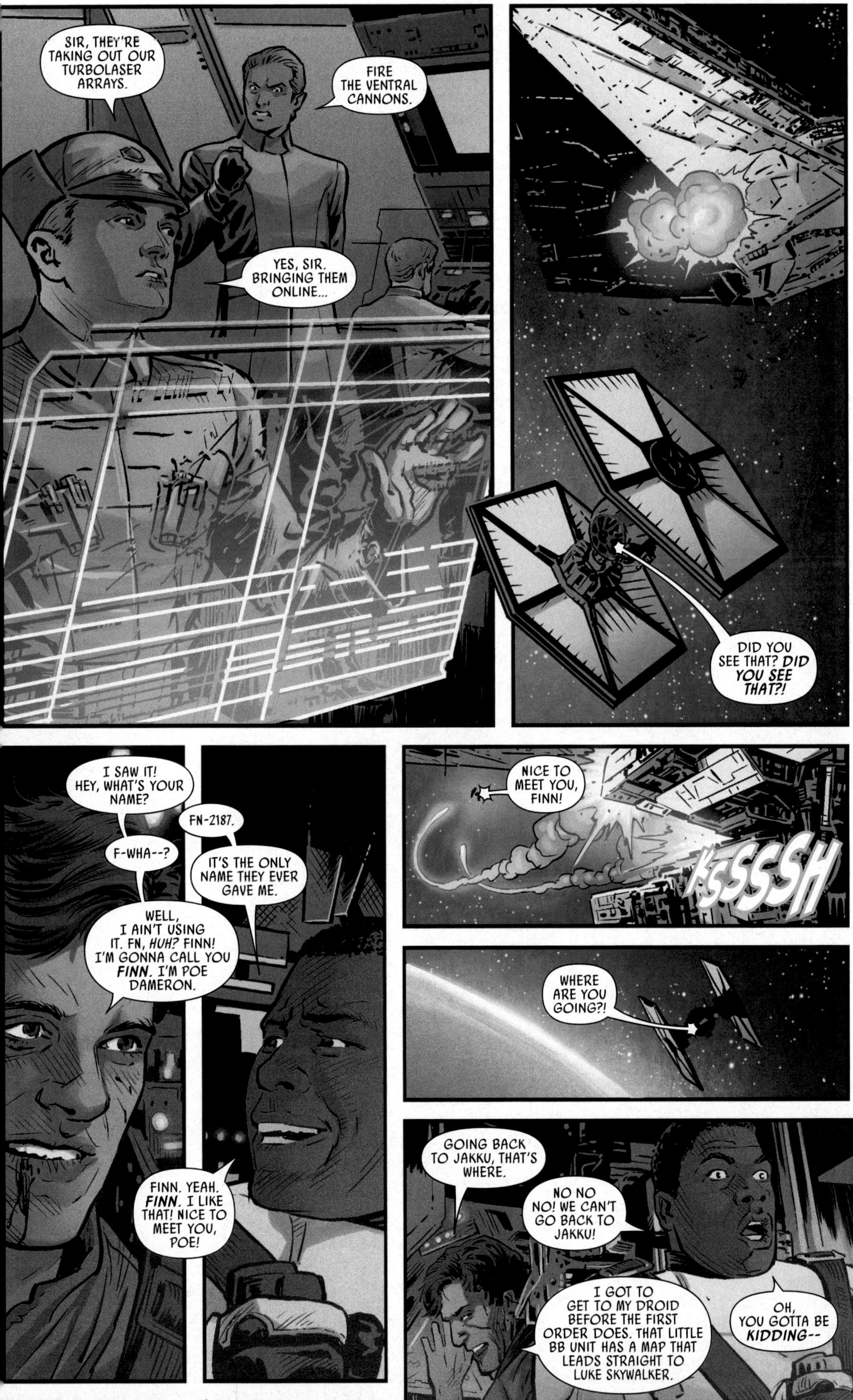

SIR, THEY'RE TAKING OUT OUR TURBOLASER ARRAYS.
FIRE THE VENTRAL CANNONS.
YES, SIR. BRINGING THEM ONLINE...
DID YOU SEE THAT? DID YOU SEE THAT?!
I SAW IT! HEY, WHAT'S YOUR NAME?
F-WHA--?
FN-2187.
IT'S THE ONLY NAME THEY EVER GAVE ME.
WELL, I AIN'T USING IT. FN, HUH? FINN! I'M GONNA CALL YOU FINN. I'M POE DAMERON.
FINN. YEAH. FINN. I LIKE THAT! NICE TO MEET YOU, POE!
NICE TO MEET YOU, FINN!
KSSSSH
WHERE ARE YOU GOING?!
GOING BACK TO JAKKU, THAT'S WHERE.
NO NO NO! WE CAN'T GO BACK TO JAKKU!
I GOT TO GET TO MY DROID BEFORE THE FIRST ORDER DOES. THAT LITTLE BB UNIT HAS A MAP THAT LEADS STRAIGHT TO LUKE SKYWALKER.
OH, YOU GOTTA BE KIDDING--

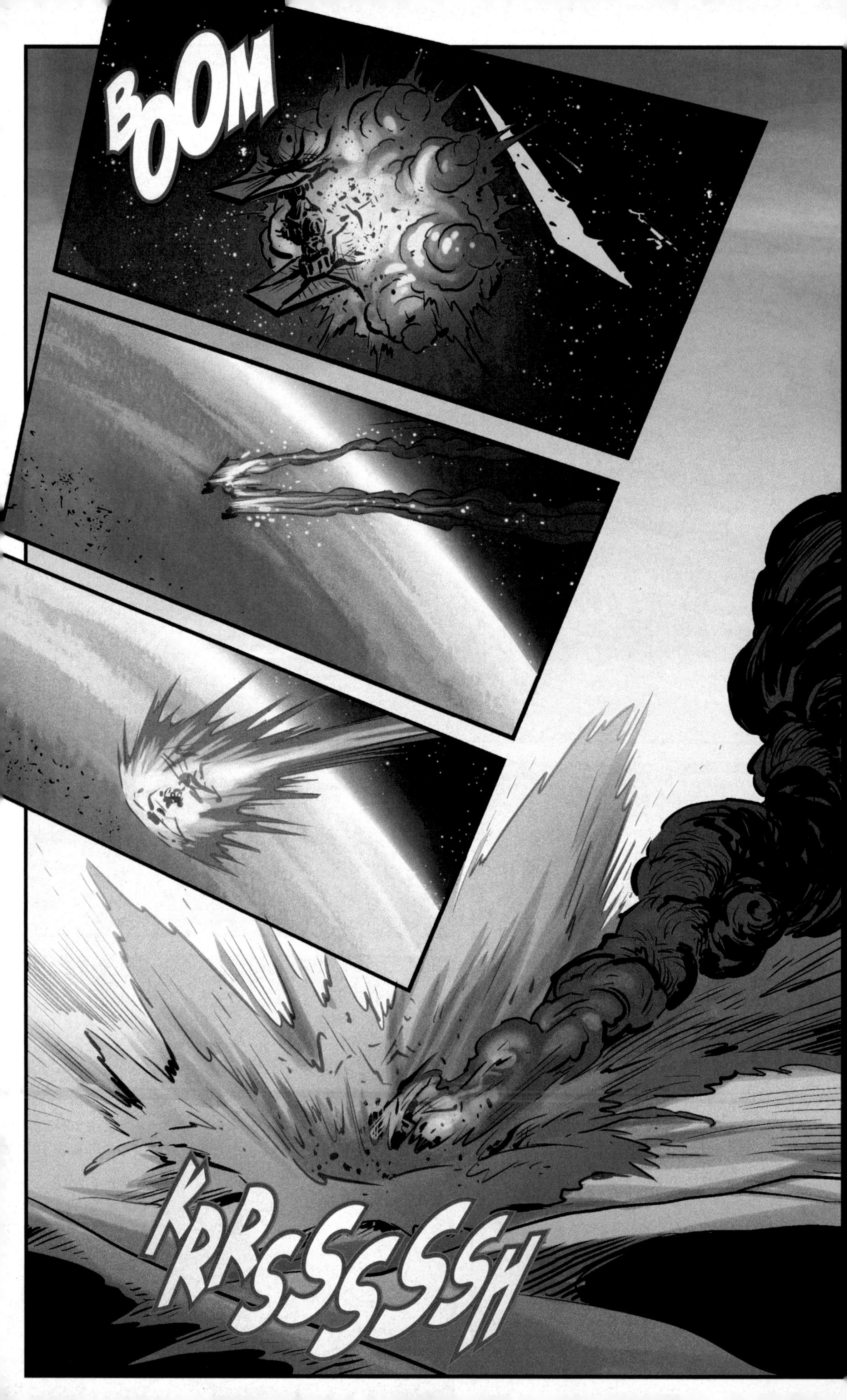
BOOM
KRRSSSSSH

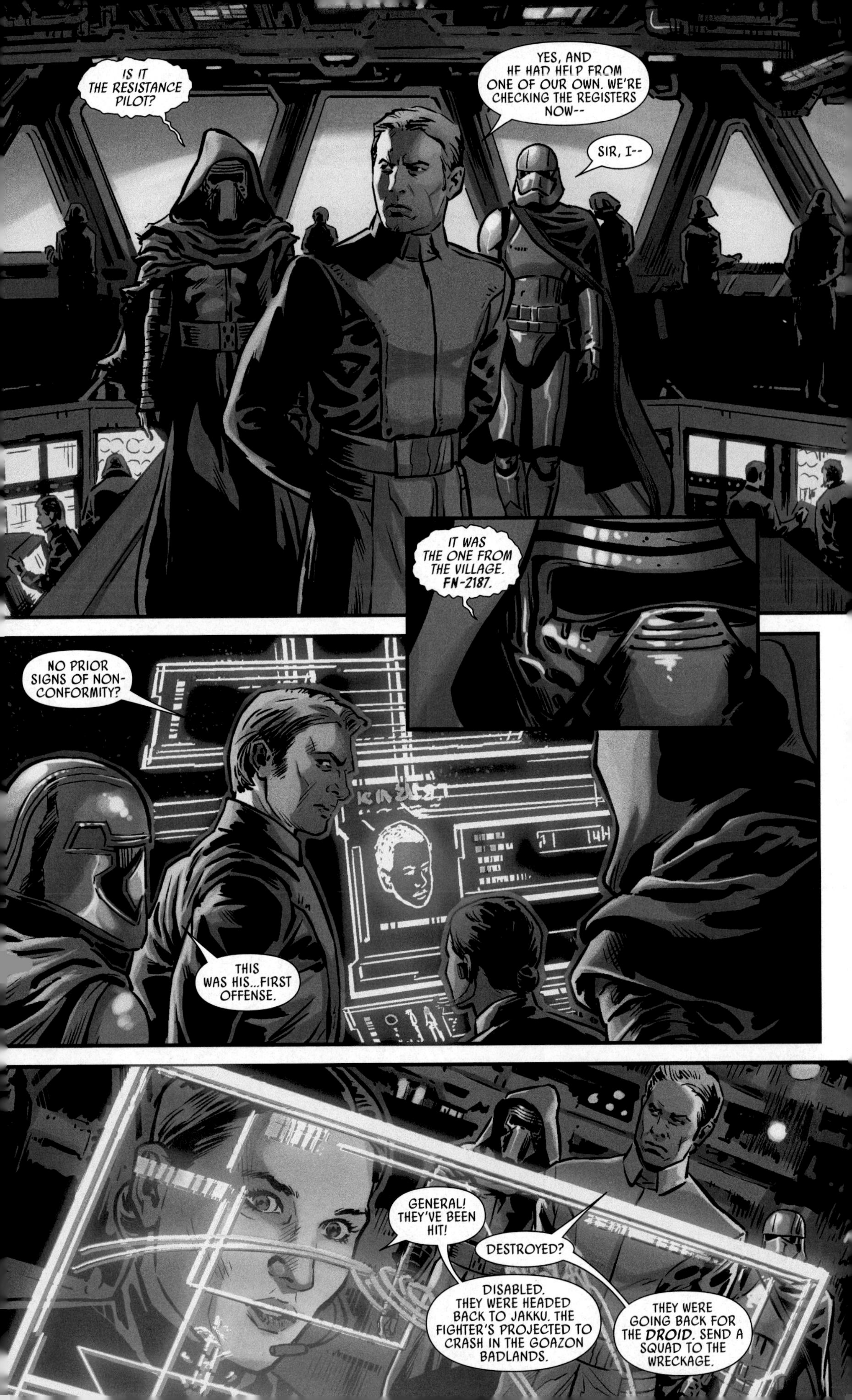
IS IT THE RESISTANCE PILOT?
YES, AND HE HAD HELP FROM ONE OF OUR OWN. WE'RE CHECKING THE REGISTERS NOW--
SIR, I--
IT WAS THE ONE FROM THE VILLAGE. **FN-2187.**
NO PRIOR SIGNS OF NON-CONFORMITY?
THIS WAS HIS...FIRST OFFENSE.
GENERAL! THEY'VE BEEN HIT!
DESTROYED?
DISABLED. THEY WERE HEADED BACK TO JAKKU. THE FIGHTER'S PROJECTED TO CRASH IN THE GOAZON BADLANDS.
THEY WERE GOING BACK FOR THE ***DROID***. SEND A SQUAD TO THE WRECKAGE.

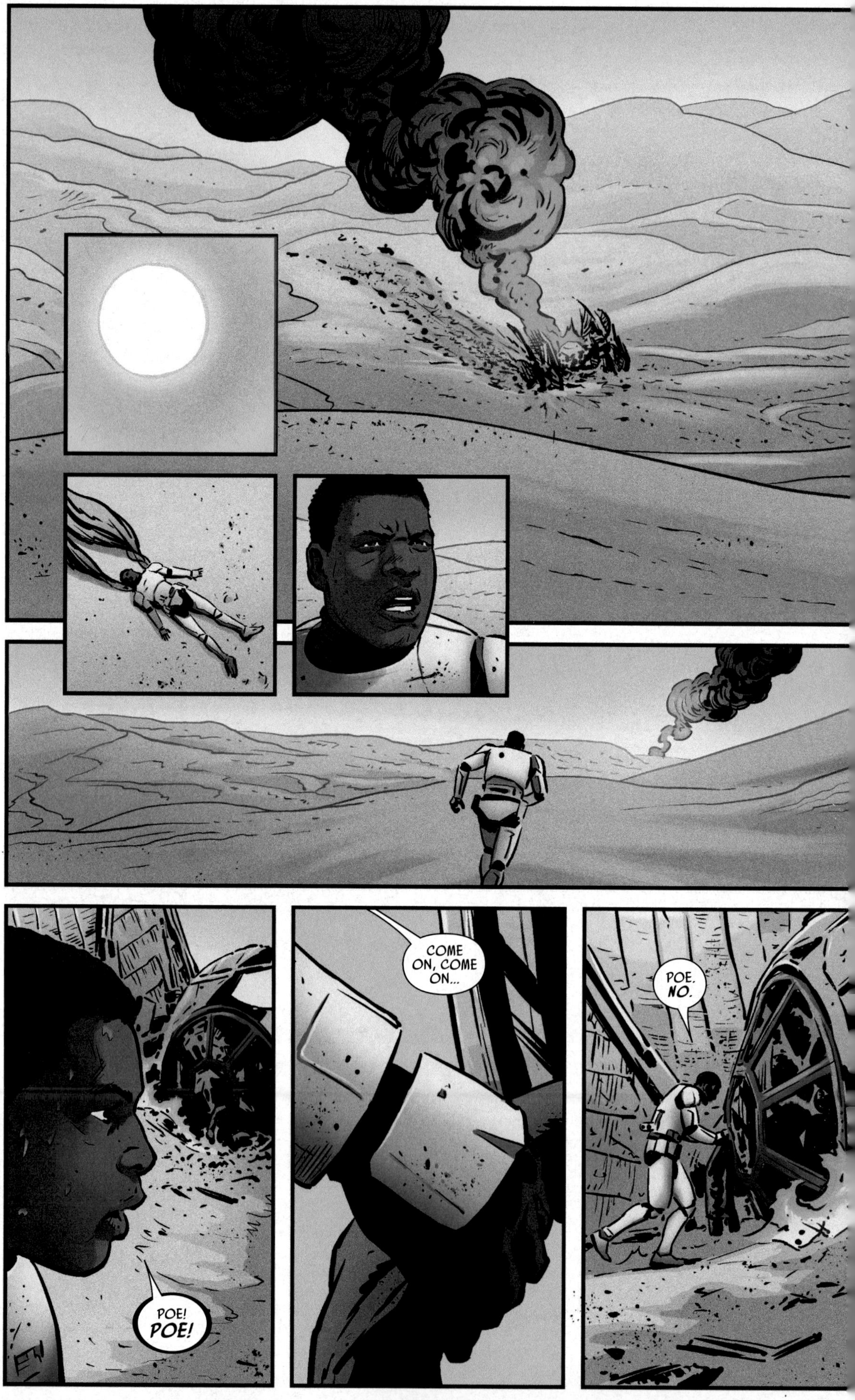
POE! POE!
COME ON, COME ON...
POE. NO.

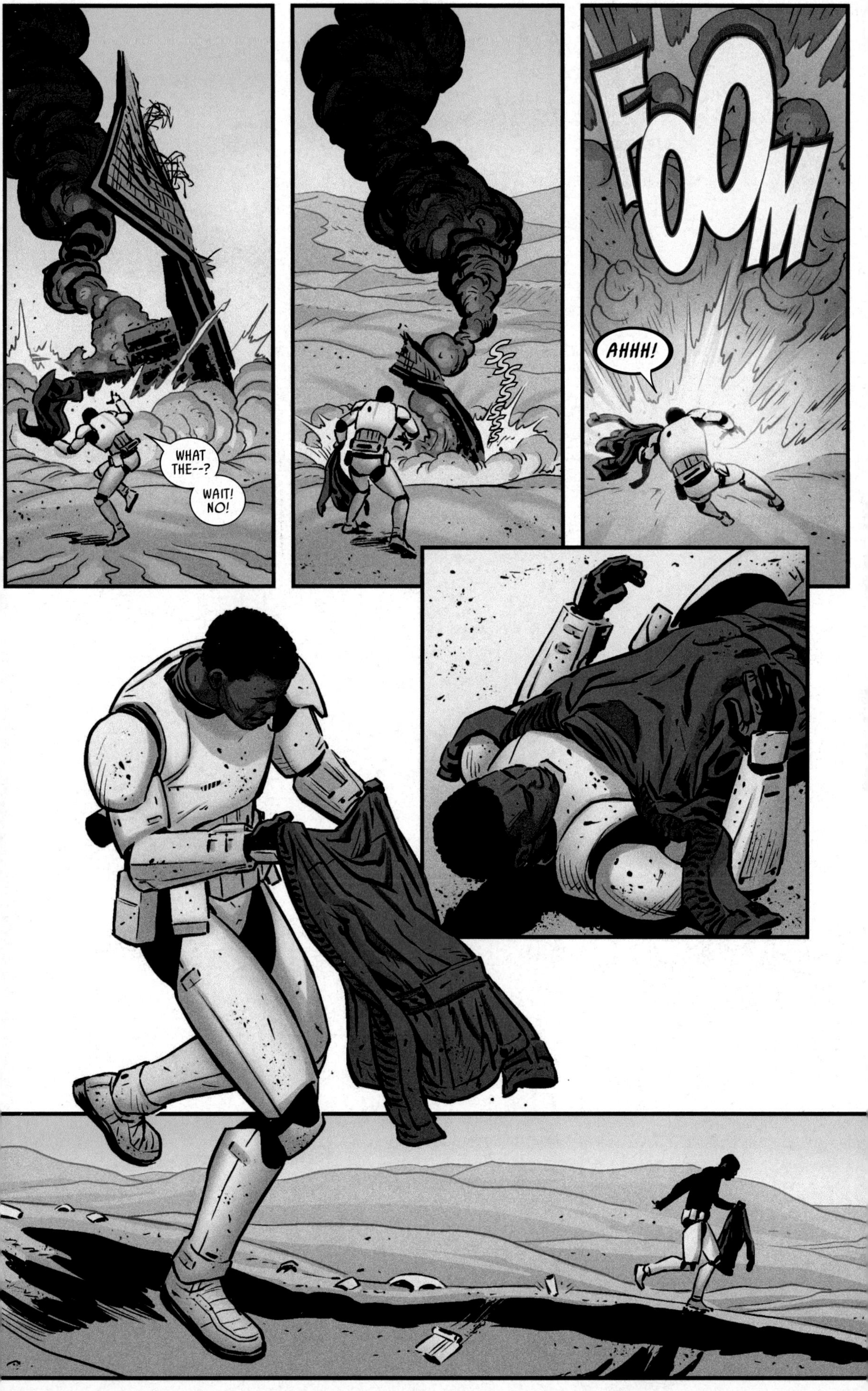
WHAT THE--?
WAIT! NO!
SSSSSSSS
FOOM
AHHH!

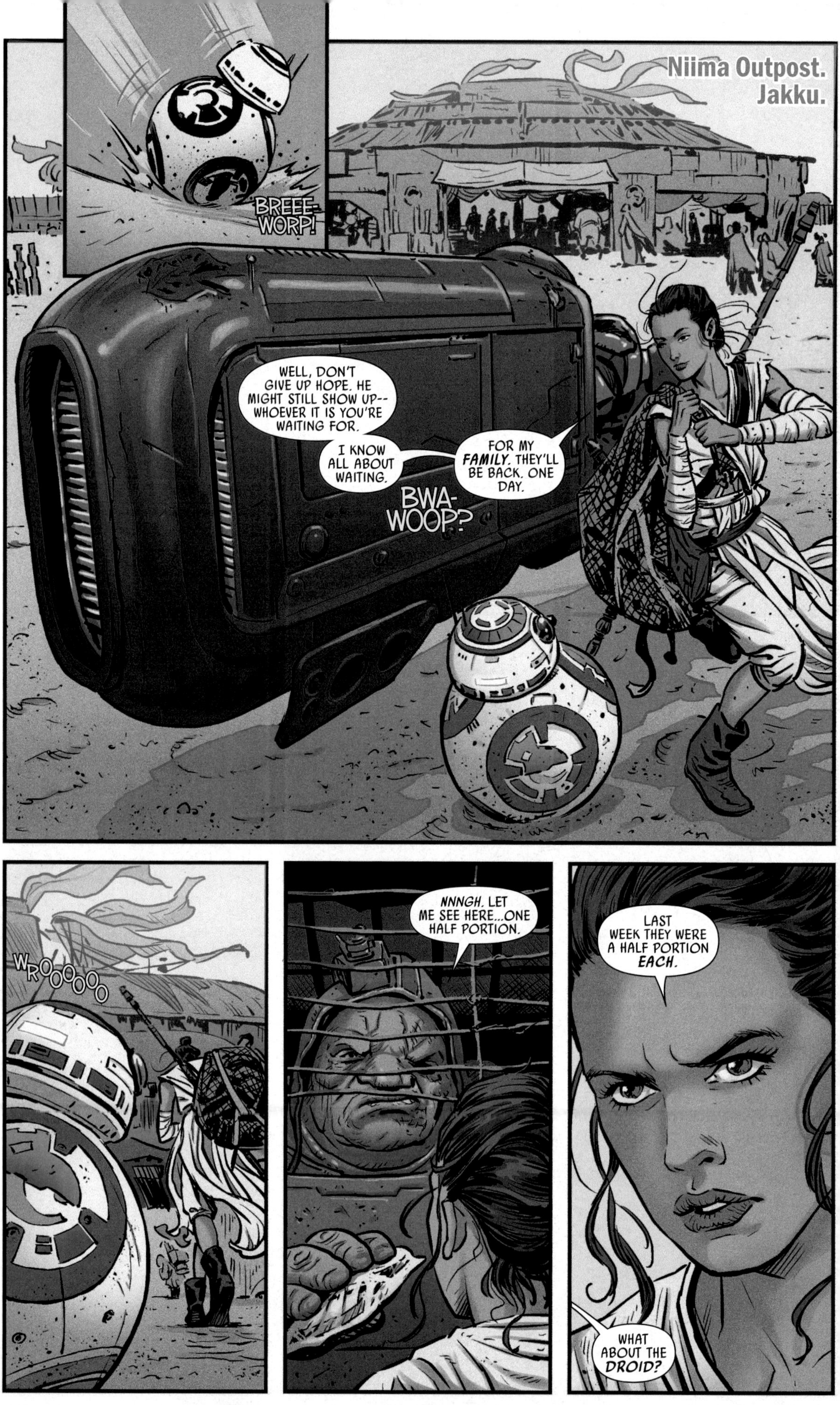
BREEE-WORP!
Niima Outpost. Jakku.
WELL, DON'T GIVE UP HOPE. HE MIGHT STILL SHOW UP--WHOEVER IT IS YOU'RE WAITING FOR.
I KNOW ALL ABOUT WAITING.
FOR MY FAMILY. THEY'LL BE BACK. ONE DAY.
BWA-WOOP?
WROOOOOO
NNNGH. LET ME SEE HERE...ONE HALF PORTION.
LAST WEEK THEY WERE A HALF PORTION EACH.
WHAT ABOUT THE DROID?

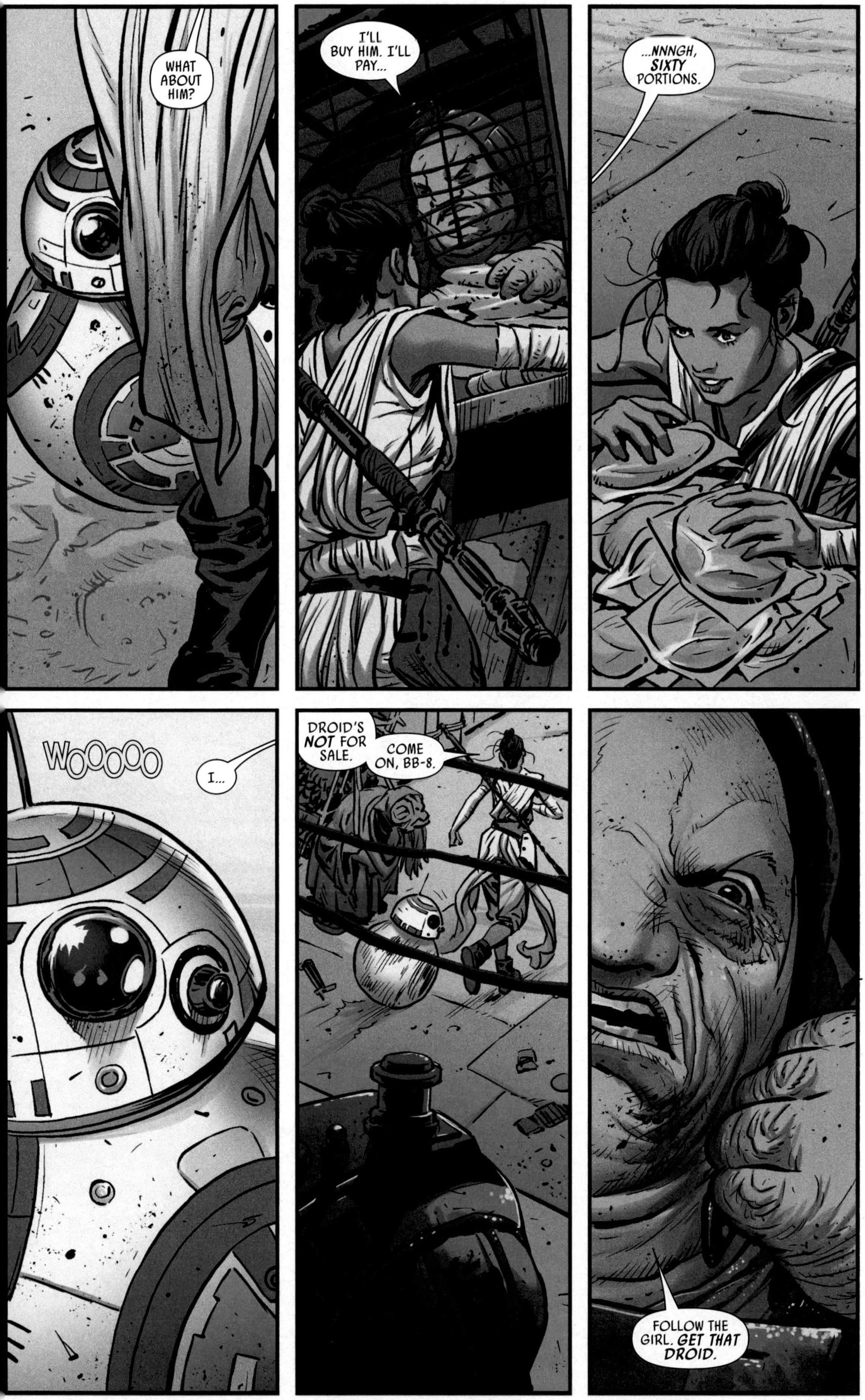
WHAT ABOUT HIM?
I'LL BUY HIM. I'LL PAY...
...NNNGH, SIXTY PORTIONS.
WOOOOO
I...
DROID'S NOT FOR SALE.
COME ON, BB-8.
FOLLOW THE GIRL. GET THAT DROID.

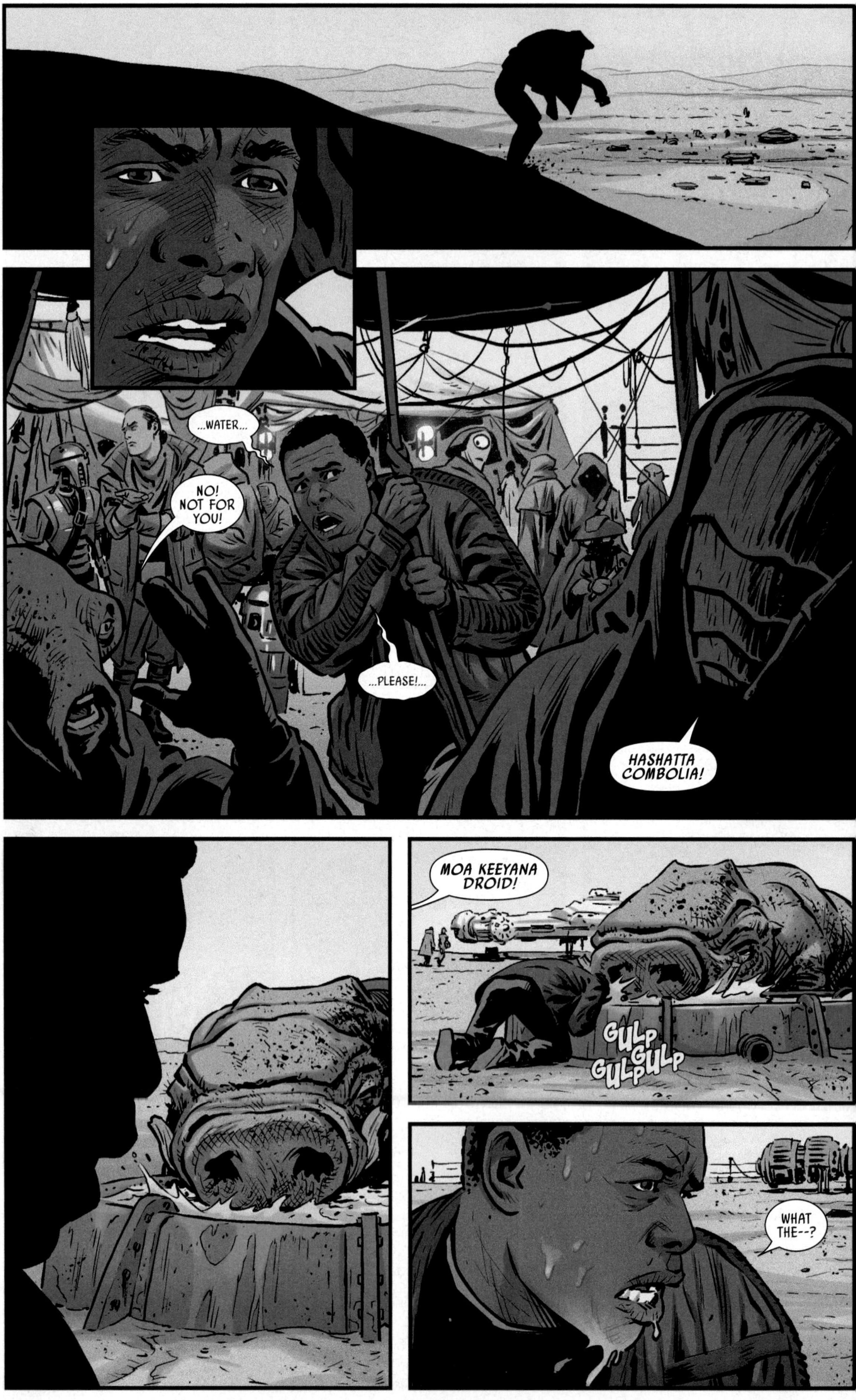
...WATER...
NO! NOT FOR YOU!
...PLEASE!...
HASHATTA COMBOLIA!
MOA KEEYANA DROID!
GULP GULP GULP GULP
WHAT THE--?

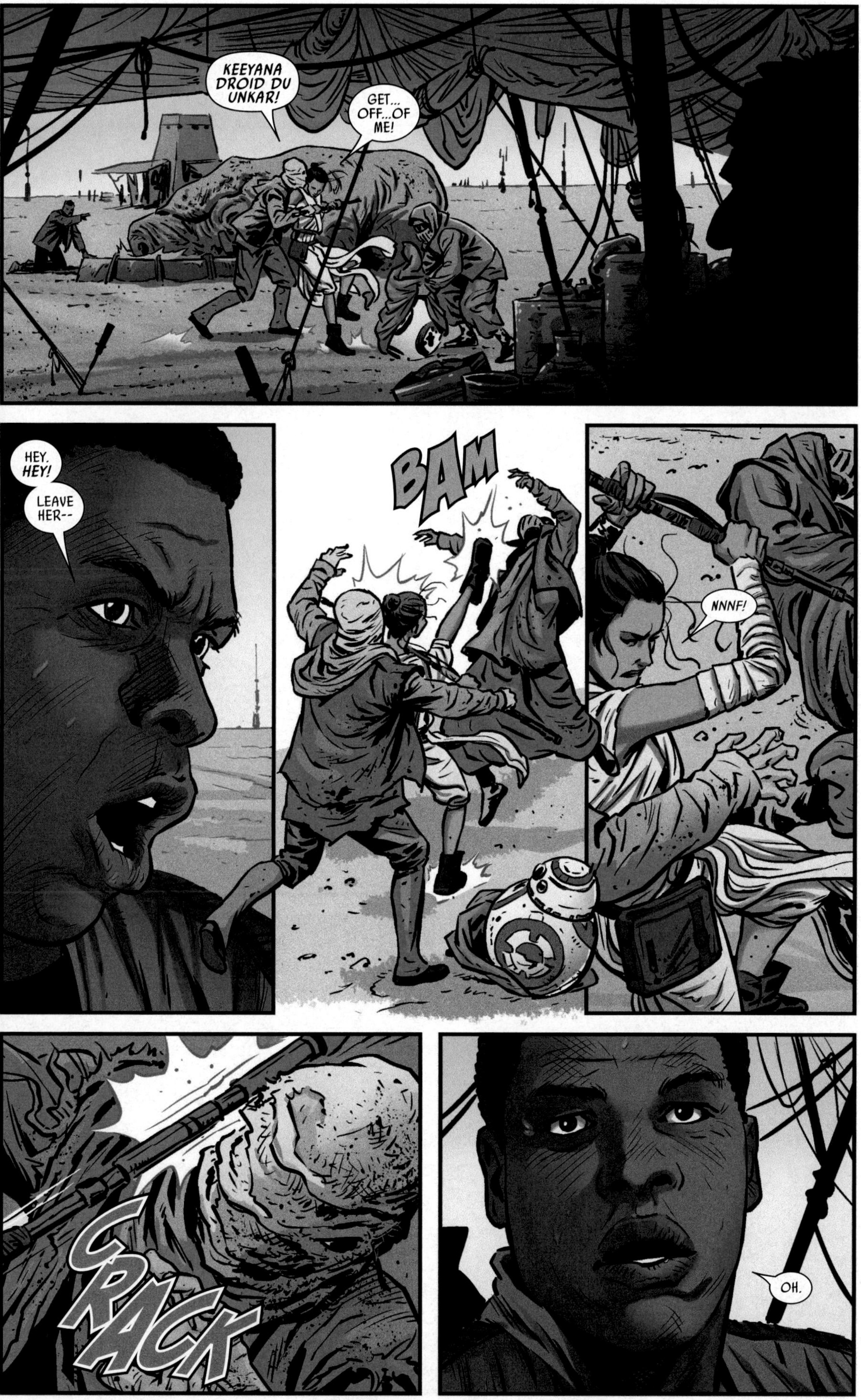
KEEYANA DROID DU UNKAR!
GET... OFF...OF ME!
HEY. HEY!
LEAVE HER--
BAM
NNNF!
CRACK
OH.

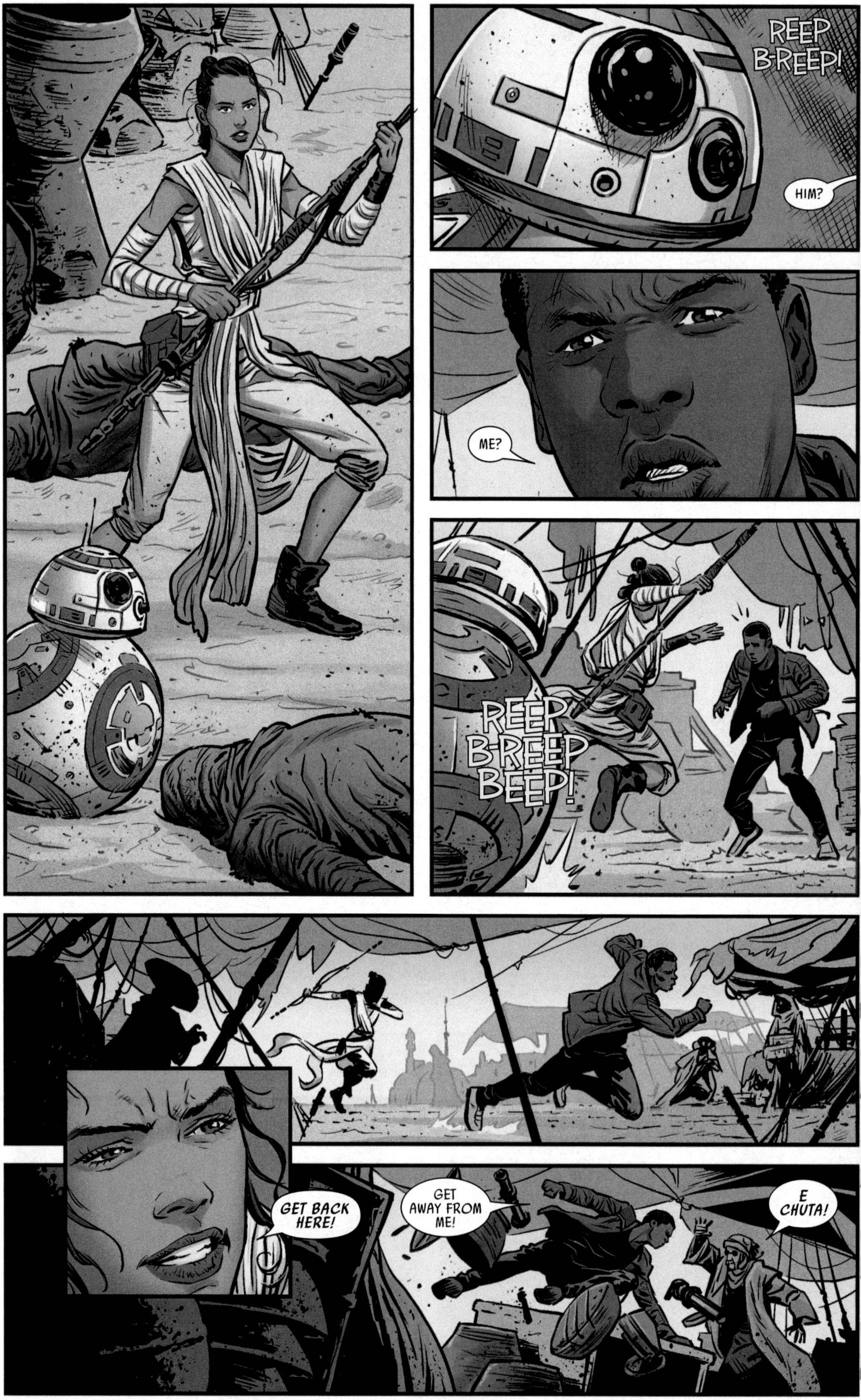
REEP B-REEP!
HIM?
ME?
REEP B-REEP BEEP!
GET BACK HERE!
GET AWAY FROM ME!
E CHUTA!

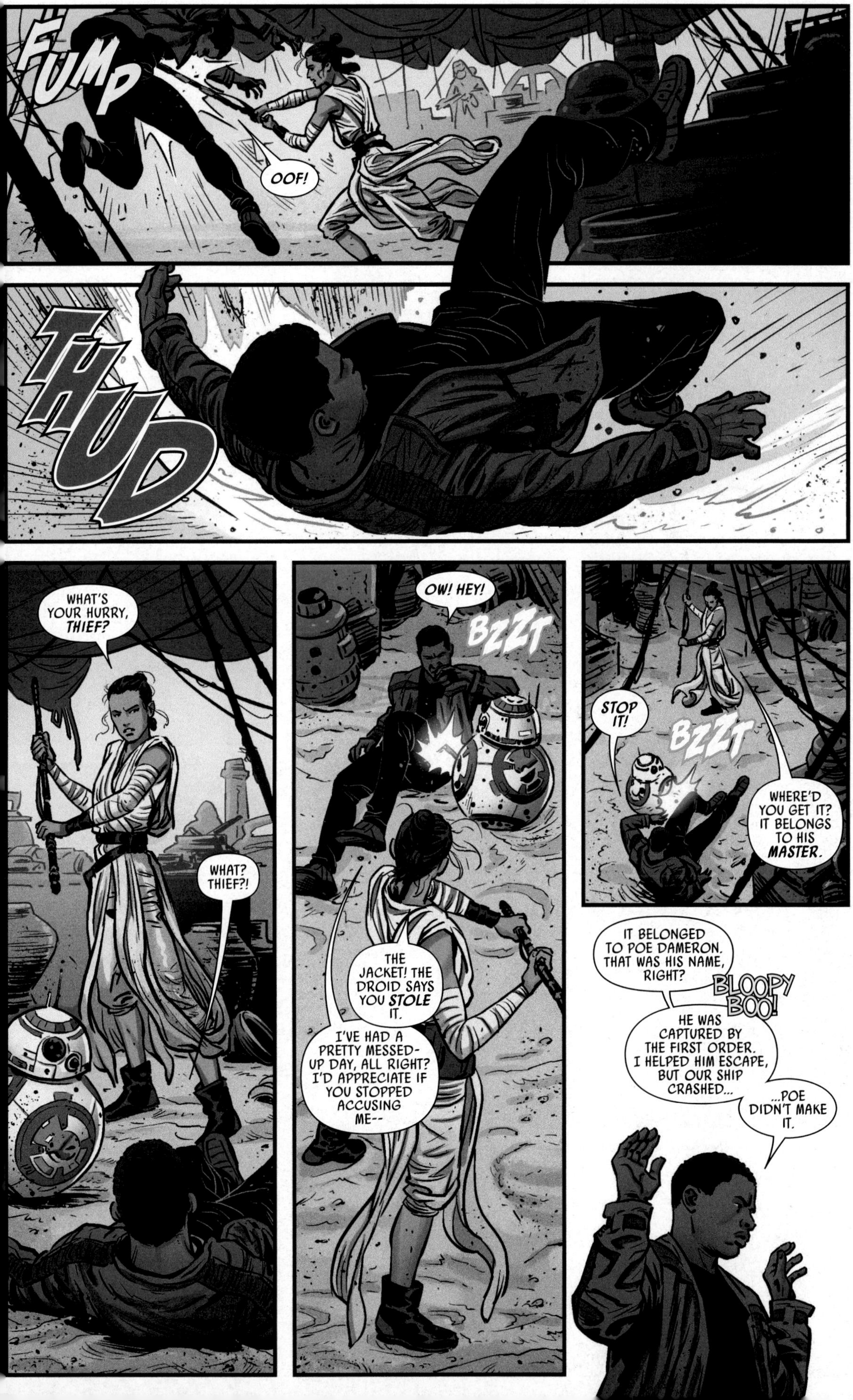
FUMP
OOF!
THUD
WHAT'S YOUR HURRY, THIEF?
WHAT? THIEF?!
OW! HEY!
BZZT
THE JACKET! THE DROID SAYS YOU STOLE IT.
I'VE HAD A PRETTY MESSED-UP DAY, ALL RIGHT? I'D APPRECIATE IF YOU STOPPED ACCUSING ME--
STOP IT!
BZZT
WHERE'D YOU GET IT? IT BELONGS TO HIS MASTER.
IT BELONGED TO POE DAMERON. THAT WAS HIS NAME, RIGHT?
BLOOPY BOO!
HE WAS CAPTURED BY THE FIRST ORDER. I HELPED HIM ESCAPE, BUT OUR SHIP CRASHED...
...POE DIDN'T MAKE IT.

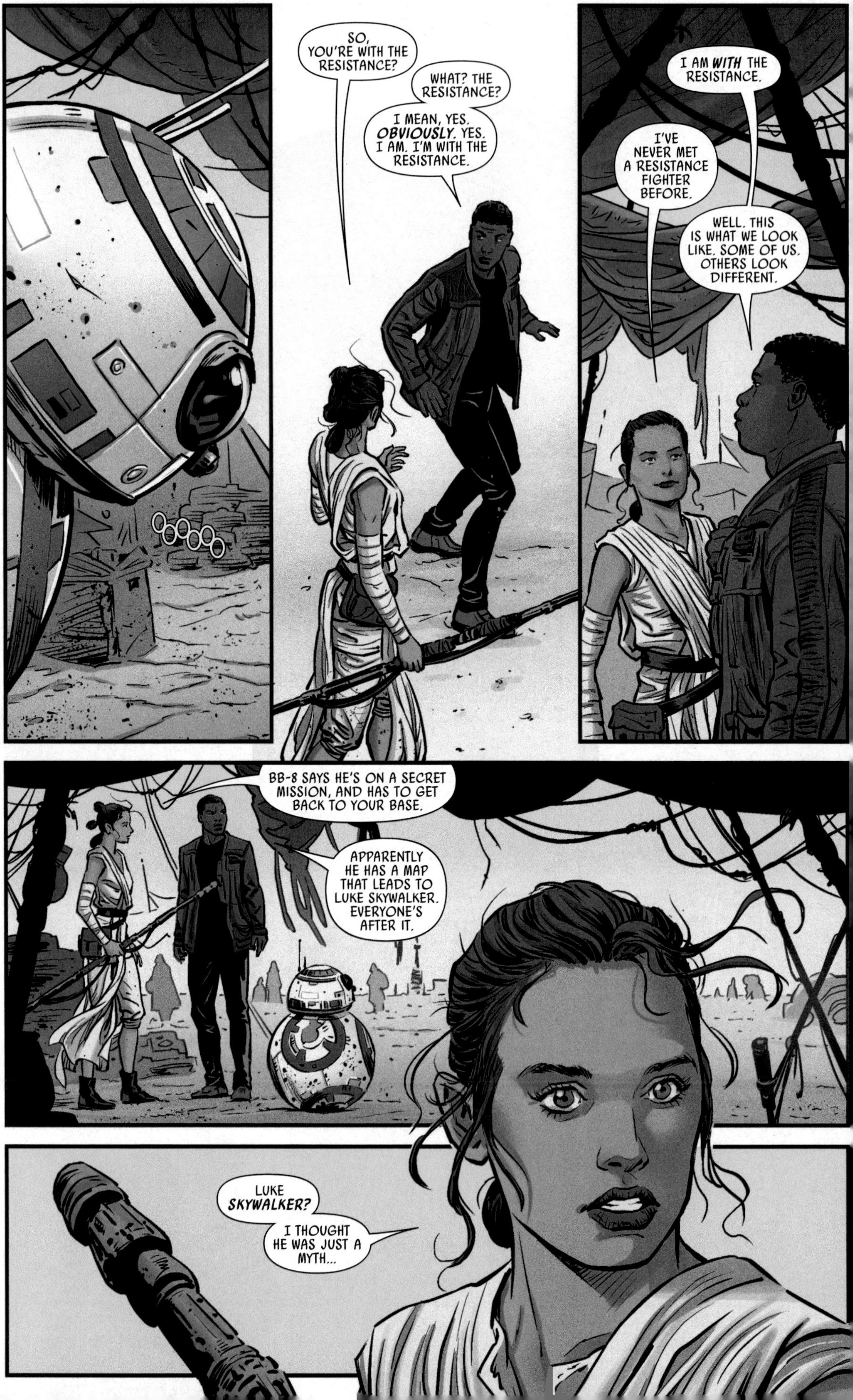
SO, YOU'RE WITH THE RESISTANCE?
WHAT? THE RESISTANCE?
I MEAN, YES. OBVIOUSLY. YES. I AM. I'M WITH THE RESISTANCE.
I AM WITH THE RESISTANCE.
I'VE NEVER MET A RESISTANCE FIGHTER BEFORE.
WELL, THIS IS WHAT WE LOOK LIKE. SOME OF US. OTHERS LOOK DIFFERENT.
BB-8 SAYS HE'S ON A SECRET MISSION, AND HAS TO GET BACK TO YOUR BASE.
APPARENTLY HE HAS A MAP THAT LEADS TO LUKE SKYWALKER. EVERYONE'S AFTER IT.
LUKE SKYWALKER?
I THOUGHT HE WAS JUST A MYTH...

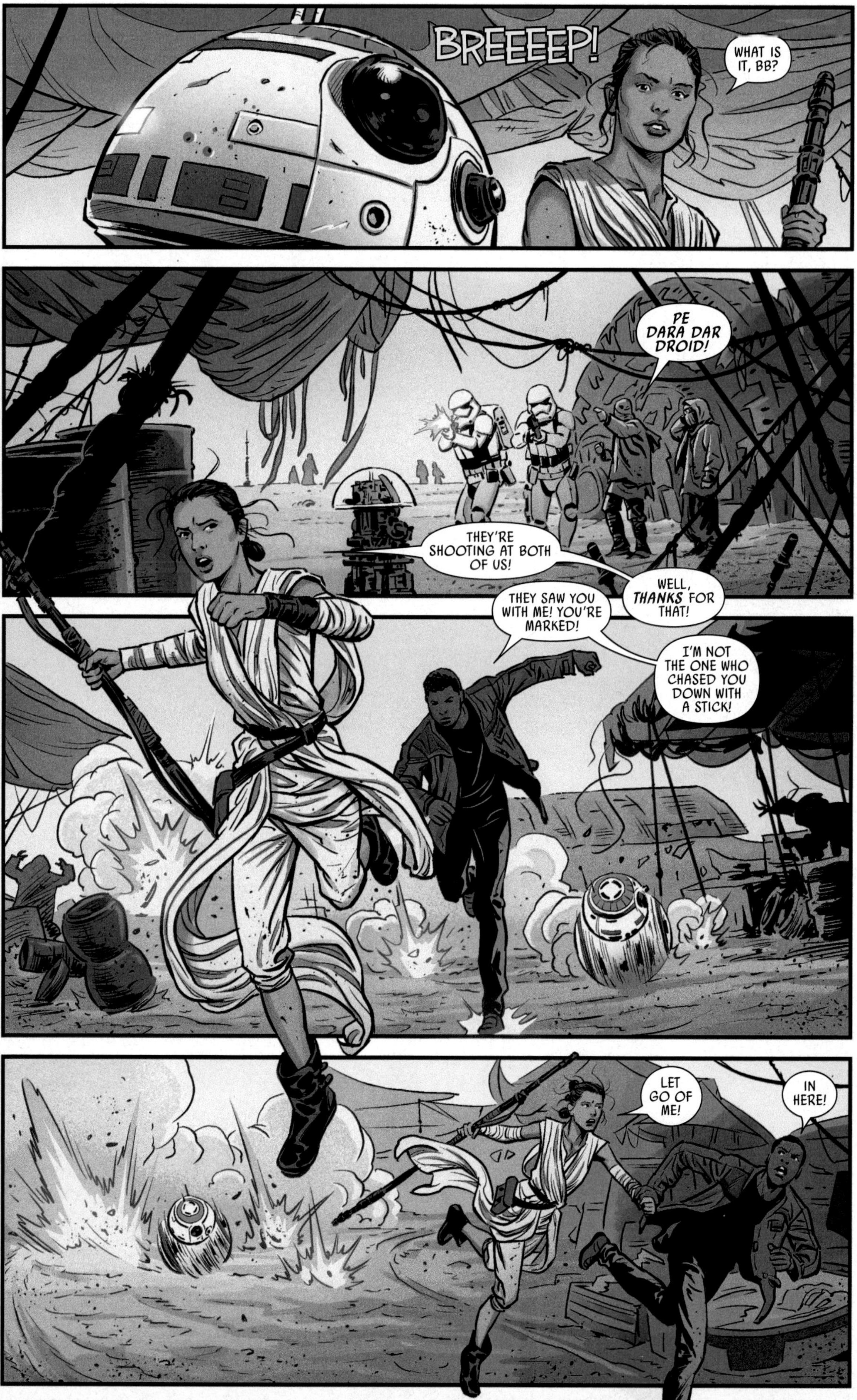
BREEEEP!
WHAT IS IT, BB?
PE DARA DAR DROID!
THEY'RE SHOOTING AT BOTH OF US!
WELL, THANKS FOR THAT!
THEY SAW YOU WITH ME! YOU'RE MARKED!
I'M NOT THE ONE WHO CHASED YOU DOWN WITH A STICK!
LET GO OF ME!
IN HERE!

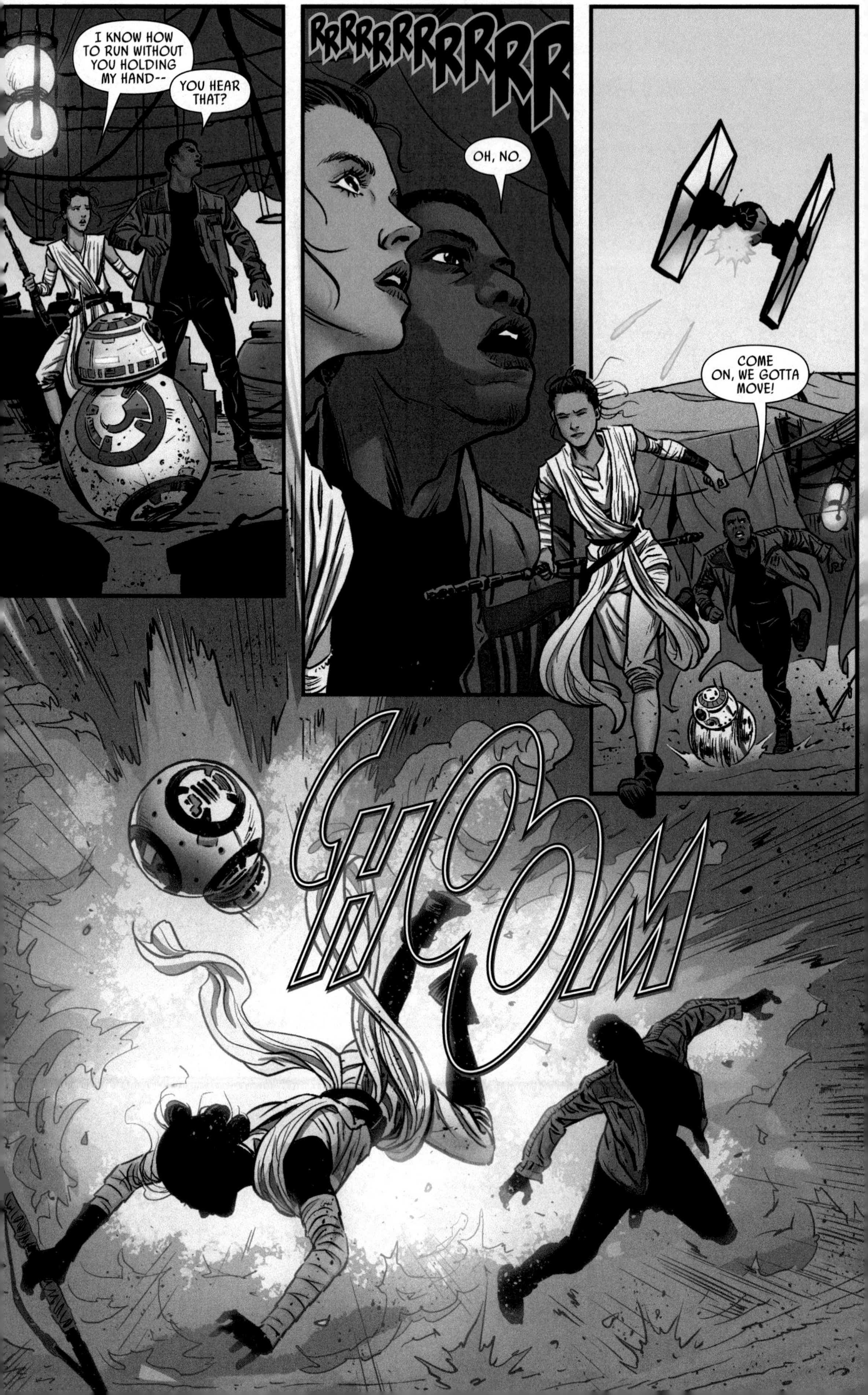
I KNOW HOW TO RUN WITHOUT YOU HOLDING MY HAND--
YOU HEAR THAT?
RRRRRRRRRRR
OH, NO.
COME ON, WE GOTTA MOVE!
CHOOM

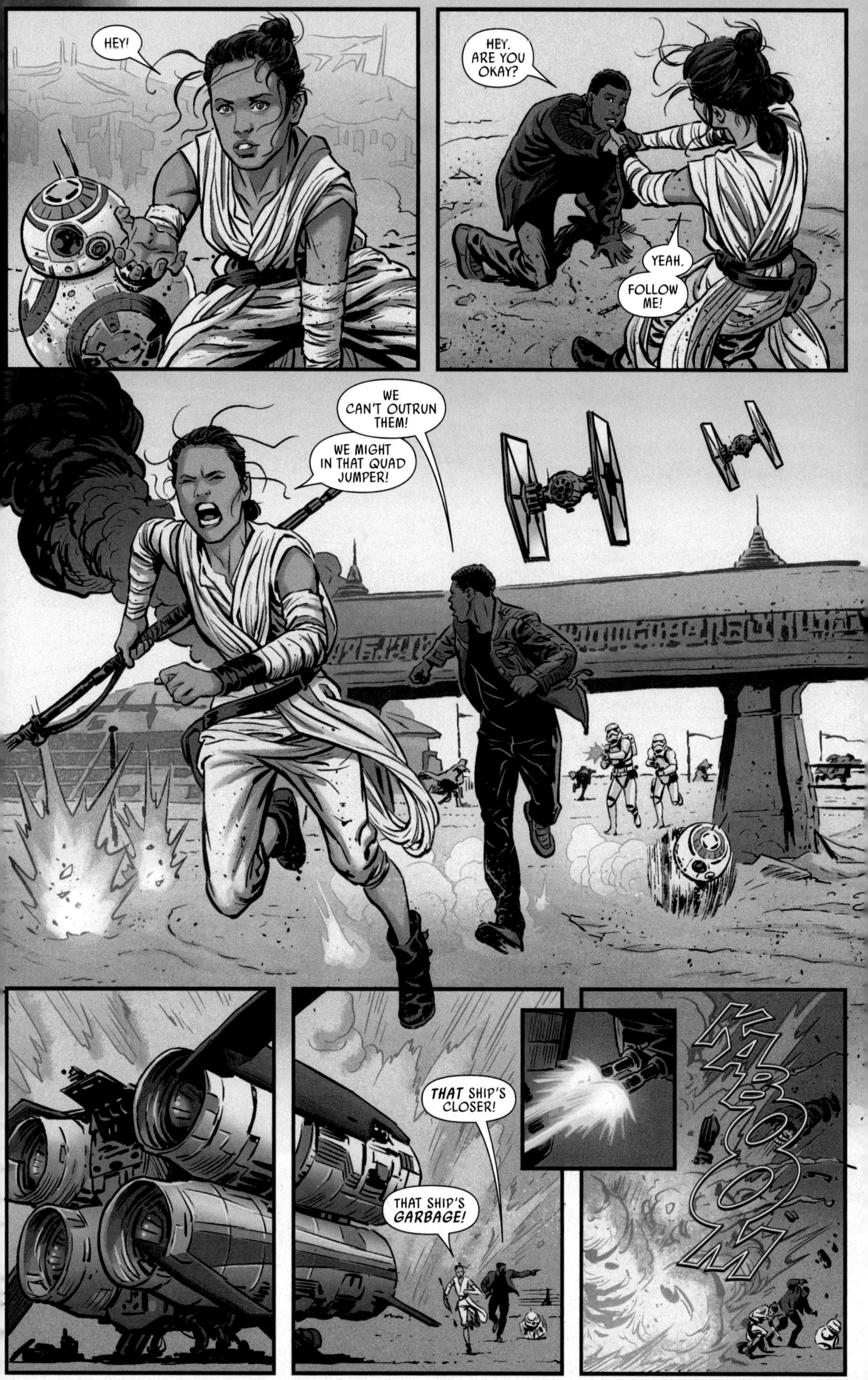
HEY!
HEY. ARE YOU OKAY?
YEAH.
FOLLOW ME!
WE CAN'T OUTRUN THEM!
WE MIGHT IN THAT QUAD JUMPER!
THAT SHIP'S CLOSER!
THAT SHIP'S *GARBAGE!*
KA-BOOM

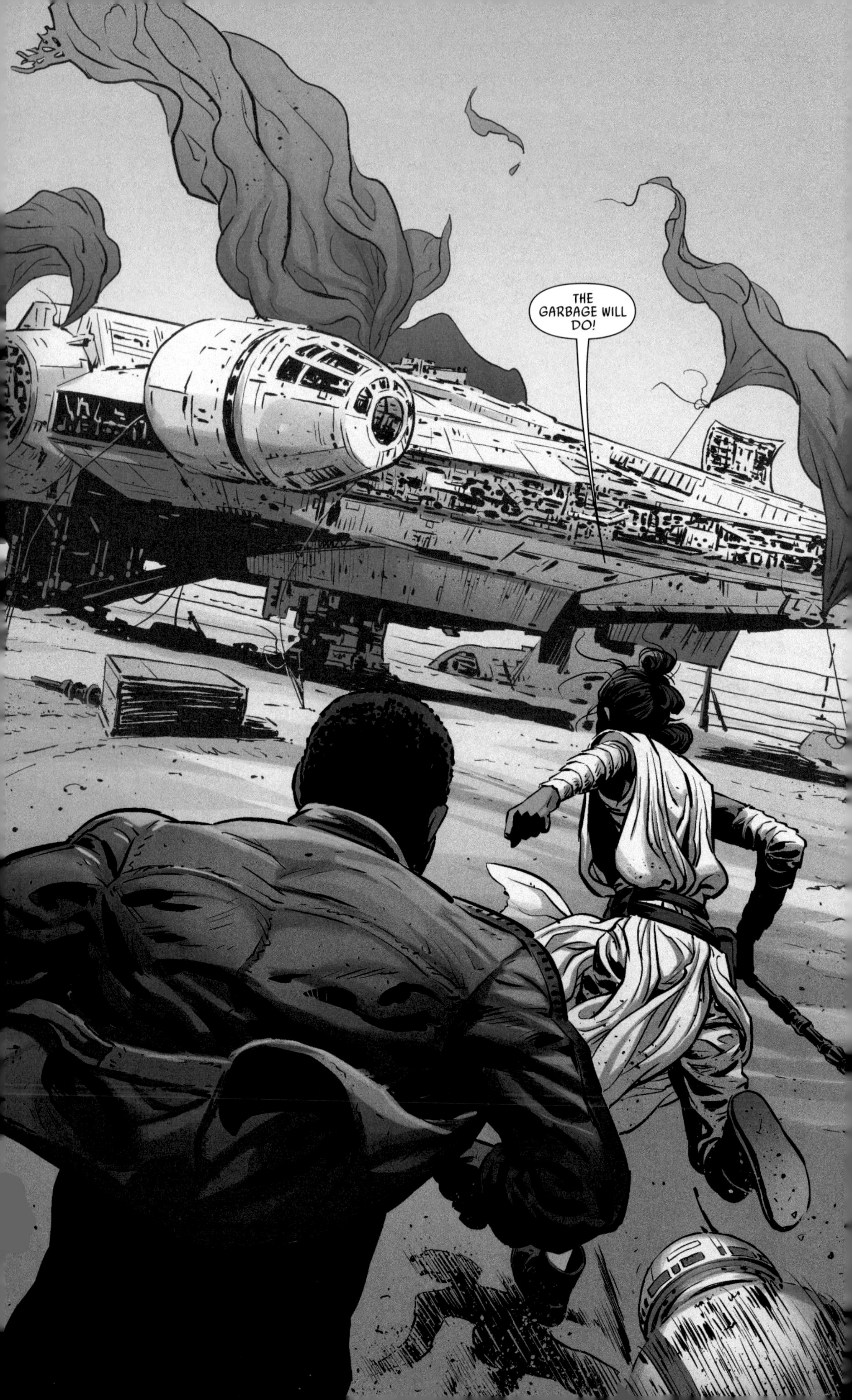
THE GARBAGE WILL DO!

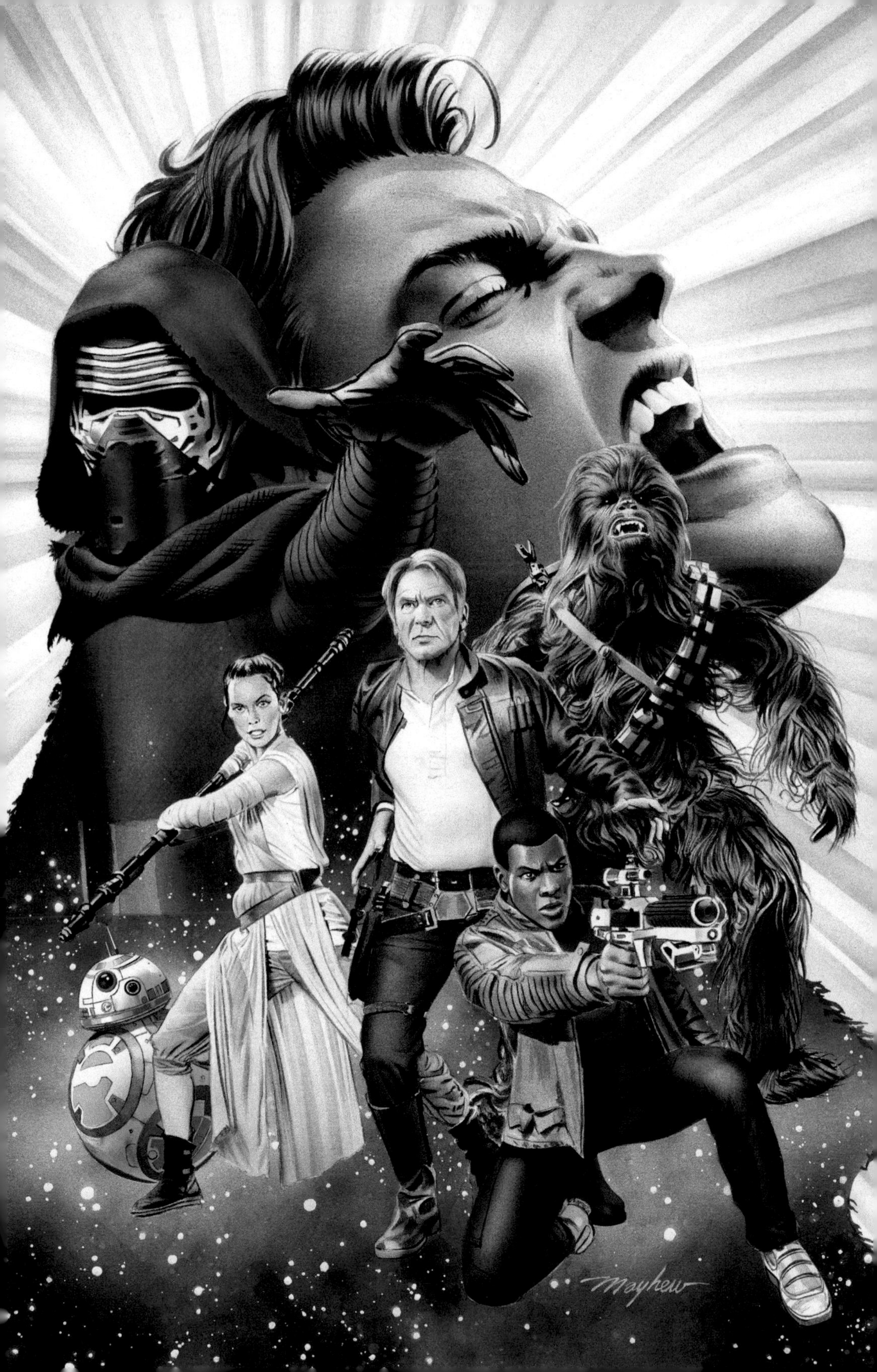
Mayhew

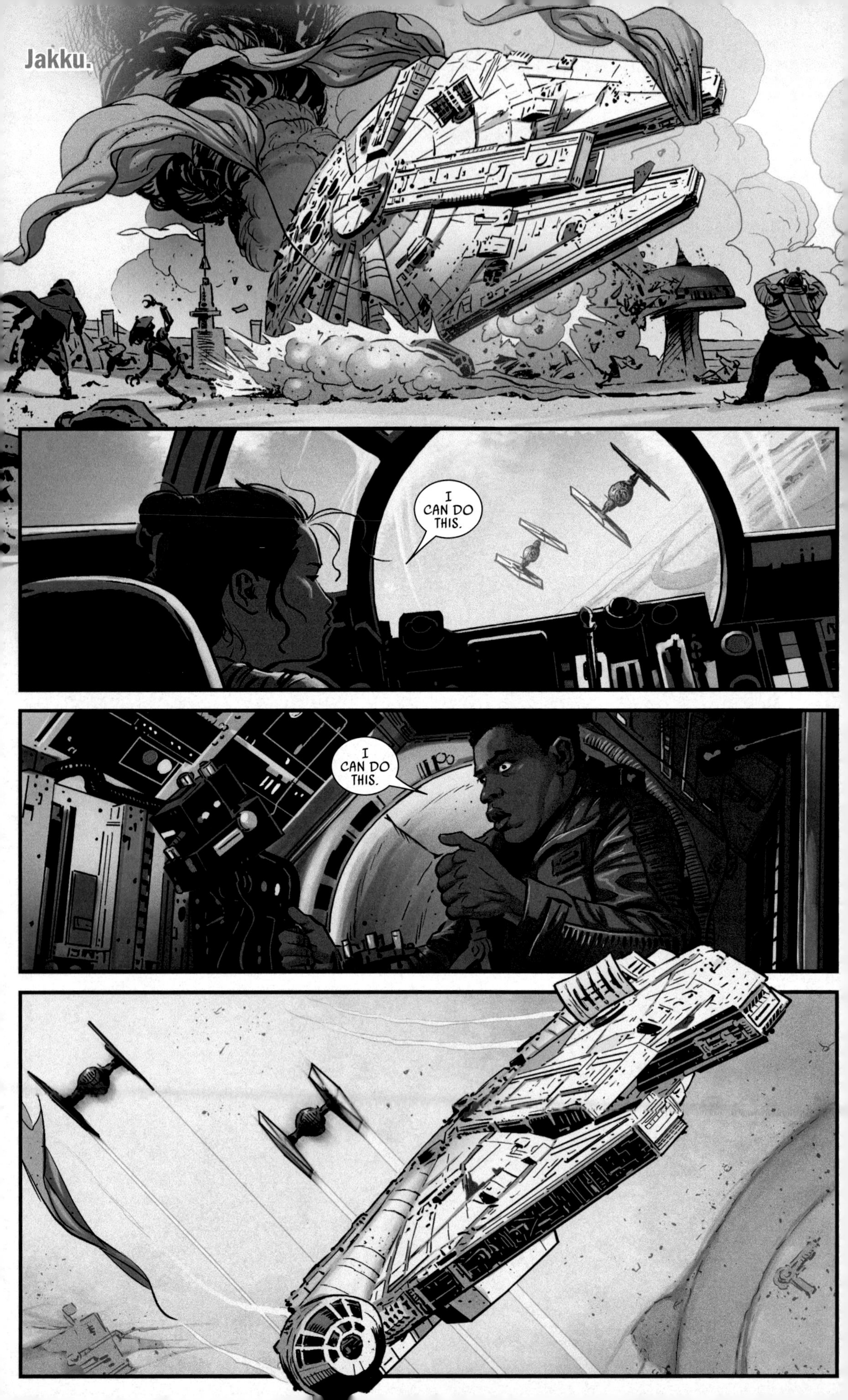
Jakku.
I CAN DO THIS.
I CAN DO THIS.

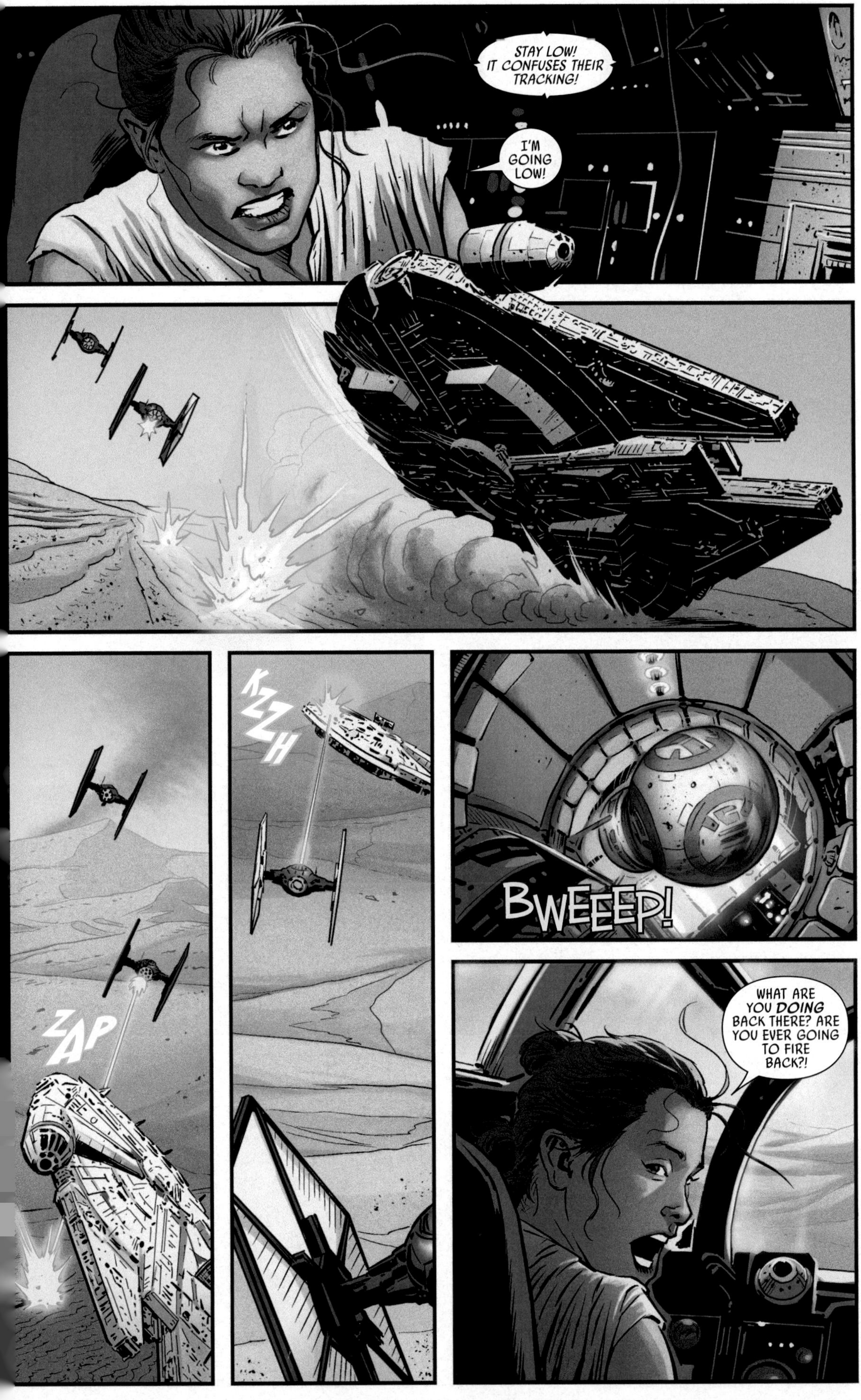
STAY LOW! IT CONFUSES THEIR TRACKING!
I'M GOING LOW!
KZZH
ZAP
BWEEEP!
WHAT ARE YOU DOING BACK THERE? ARE YOU EVER GOING TO FIRE BACK?!

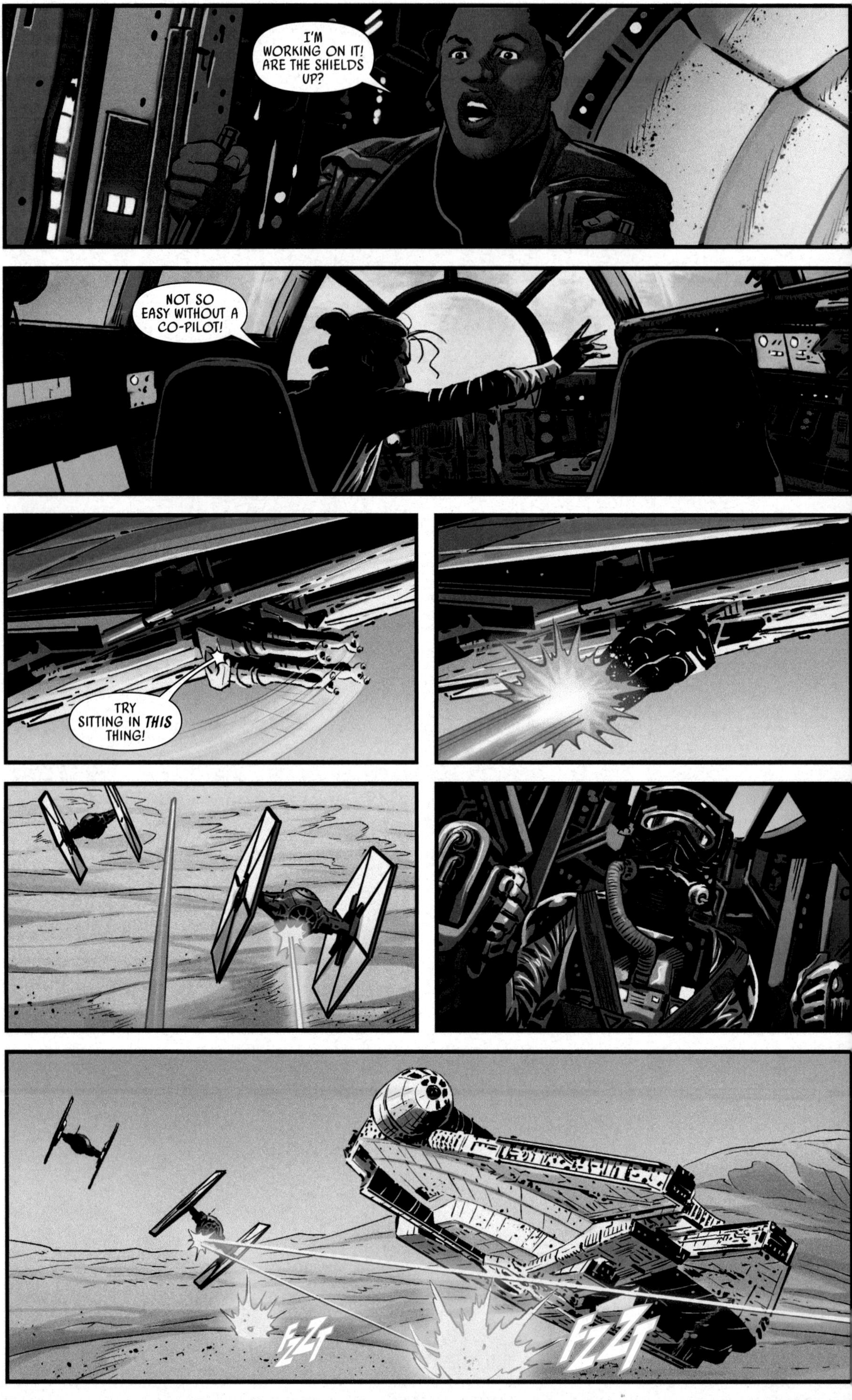
I'M WORKING ON IT! ARE THE SHIELDS UP?
NOT SO EASY WITHOUT A CO-PILOT!
TRY SITTING IN *THIS* THING!
FZZT
FZZT

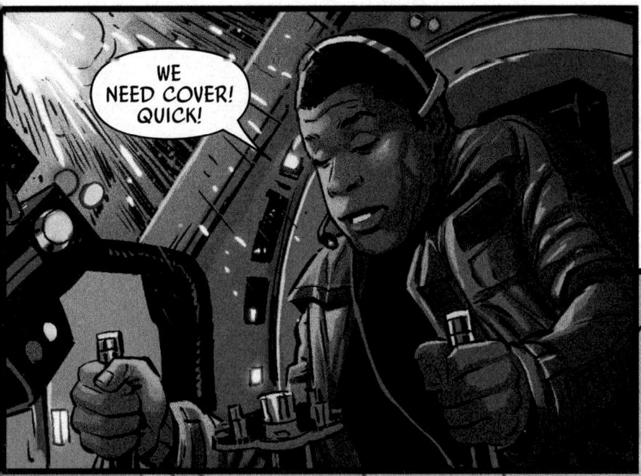
WE NEED COVER! QUICK!

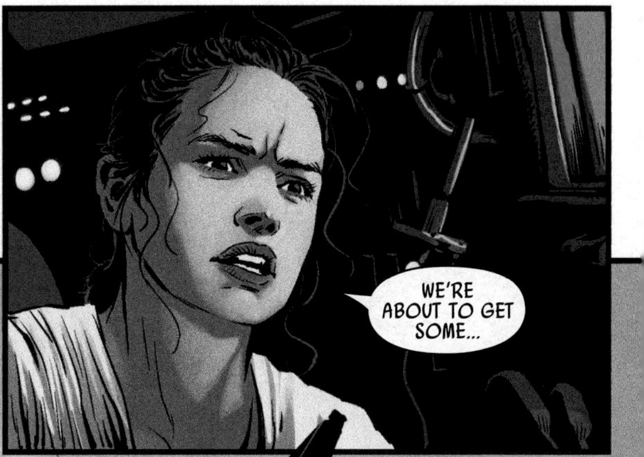
WE'RE ABOUT TO GET SOME...

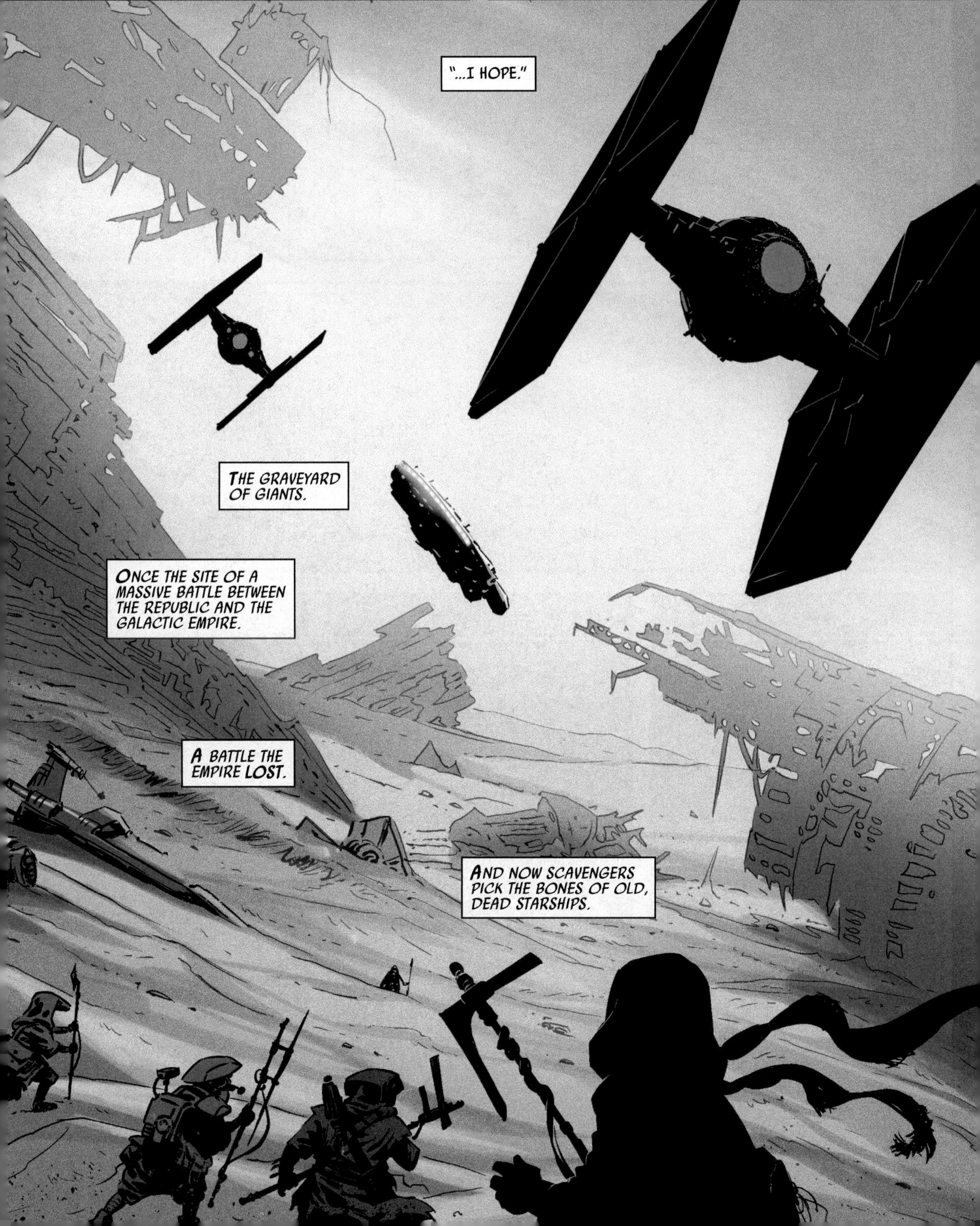
"...I HOPE."
THE GRAVEYARD OF GIANTS.
ONCE THE SITE OF A MASSIVE BATTLE BETWEEN THE REPUBLIC AND THE GALACTIC EMPIRE.
A BATTLE THE EMPIRE LOST.
AND NOW SCAVENGERS PICK THE BONES OF OLD, DEAD STARSHIPS.

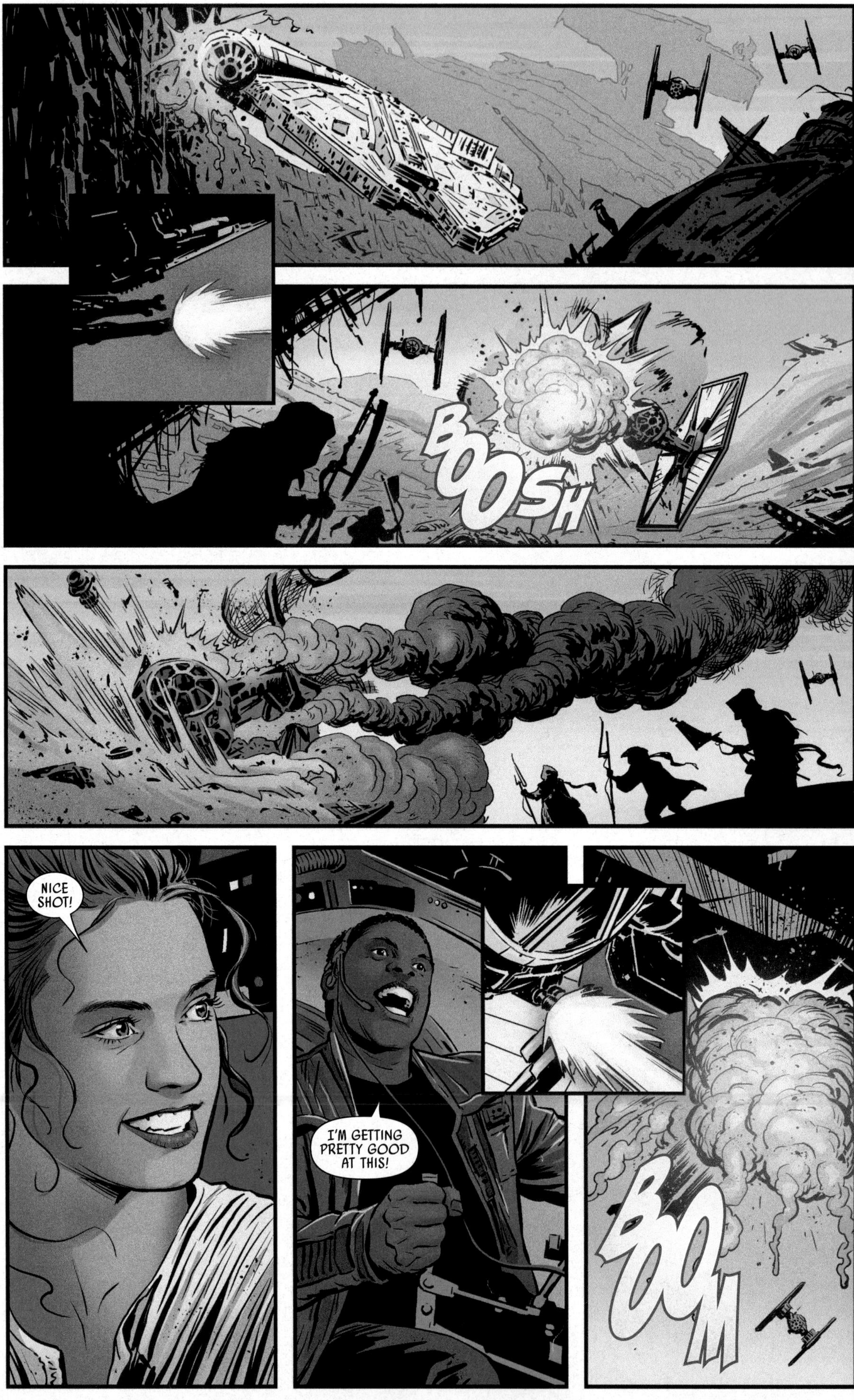
BOOSH
NICE SHOT!
I'M GETTING PRETTY GOOD AT THIS!
BOOM

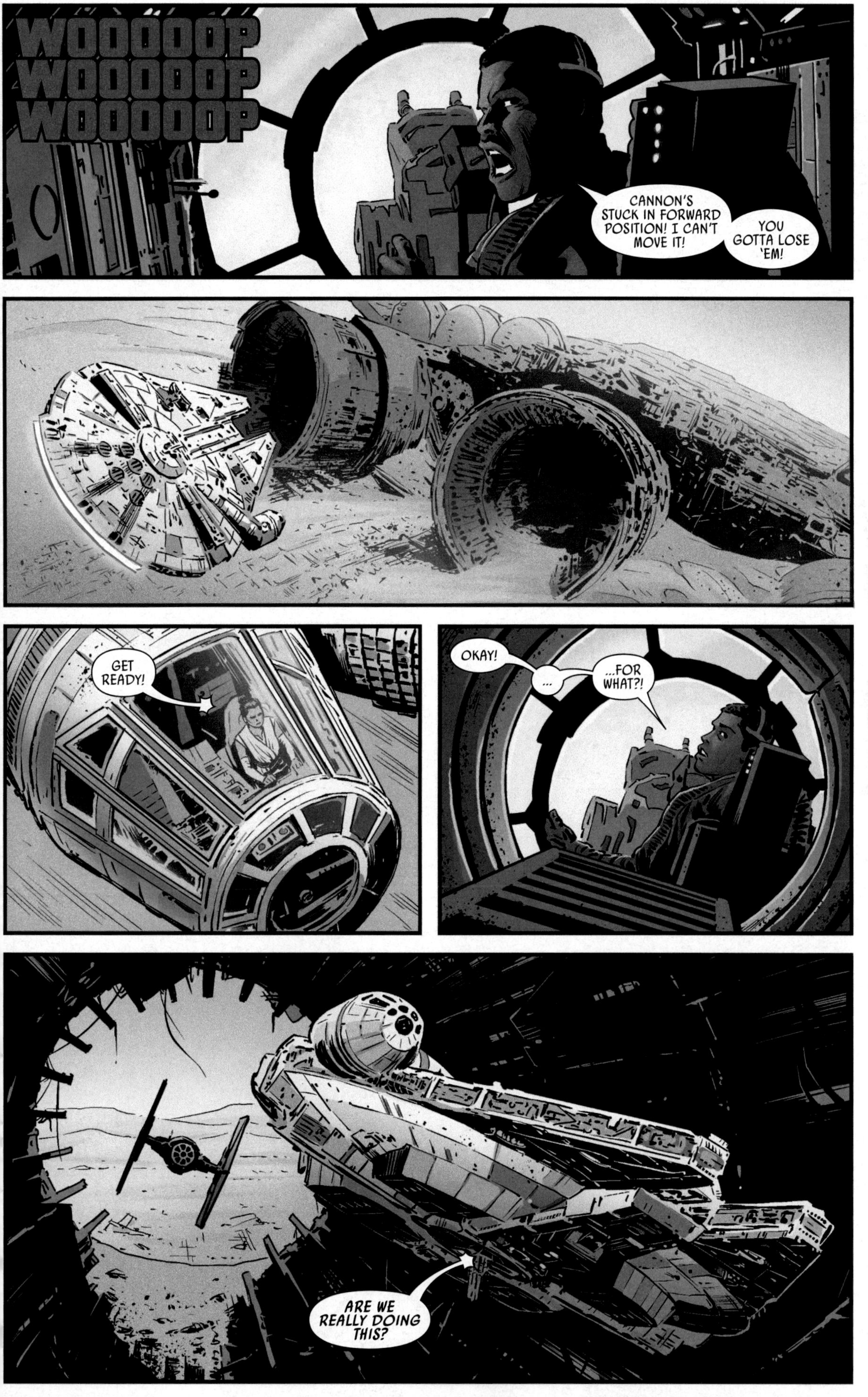
WOOOOOP
WOOOOOP
WOOOOOP
CANNON'S STUCK IN FORWARD POSITION! I CAN'T MOVE IT!
YOU GOTTA LOSE 'EM!
GET READY!
OKAY!
...
...FOR WHAT?!
ARE WE REALLY DOING THIS?

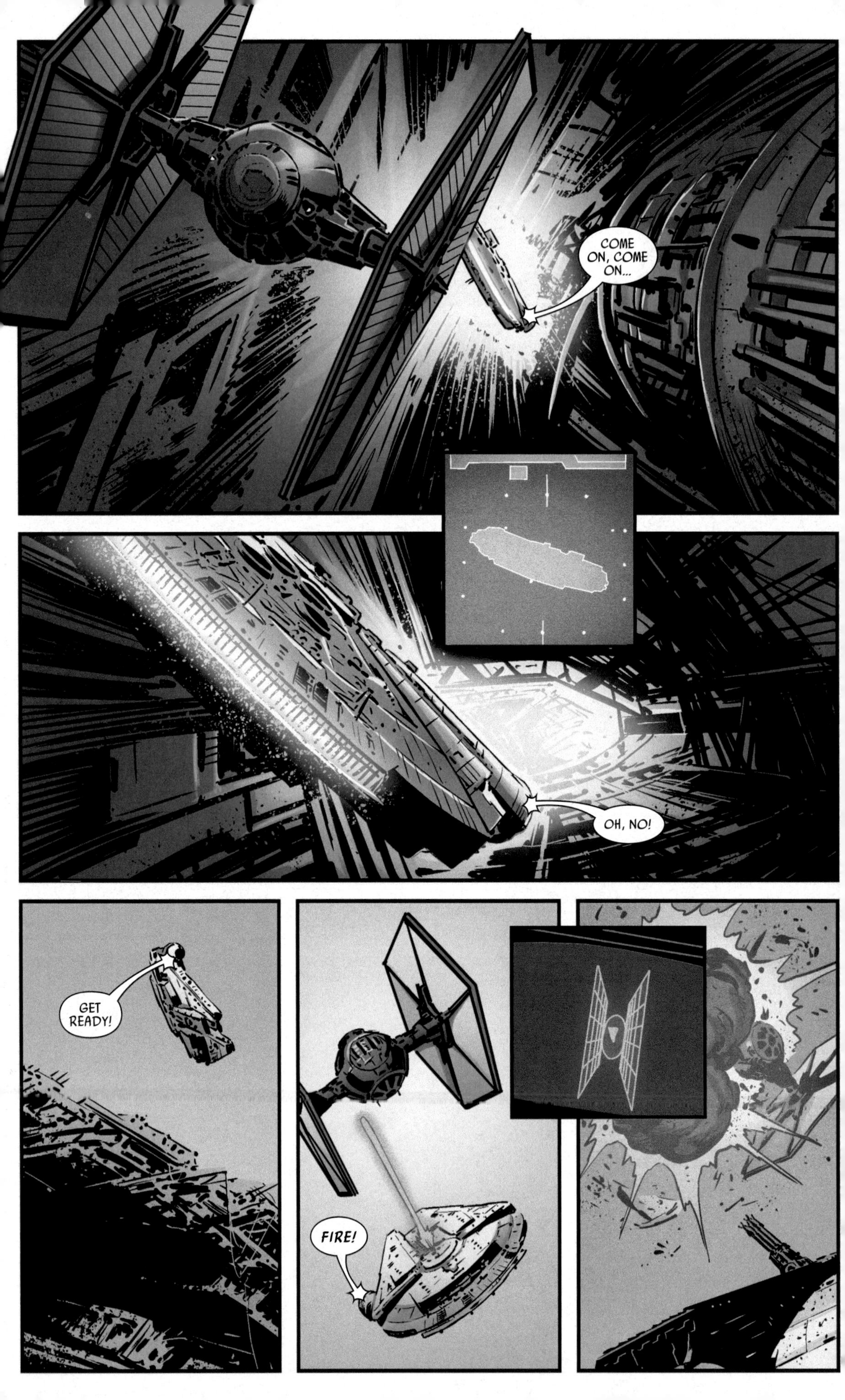
COME ON, COME ON...
OH, NO!
GET READY!
FIRE!

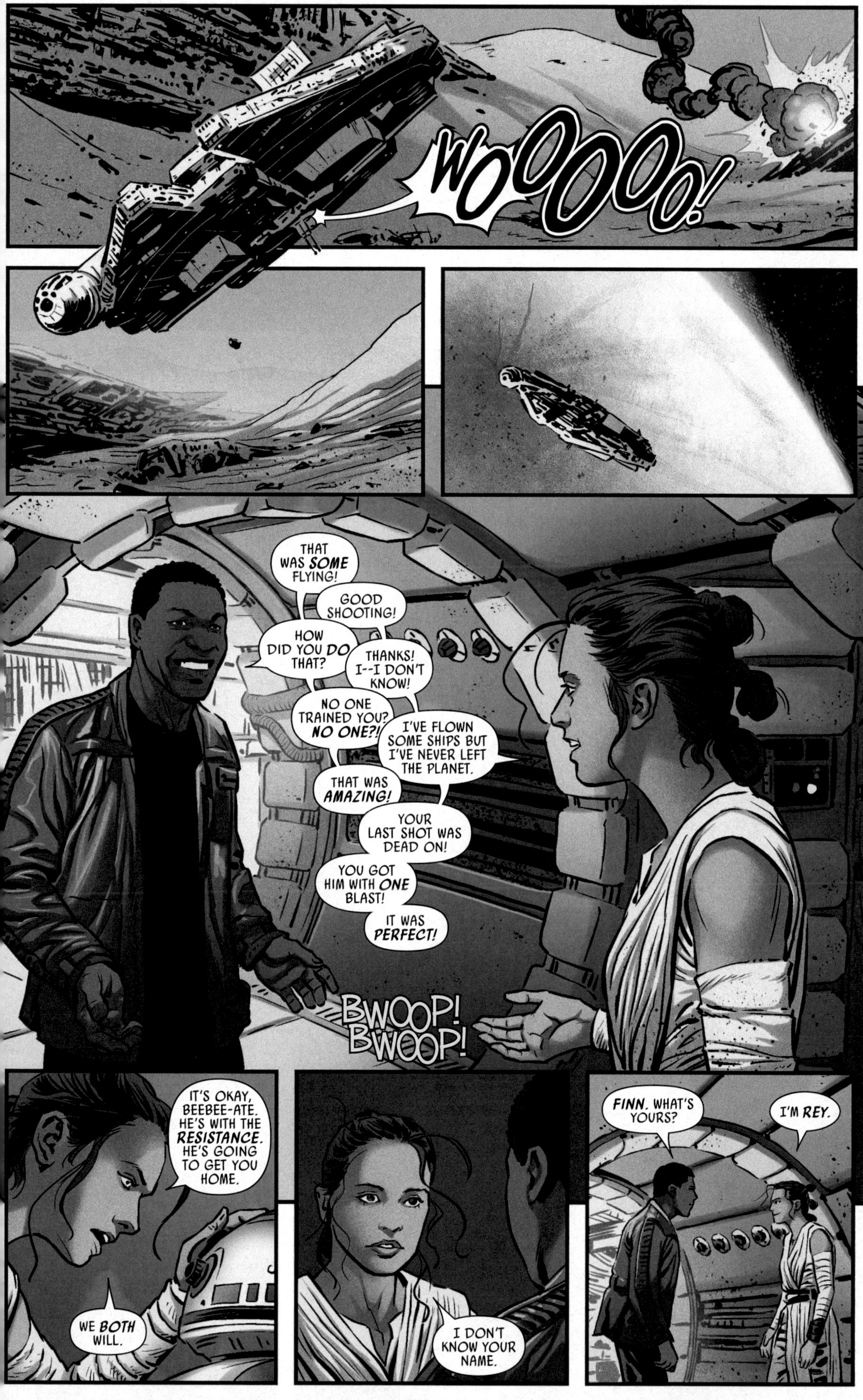

WOOOOOO!
THAT WAS SOME FLYING!
GOOD SHOOTING!
HOW DID YOU DO THAT?
THANKS! I--I DON'T KNOW!
NO ONE TRAINED YOU? NO ONE?!
I'VE FLOWN SOME SHIPS BUT I'VE NEVER LEFT THE PLANET.
THAT WAS AMAZING!
YOUR LAST SHOT WAS DEAD ON!
YOU GOT HIM WITH ONE BLAST!
IT WAS PERFECT!
BWOOP! BWOOP!
IT'S OKAY, BEEBEE-ATE. HE'S WITH THE RESISTANCE. HE'S GOING TO GET YOU HOME.
WE BOTH WILL.
I DON'T KNOW YOUR NAME.
FINN. WHAT'S YOURS?
I'M REY.

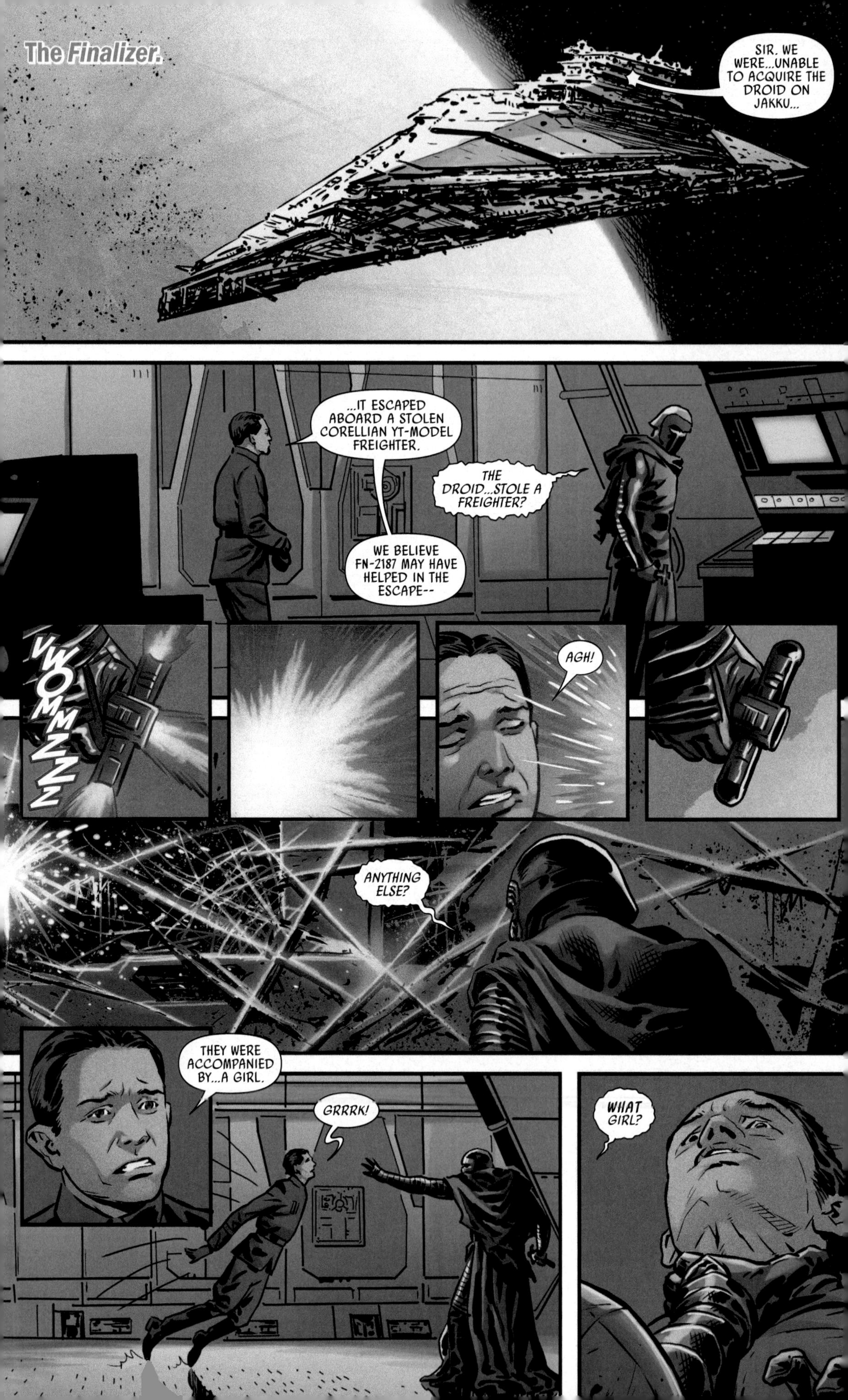
The Finalizer.
SIR. WE WERE...UNABLE TO ACQUIRE THE DROID ON JAKKU...
...IT ESCAPED ABOARD A STOLEN CORELLIAN YT-MODEL FREIGHTER.
THE DROID...STOLE A FREIGHTER?
WE BELIEVE FN-2187 MAY HAVE HELPED IN THE ESCAPE--
VWOMMZZZ
AGH!
ANYTHING ELSE?
THEY WERE ACCOMPANIED BY...A GIRL.
GRRRK!
WHAT GIRL?

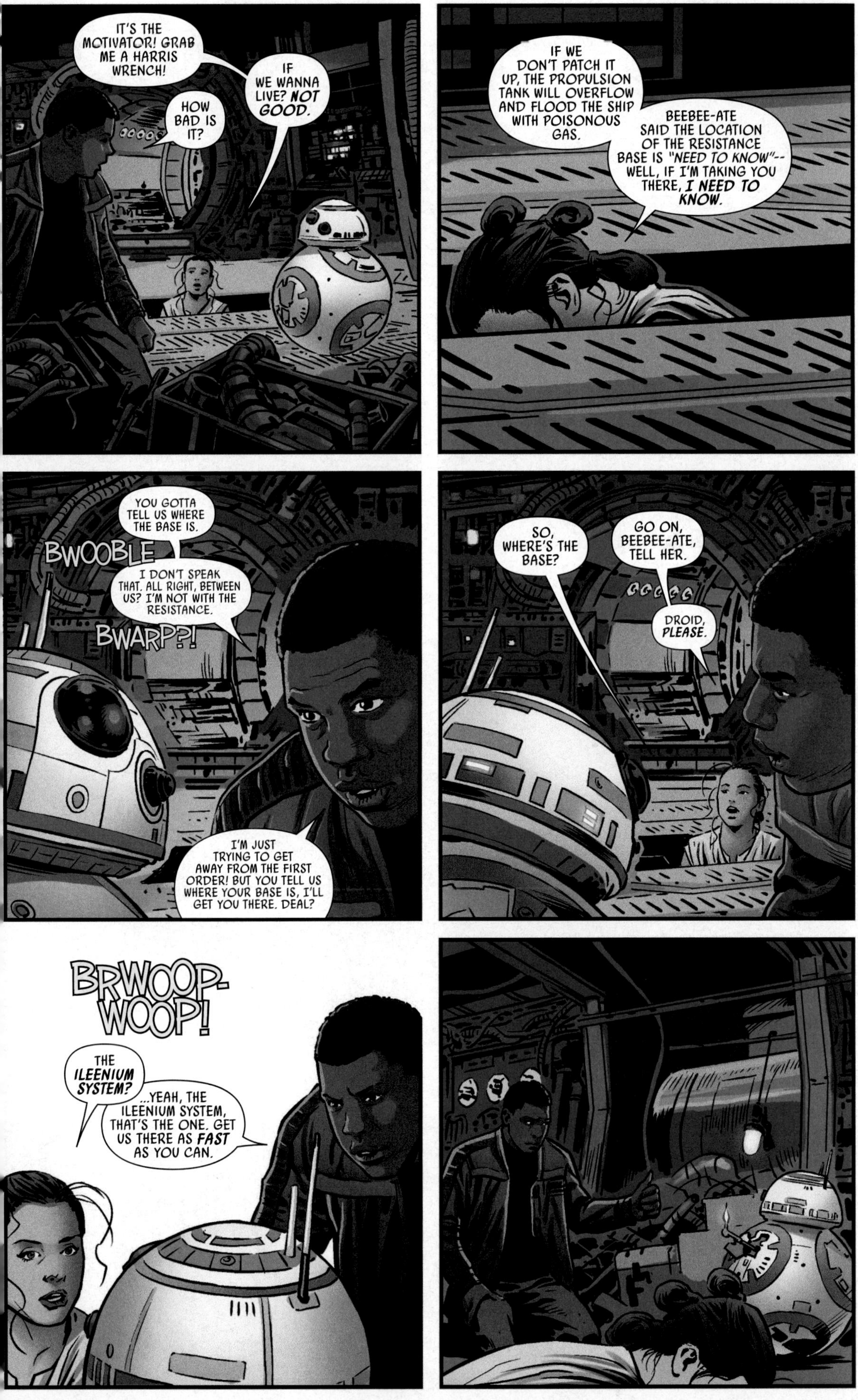
IT'S THE MOTIVATOR! GRAB ME A HARRIS WRENCH!
HOW BAD IS IT?
IF WE WANNA LIVE? NOT GOOD.
IF WE DON'T PATCH IT UP, THE PROPULSION TANK WILL OVERFLOW AND FLOOD THE SHIP WITH POISONOUS GAS.
BEEBEE-ATE SAID THE LOCATION OF THE RESISTANCE BASE IS "NEED TO KNOW"-- WELL, IF I'M TAKING YOU THERE, I NEED TO KNOW.
YOU GOTTA TELL US WHERE THE BASE IS.
BWOOBLE
I DON'T SPEAK THAT. ALL RIGHT, BETWEEN US? I'M NOT WITH THE RESISTANCE.
BWARP?!
I'M JUST TRYING TO GET AWAY FROM THE FIRST ORDER! BUT YOU TELL US WHERE YOUR BASE IS, I'LL GET YOU THERE. DEAL?
SO, WHERE'S THE BASE?
GO ON, BEEBEE-ATE, TELL HER.
DROID, PLEASE.
BRWOOP-WOOP!
THE ILEENIUM SYSTEM?
...YEAH, THE ILEENIUM SYSTEM, THAT'S THE ONE. GET US THERE AS FAST AS YOU CAN.

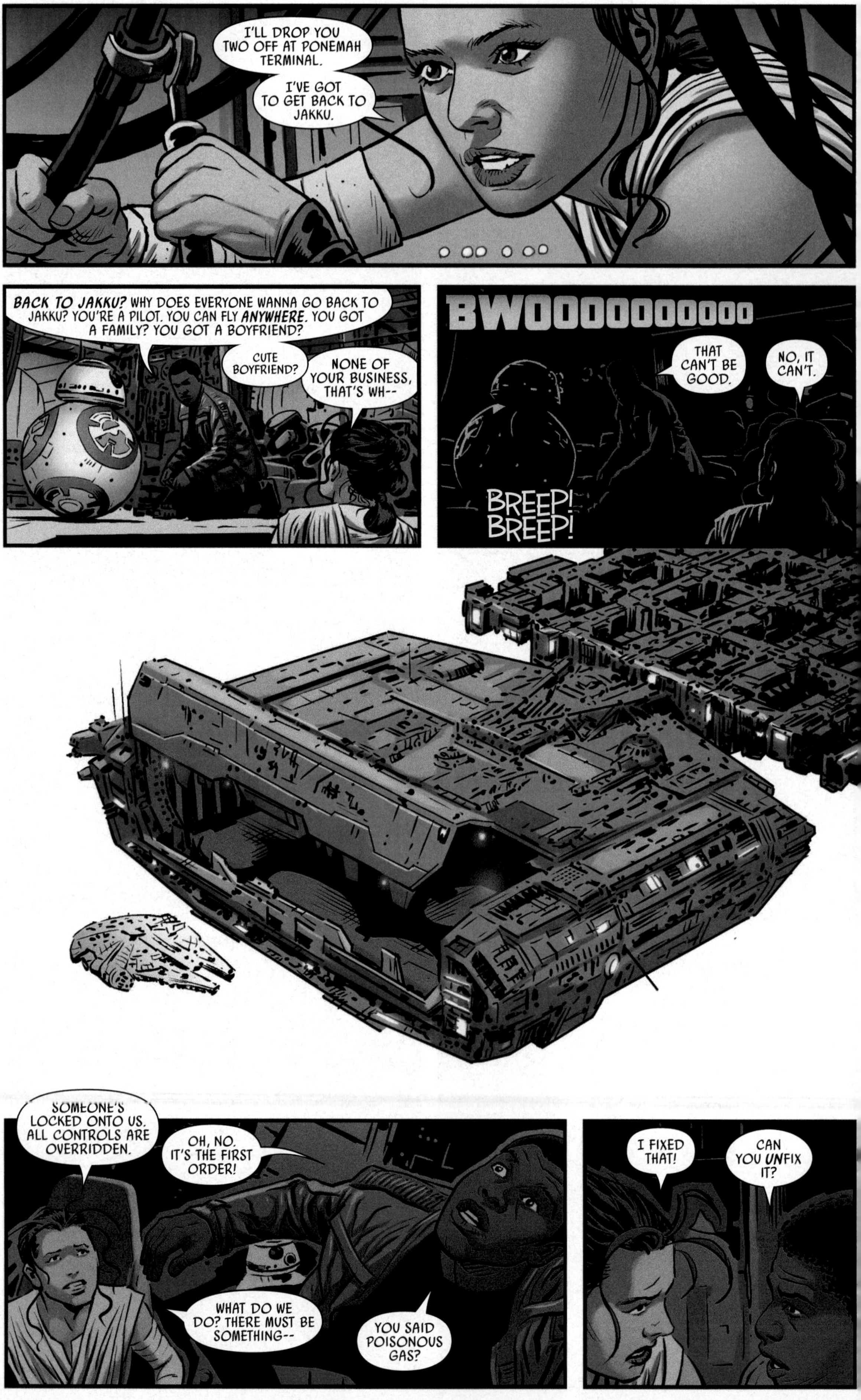

I'LL DROP YOU TWO OFF AT PONEMAH TERMINAL.
I'VE GOT TO GET BACK TO JAKKU.
BACK TO JAKKU? WHY DOES EVERYONE WANNA GO BACK TO JAKKU? YOU'RE A PILOT. YOU CAN FLY ANYWHERE. YOU GOT A FAMILY? YOU GOT A BOYFRIEND?
CUTE BOYFRIEND?
NONE OF YOUR BUSINESS, THAT'S WH--
BWOOOOOOOOOO
THAT CAN'T BE GOOD.
NO, IT CAN'T.
BREEP! BREEP!
SOMEONE'S LOCKED ONTO US. ALL CONTROLS ARE OVERRIDDEN.
OH, NO. IT'S THE FIRST ORDER!
WHAT DO WE DO? THERE MUST BE SOMETHING--
YOU SAID POISONOUS GAS?
I FIXED THAT!
CAN YOU UNFIX IT?

HISSSSS
CHEWIE... WE'RE HOME.
RRRRAARWRR!

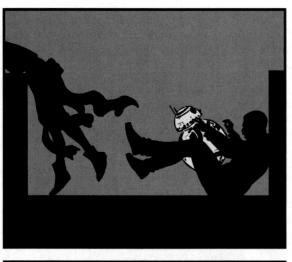

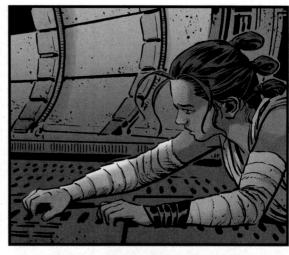

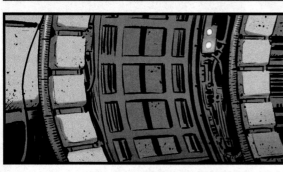

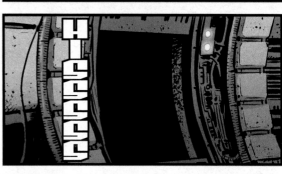

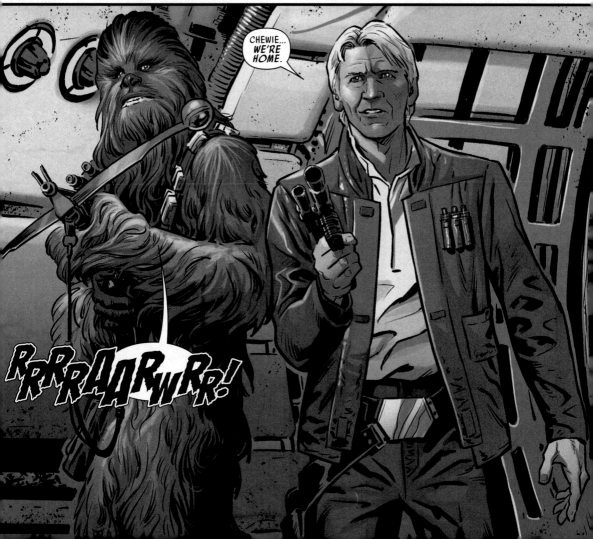

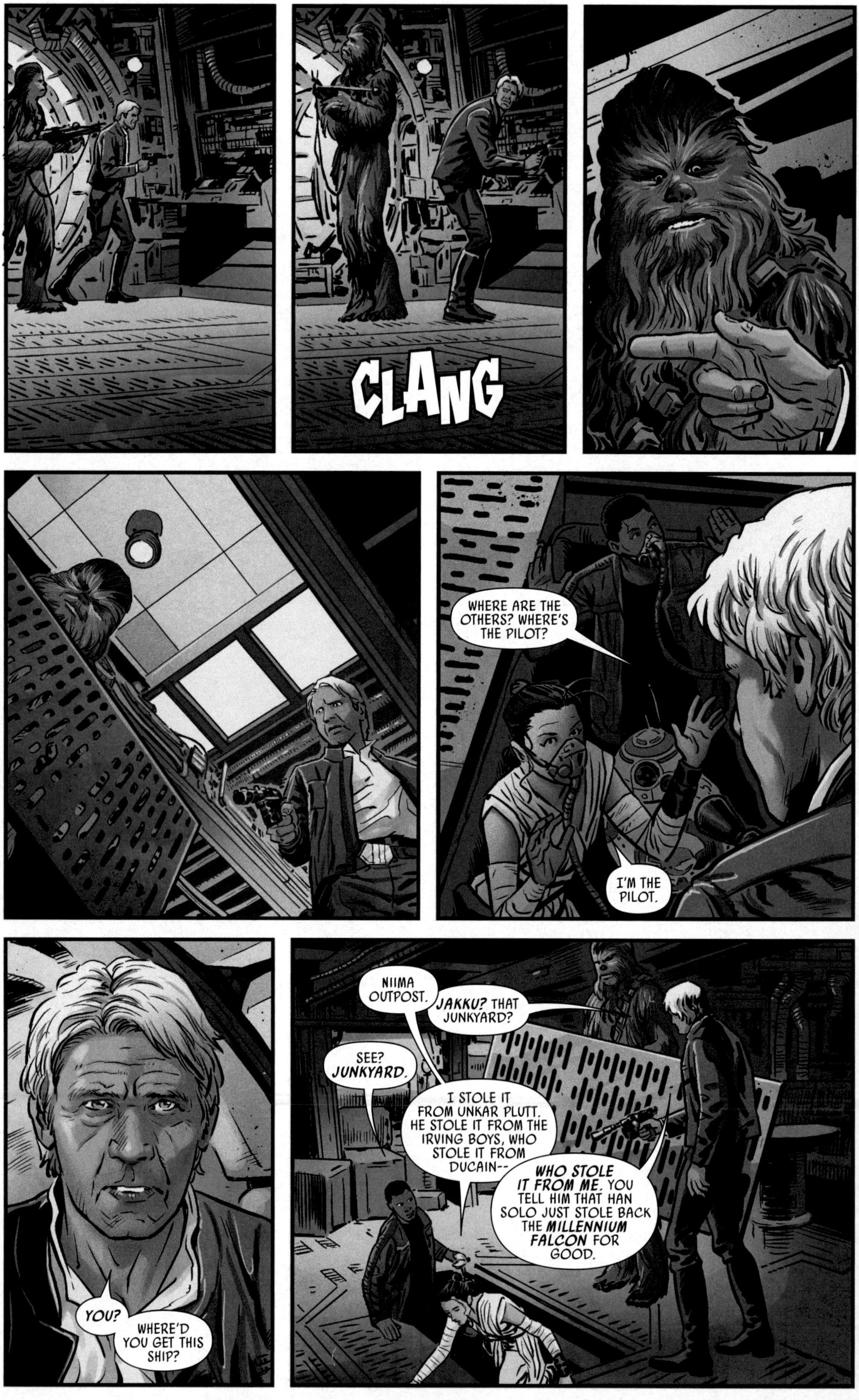
CLANG
WHERE ARE THE OTHERS? WHERE'S THE PILOT?
I'M THE PILOT.
YOU?
WHERE'D YOU GET THIS SHIP?
NIIMA OUTPOST.
JAKKU? THAT JUNKYARD?
SEE? JUNKYARD.
I STOLE IT FROM UNKAR PLUTT. HE STOLE IT FROM THE IRVING BOYS, WHO STOLE IT FROM DUCAIN--
WHO STOLE IT FROM ME. YOU TELL HIM THAT HAN SOLO JUST STOLE BACK THE MILLENNIUM FALCON FOR GOOD.

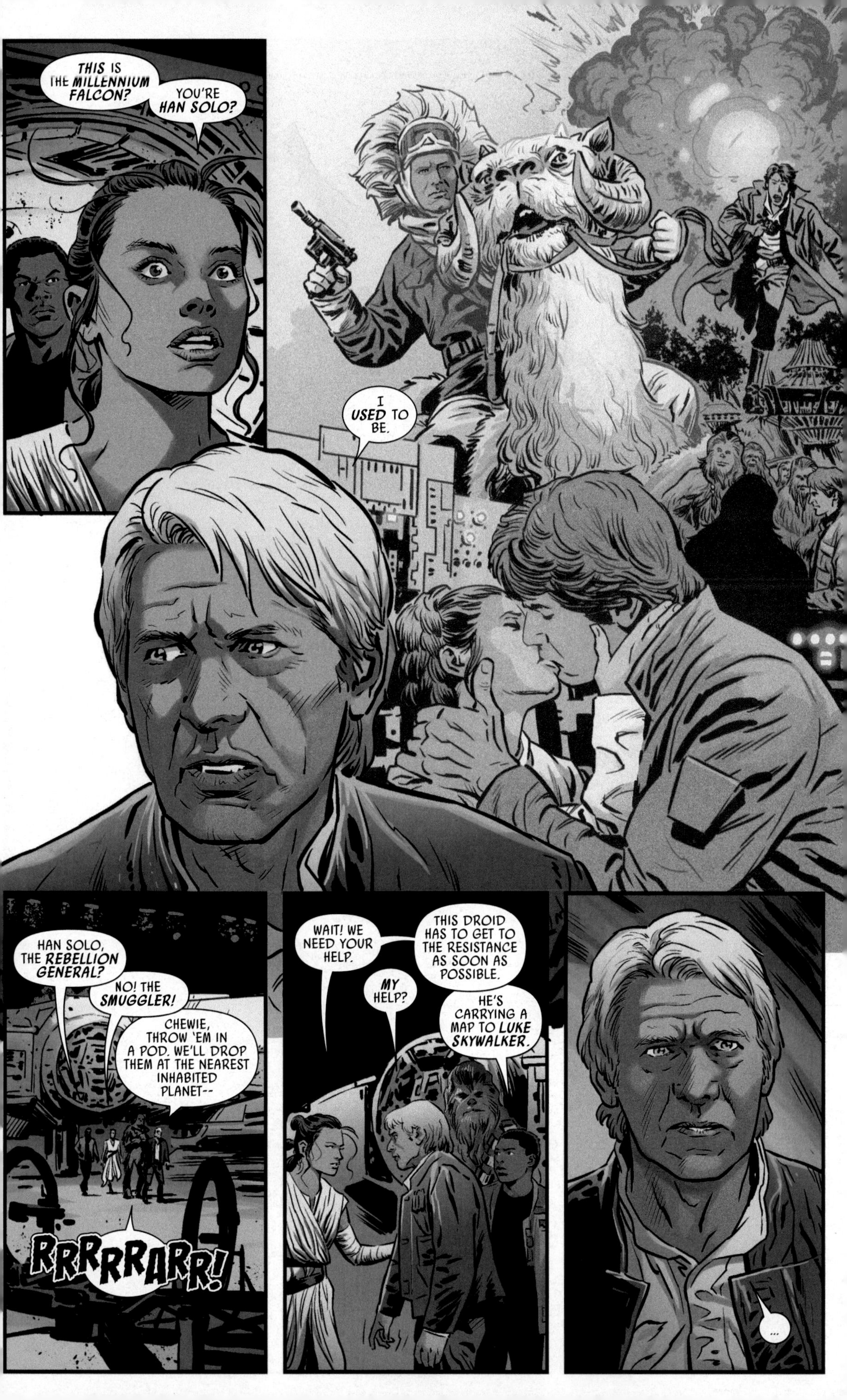
THIS IS THE MILLENNIUM FALCON?
YOU'RE HAN SOLO?
I USED TO BE.
HAN SOLO, THE REBELLION GENERAL?
NO! THE SMUGGLER!
CHEWIE, THROW 'EM IN A POD. WE'LL DROP THEM AT THE NEAREST INHABITED PLANET--
RRRRRARR!
WAIT! WE NEED YOUR HELP.
THIS DROID HAS TO GET TO THE RESISTANCE AS SOON AS POSSIBLE.
MY HELP?
HE'S CARRYING A MAP TO LUKE SKYWALKER.
...

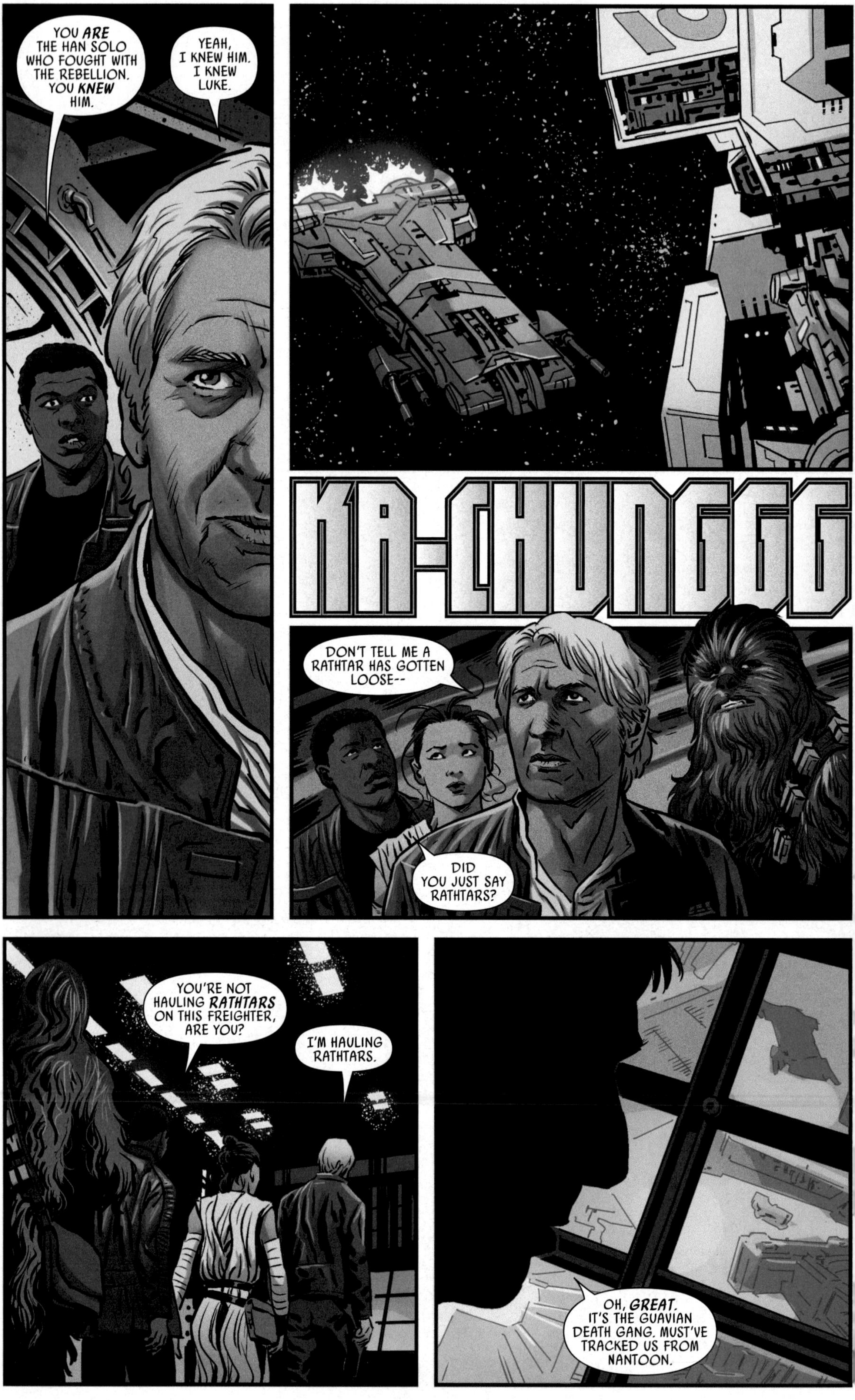
YOU ARE THE HAN SOLO WHO FOUGHT WITH THE REBELLION. YOU KNEW HIM.
YEAH, I KNEW HIM. I KNEW LUKE.
KA-CHUNGGG
DON'T TELL ME A RATHTAR HAS GOTTEN LOOSE--
DID YOU JUST SAY RATHTARS?
YOU'RE NOT HAULING RATHTARS ON THIS FREIGHTER, ARE YOU?
I'M HAULING RATHTARS.
OH, GREAT. IT'S THE GUAVIAN DEATH GANG. MUST'VE TRACKED US FROM NANTOON.

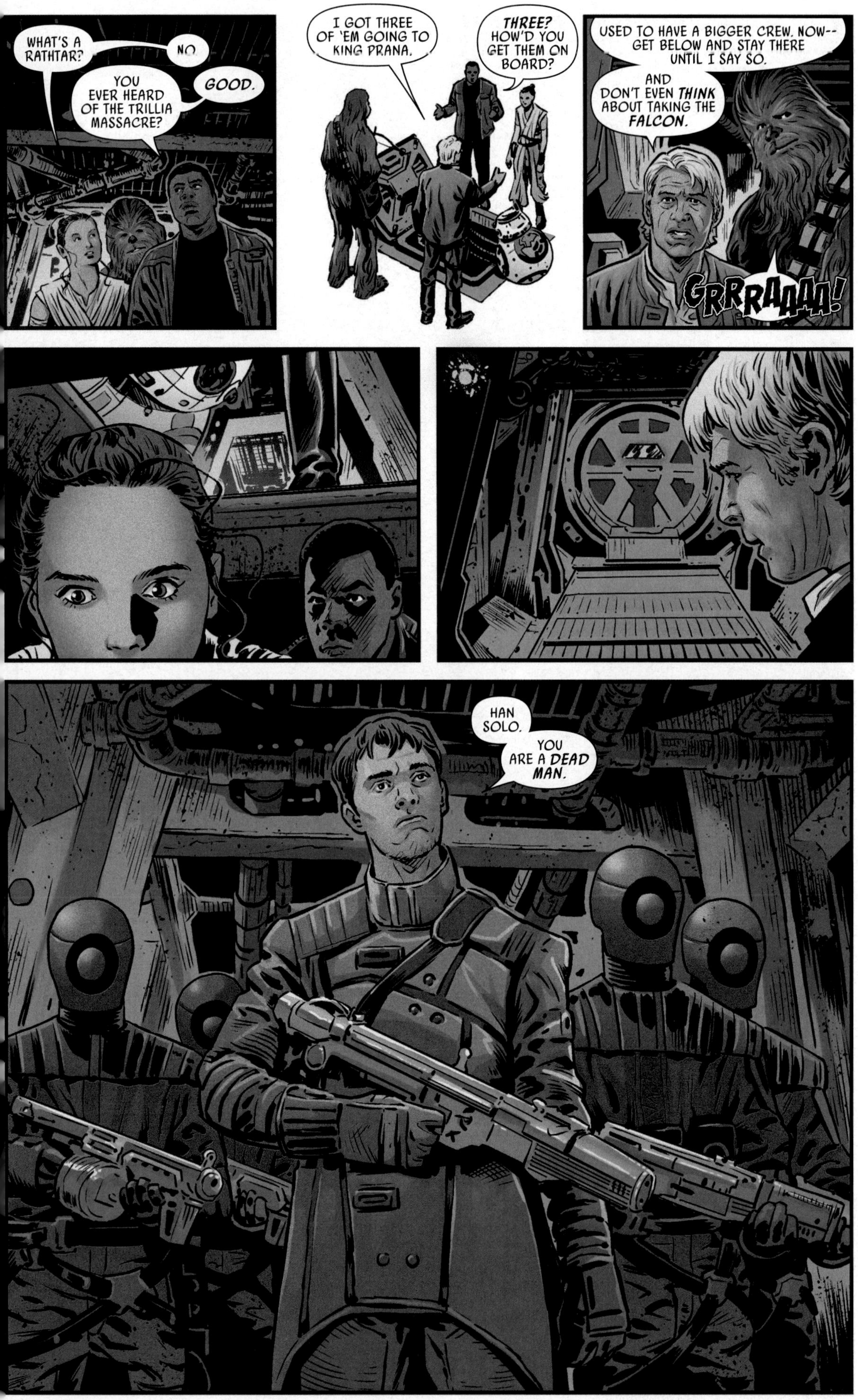
WHAT'S A RATHTAR?
NO.
YOU EVER HEARD OF THE TRILLIA MASSACRE?
GOOD.
I GOT THREE OF 'EM GOING TO KING PRANA.
THREE? HOW'D YOU GET THEM ON BOARD?
USED TO HAVE A BIGGER CREW. NOW-- GET BELOW AND STAY THERE UNTIL I SAY SO.
AND DON'T EVEN THINK ABOUT TAKING THE FALCON.
GRRRAAAA!
HAN SOLO.
YOU ARE A DEAD MAN.

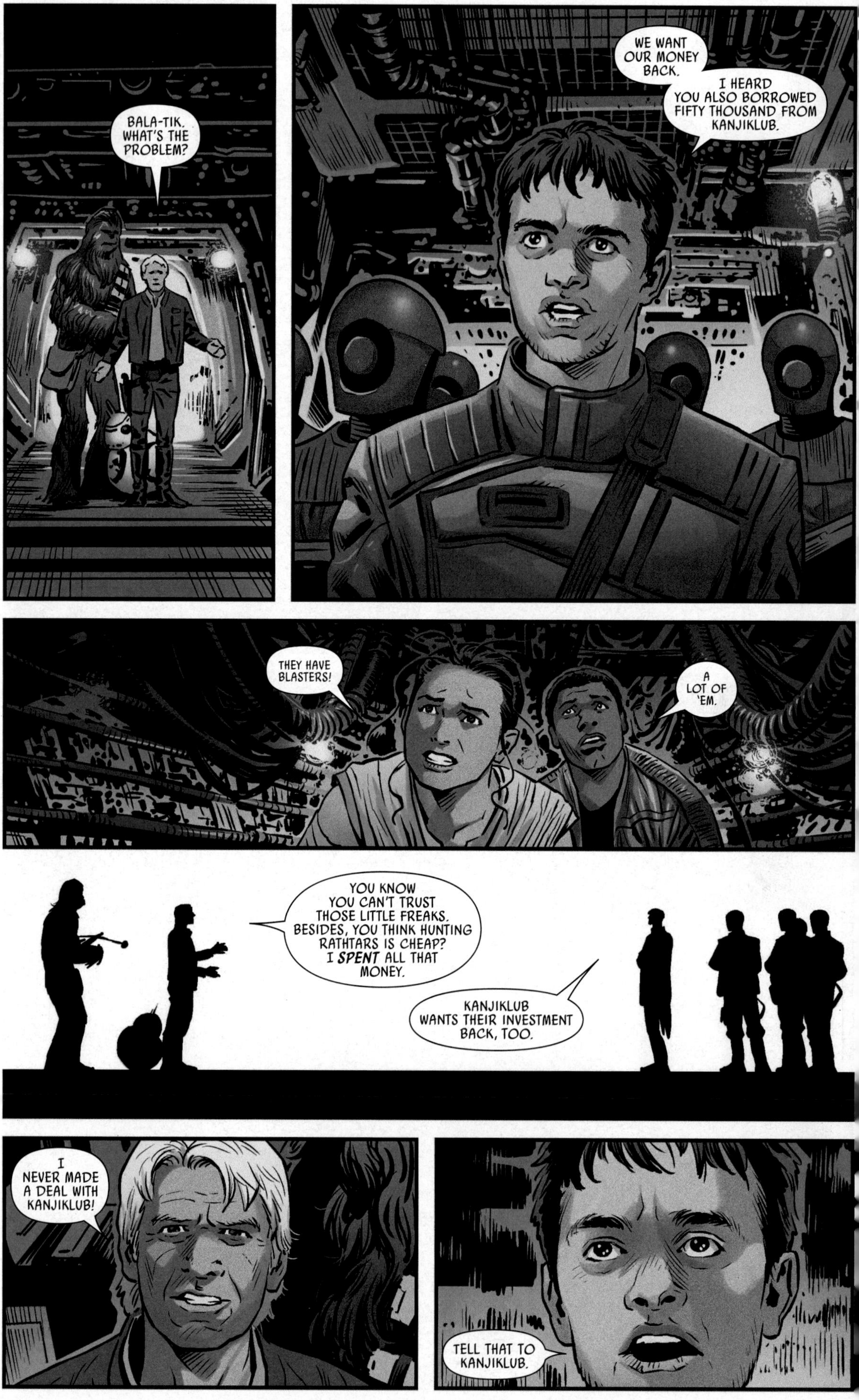
BALA-TIK. WHAT'S THE PROBLEM?
WE WANT OUR MONEY BACK.
I HEARD YOU ALSO BORROWED FIFTY THOUSAND FROM KANJIKLUB.
THEY HAVE BLASTERS!
A LOT OF 'EM.
YOU KNOW YOU CAN'T TRUST THOSE LITTLE FREAKS. BESIDES, YOU THINK HUNTING RATHTARS IS CHEAP? I *SPENT* ALL THAT MONEY.
KANJIKLUB WANTS THEIR INVESTMENT BACK, TOO.
I NEVER MADE A DEAL WITH KANJIKLUB!
TELL THAT TO KANJIKLUB.

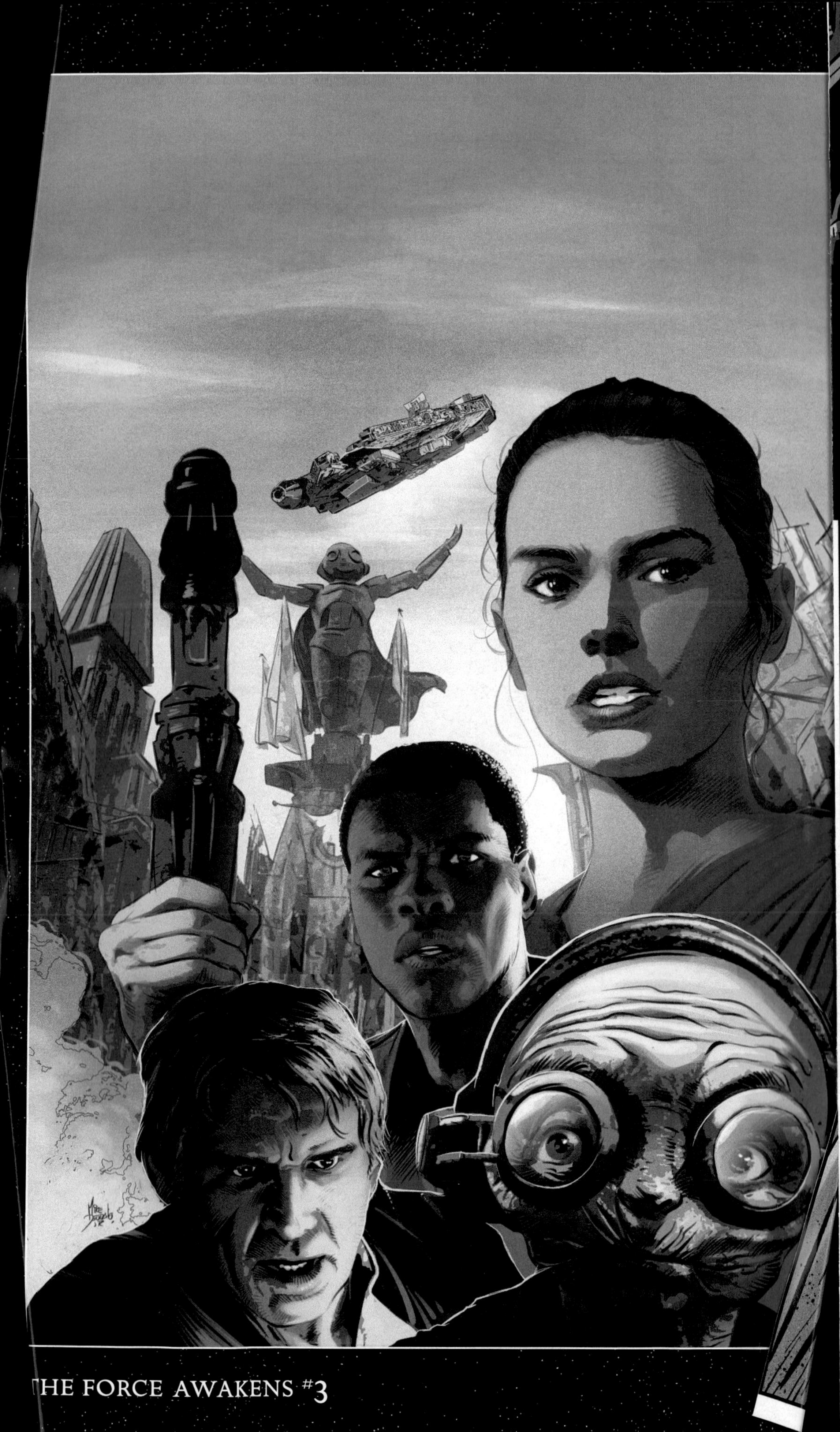
THE FORCE AWAKENS #3

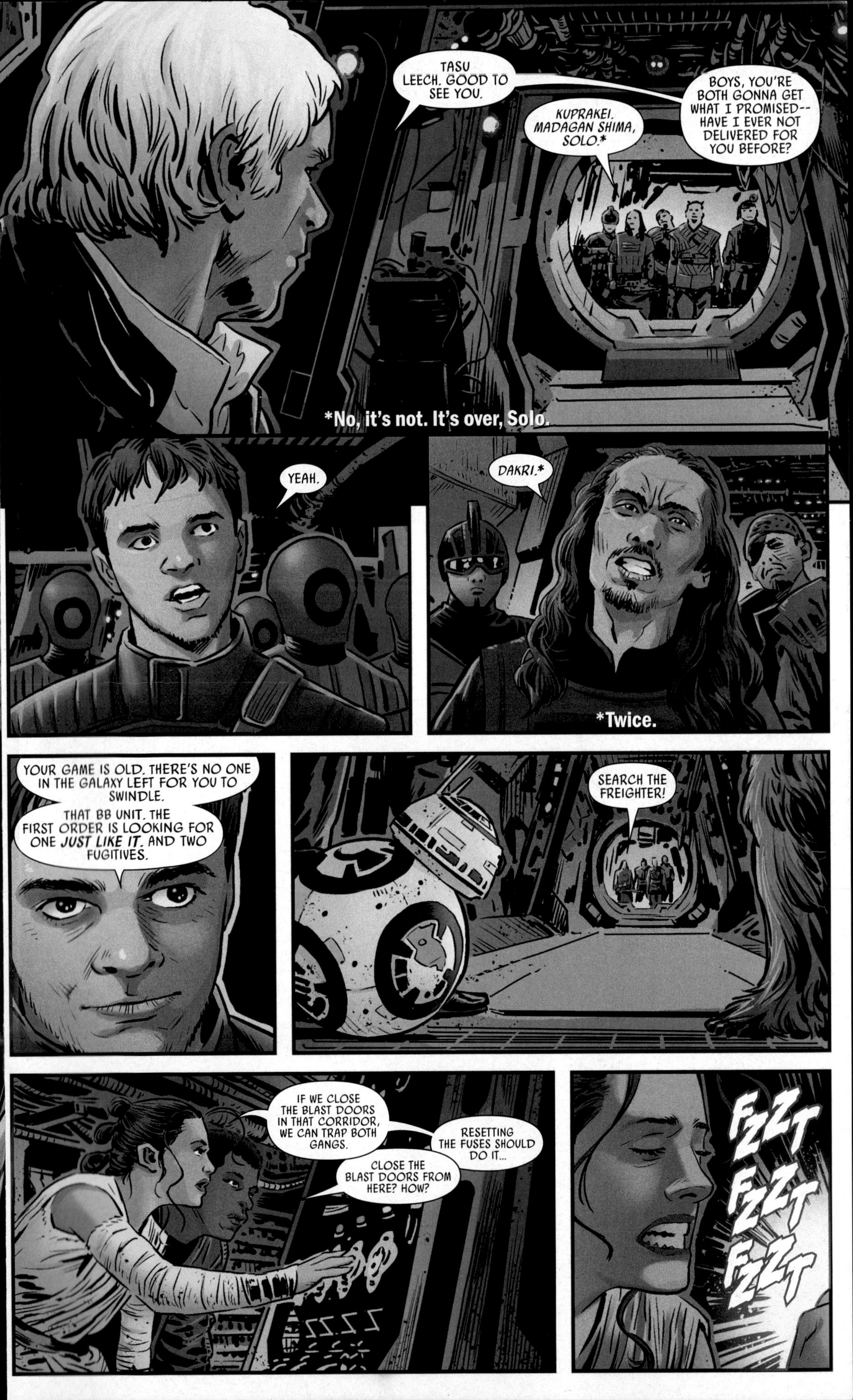
TASU LEECH. GOOD TO SEE YOU.
KUPRAKEI. MADAGAN SHIMA, SOLO.*
BOYS, YOU'RE BOTH GONNA GET WHAT I PROMISED-- HAVE I EVER NOT DELIVERED FOR YOU BEFORE?
*No, it's not. It's over, Solo.
YEAH.
DAKRI.*
*Twice.
YOUR GAME IS OLD. THERE'S NO ONE IN THE GALAXY LEFT FOR YOU TO SWINDLE.
THAT BB UNIT. THE FIRST ORDER IS LOOKING FOR ONE JUST LIKE IT. AND TWO FUGITIVES.
SEARCH THE FREIGHTER!
IF WE CLOSE THE BLAST DOORS IN THAT CORRIDOR, WE CAN TRAP BOTH GANGS.
CLOSE THE BLAST DOORS FROM HERE? HOW?
RESETTING THE FUSES SHOULD DO IT...
FZZT FZZT FZZT

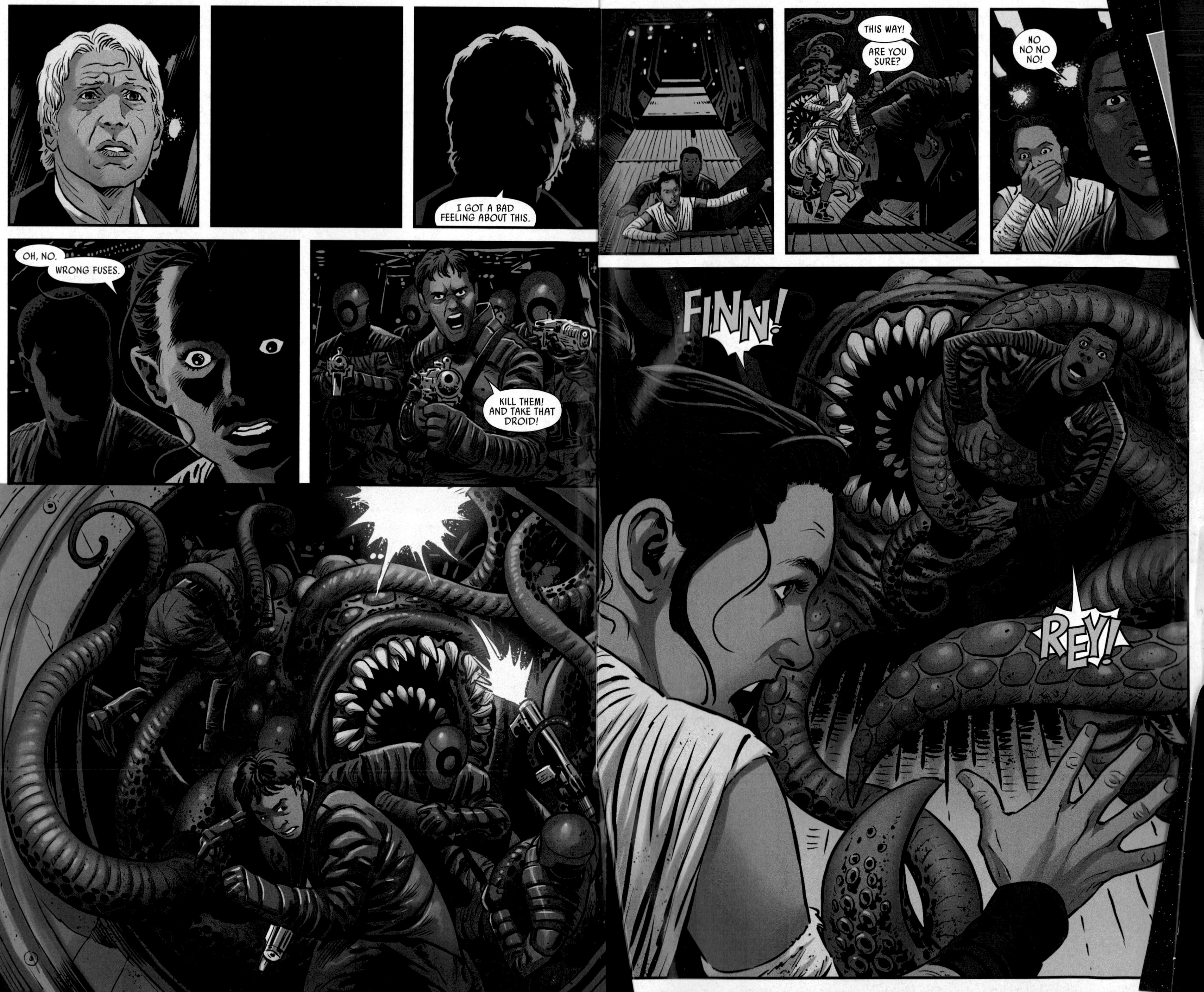
I GOT A BAD FEELING ABOUT THIS.
OH, NO.
WRONG FUSES.
KILL THEM! AND TAKE THAT DROID!
THIS WAY!
ARE YOU SURE?
NO NO NO NO!
FINN!
REY!

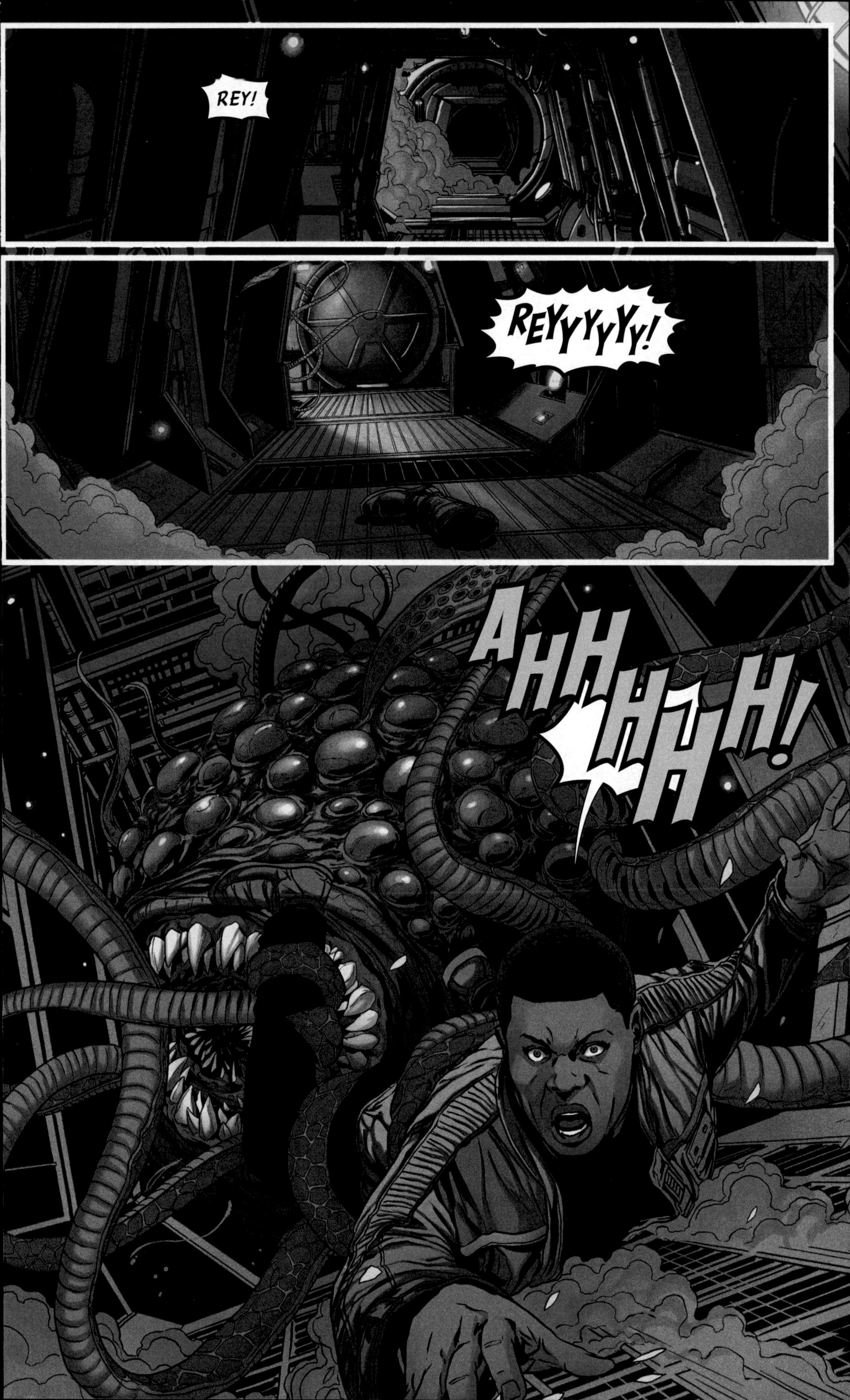
REY!
REYYYYYY!
AHHHHHH!

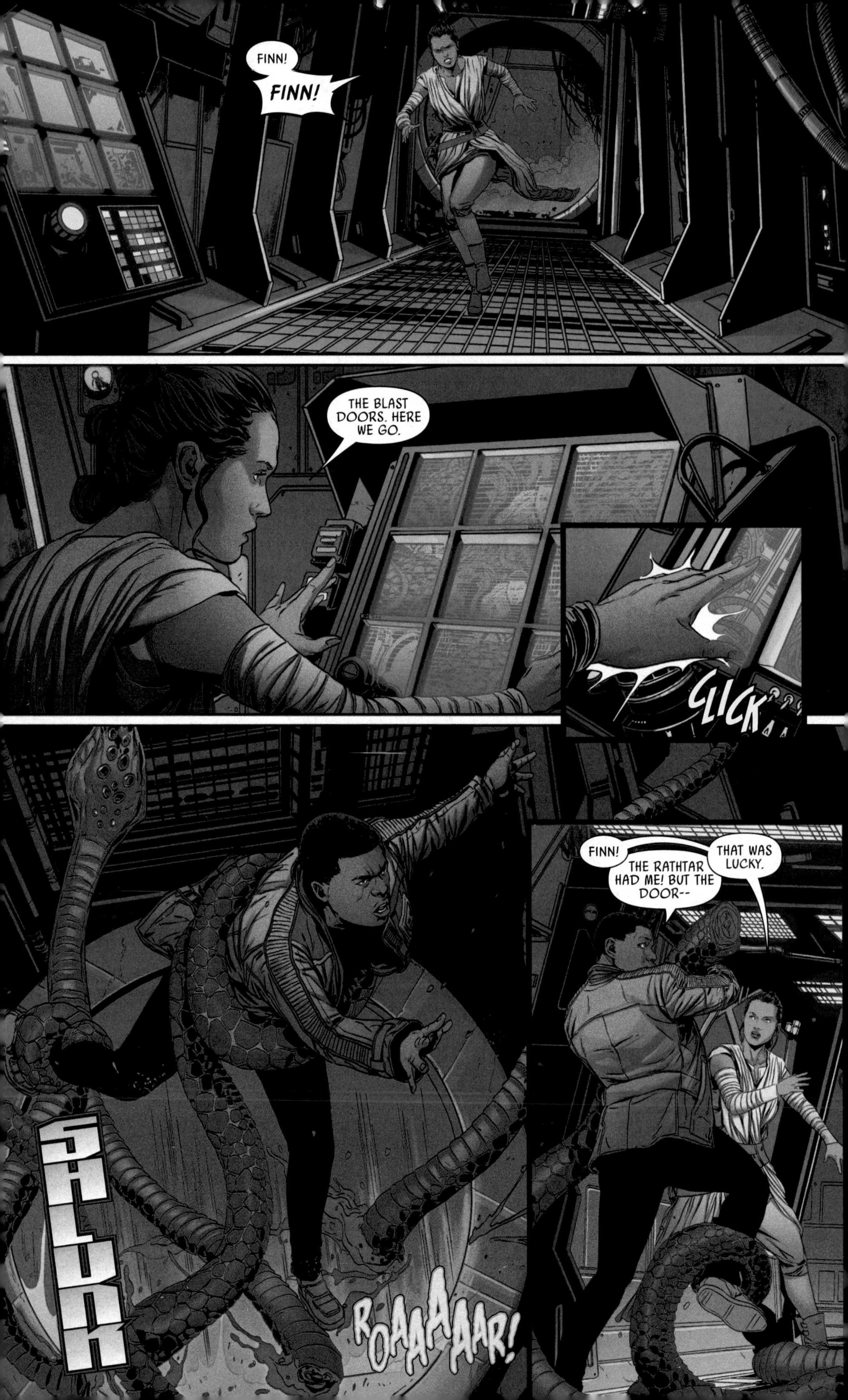
FINN!
FINN!
THE BLAST DOORS. HERE WE GO.
CLICK
SHLUK
ROAAAAAR!
FINN!
THE RATHTAR HAD ME! BUT THE DOOR--
THAT WAS LUCKY.

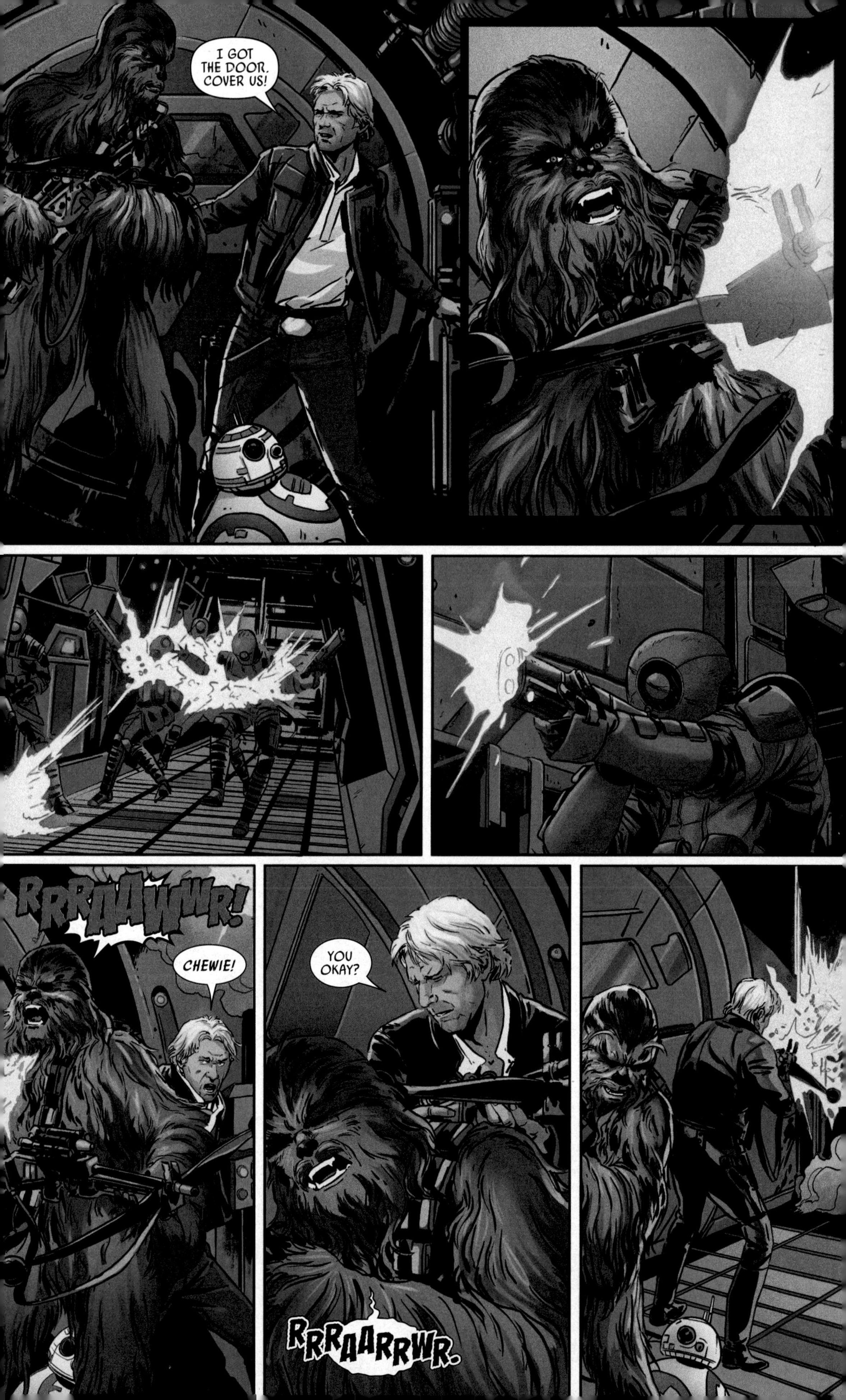
I GOT THE DOOR. COVER US!
RRRAAWWR!
CHEWIE!
YOU OKAY?
RRRAARRRWR.

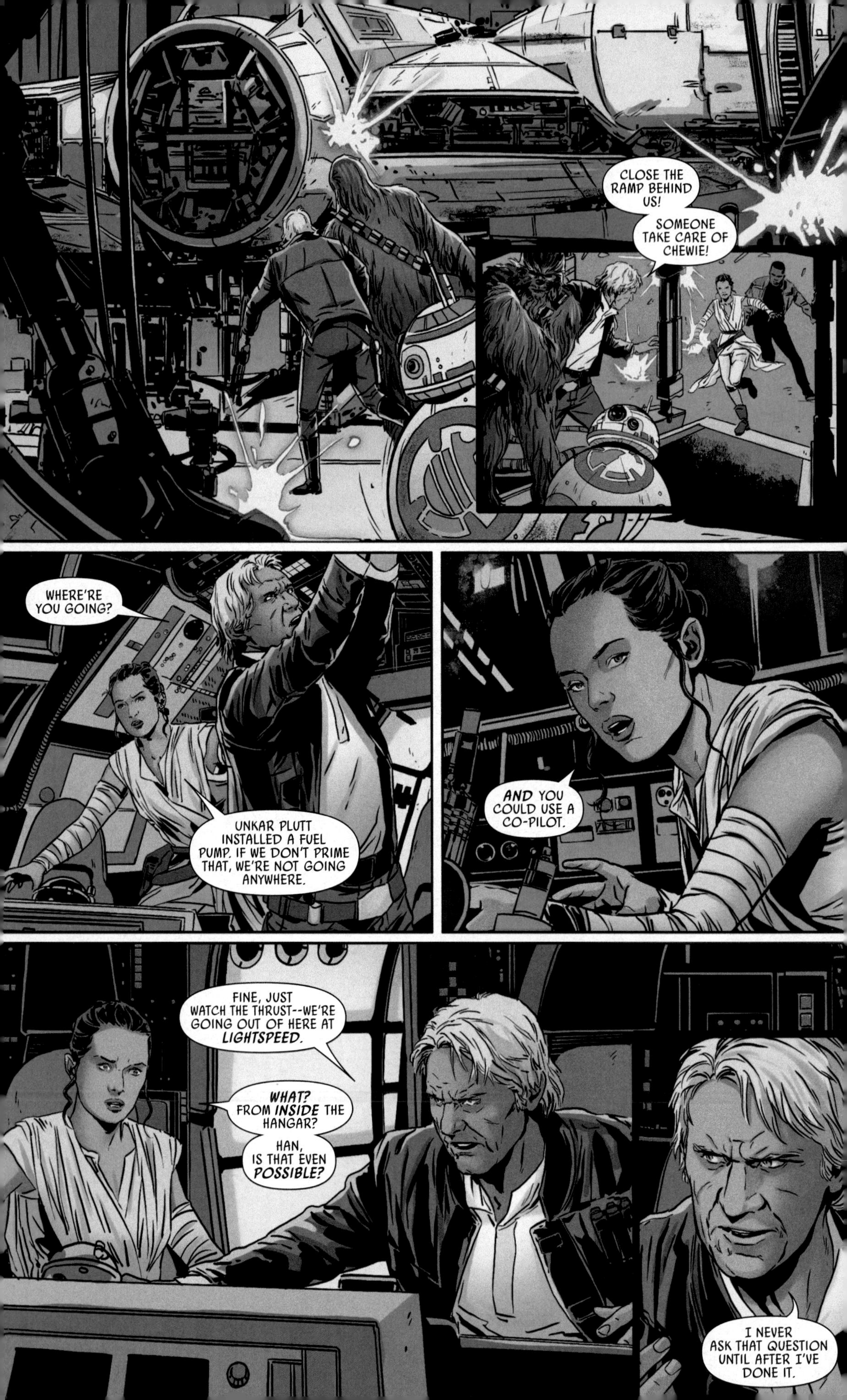
CLOSE THE RAMP BEHIND US!
SOMEONE TAKE CARE OF CHEWIE!
WHERE'RE YOU GOING?
UNKAR PLUTT INSTALLED A FUEL PUMP. IF WE DON'T PRIME THAT, WE'RE NOT GOING ANYWHERE.
AND YOU COULD USE A CO-PILOT.
FINE, JUST WATCH THE THRUST--WE'RE GOING OUT OF HERE AT LIGHTSPEED.
WHAT? FROM INSIDE THE HANGAR?
HAN, IS THAT EVEN POSSIBLE?
I NEVER ASK THAT QUESTION UNTIL AFTER I'VE DONE IT.

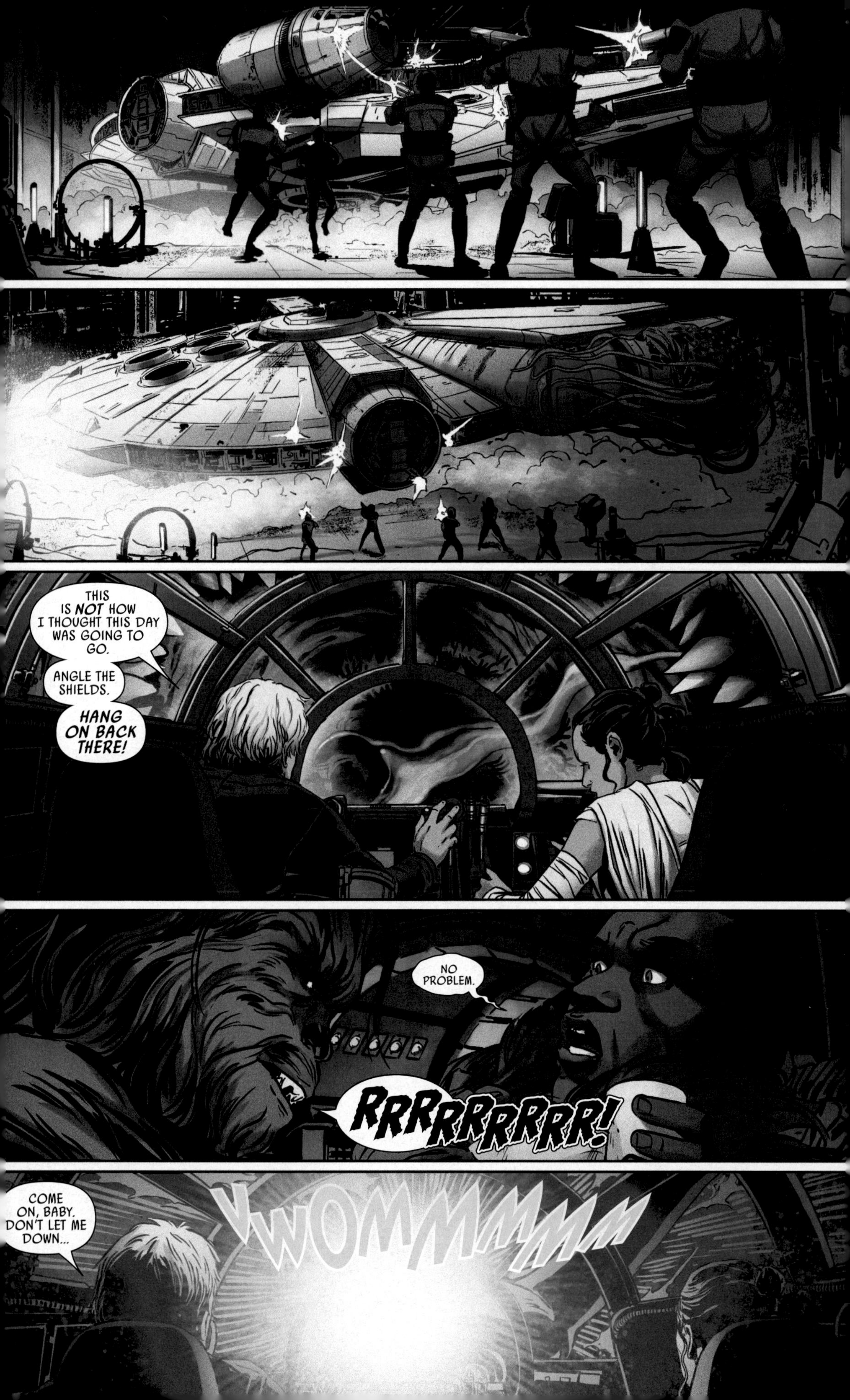
THIS IS **NOT** HOW I THOUGHT THIS DAY WAS GOING TO GO.
ANGLE THE SHIELDS.
HANG ON BACK THERE!
NO PROBLEM.
RRRRRRRRRR!
COME ON, BABY. DON'T LET ME DOWN...
VWOMMMMMM

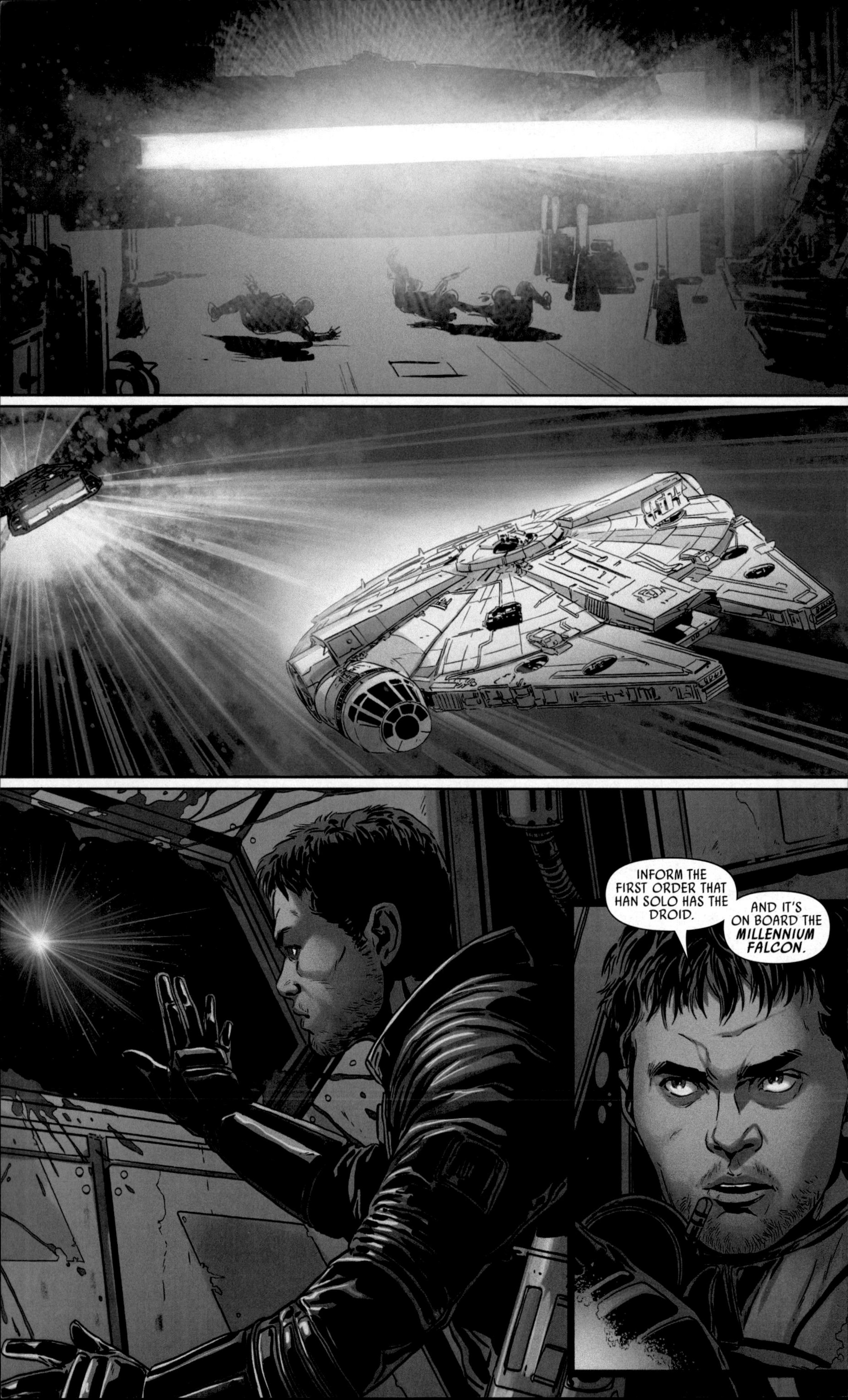
INFORM THE FIRST ORDER THAT HAN SOLO HAS THE DROID.
AND IT'S ON BOARD THE *MILLENNIUM FALCON*.

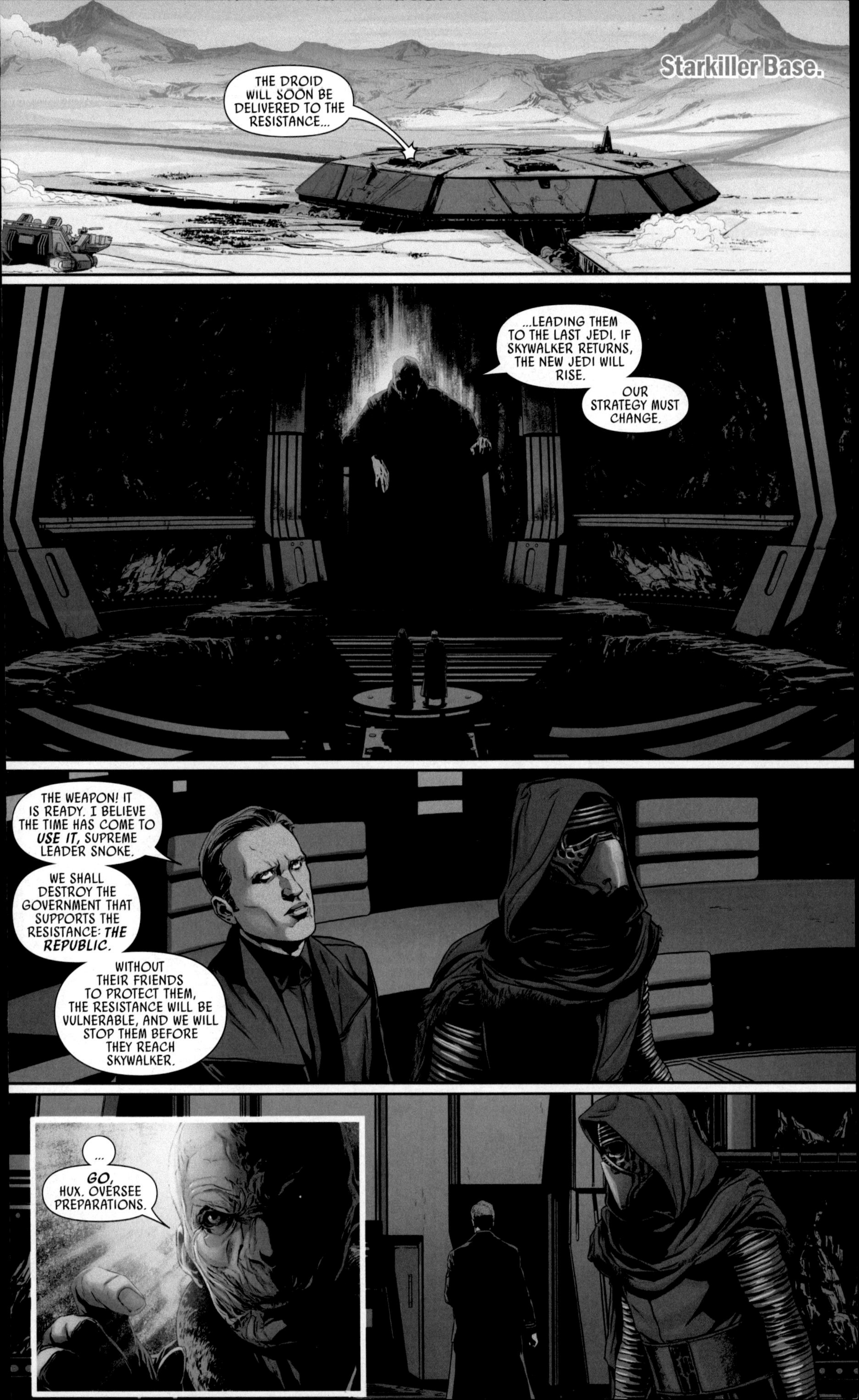
Starkiller Base.
THE DROID WILL SOON BE DELIVERED TO THE RESISTANCE...
...LEADING THEM TO THE LAST JEDI. IF SKYWALKER RETURNS, THE NEW JEDI WILL RISE.
OUR STRATEGY MUST CHANGE.
THE WEAPON! IT IS READY. I BELIEVE THE TIME HAS COME TO USE IT, SUPREME LEADER SNOKE.
WE SHALL DESTROY THE GOVERNMENT THAT SUPPORTS THE RESISTANCE: THE REPUBLIC.
WITHOUT THEIR FRIENDS TO PROTECT THEM, THE RESISTANCE WILL BE VULNERABLE, AND WE WILL STOP THEM BEFORE THEY REACH SKYWALKER.
...
GO, HUX. OVERSEE PREPARATIONS.

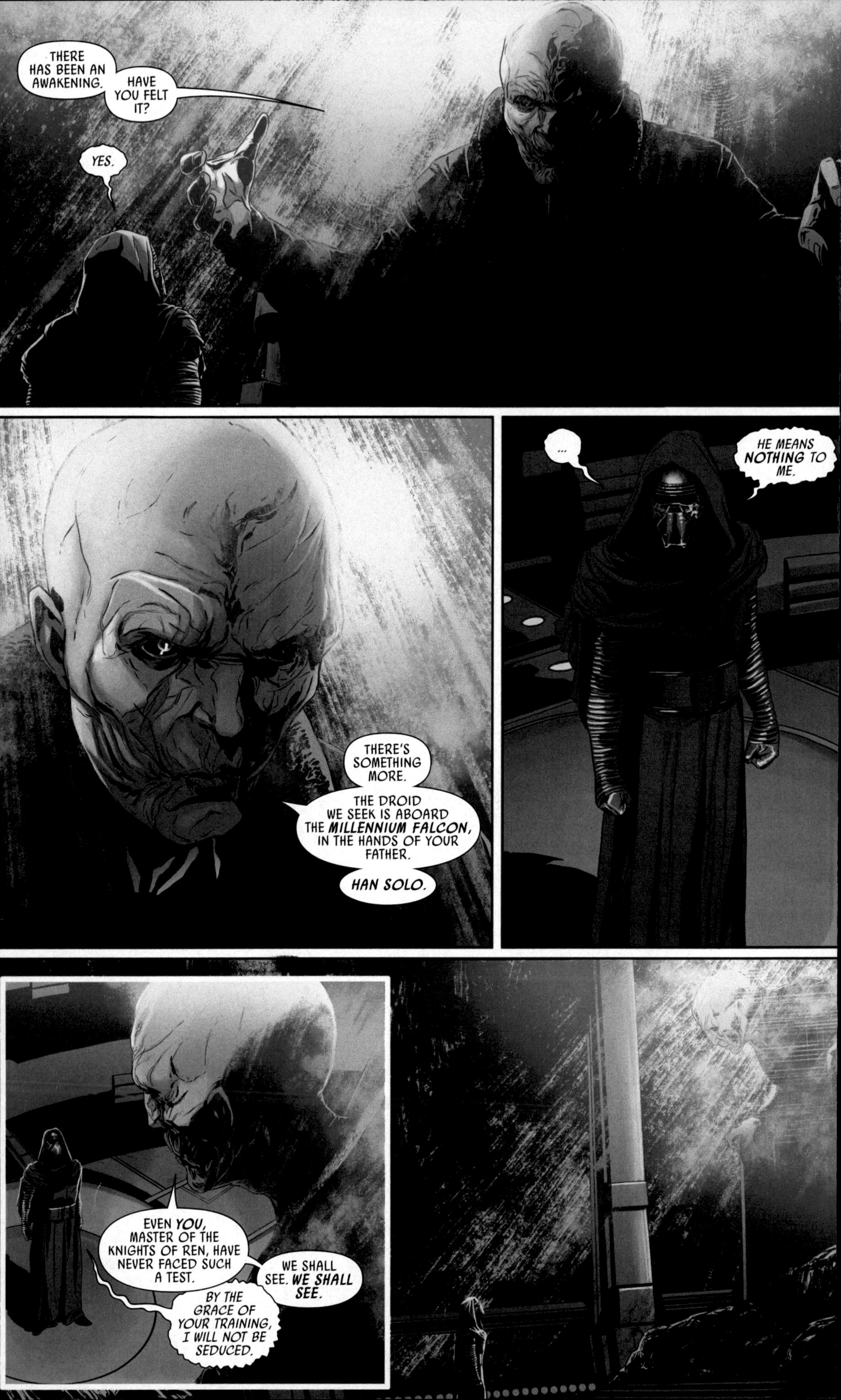
THERE HAS BEEN AN AWAKENING.
HAVE YOU FELT IT?
YES.
THERE'S SOMETHING MORE.
THE DROID WE SEEK IS ABOARD THE MILLENNIUM FALCON, IN THE HANDS OF YOUR FATHER.
HAN SOLO.
...
HE MEANS NOTHING TO ME.
EVEN YOU, MASTER OF THE KNIGHTS OF REN, HAVE NEVER FACED SUCH A TEST.
BY THE GRACE OF YOUR TRAINING, I WILL NOT BE SEDUCED.
WE SHALL SEE. WE SHALL SEE.

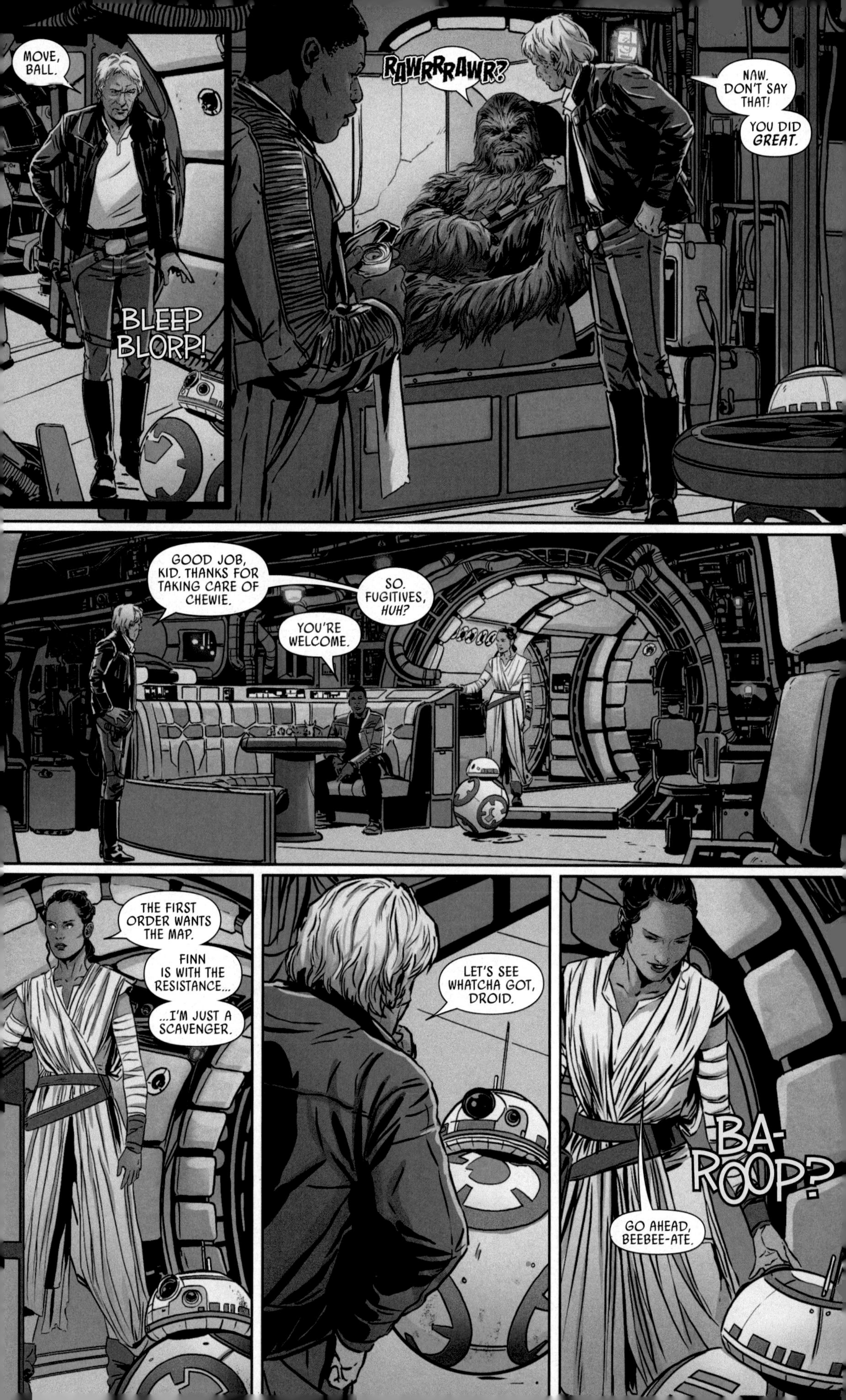
MOVE, BALL.
BLEEP BLORP!
RAWRRRAWR?
NAW. DON'T SAY THAT!
YOU DID GREAT.
GOOD JOB, KID. THANKS FOR TAKING CARE OF CHEWIE.
YOU'RE WELCOME.
SO. FUGITIVES, HUH?
THE FIRST ORDER WANTS THE MAP.
FINN IS WITH THE RESISTANCE...
...I'M JUST A SCAVENGER.
LET'S SEE WHATCHA GOT, DROID.
BA-ROOP?
GO AHEAD, BEEBEE-ATE.

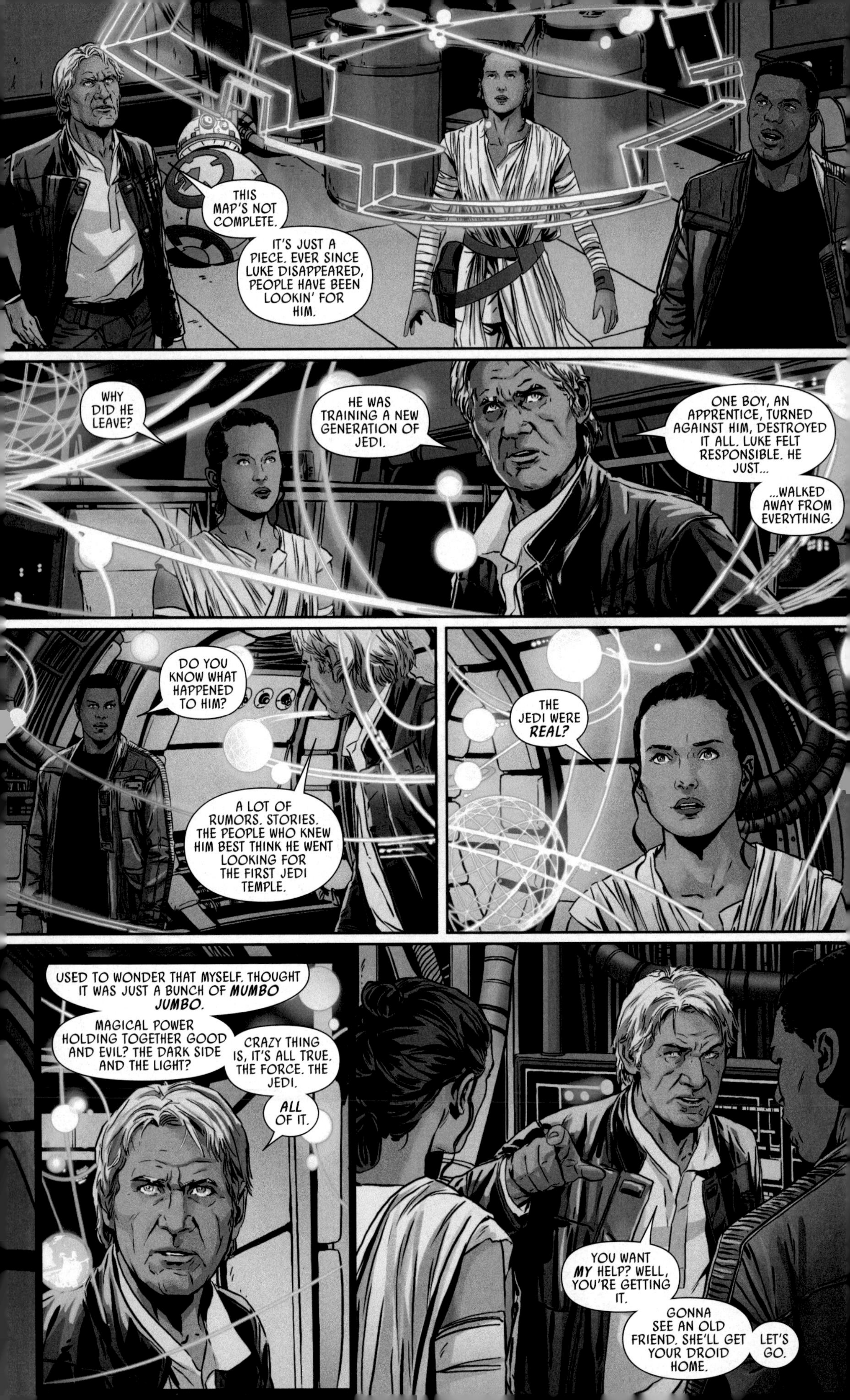
THIS MAP'S NOT COMPLETE.
IT'S JUST A PIECE. EVER SINCE LUKE DISAPPEARED, PEOPLE HAVE BEEN LOOKIN' FOR HIM.
WHY DID HE LEAVE?
HE WAS TRAINING A NEW GENERATION OF JEDI.
ONE BOY, AN APPRENTICE, TURNED AGAINST HIM, DESTROYED IT ALL. LUKE FELT RESPONSIBLE. HE JUST...
...WALKED AWAY FROM EVERYTHING.
DO YOU KNOW WHAT HAPPENED TO HIM?
A LOT OF RUMORS. STORIES. THE PEOPLE WHO KNEW HIM BEST THINK HE WENT LOOKING FOR THE FIRST JEDI TEMPLE.
THE JEDI WERE *REAL?*
USED TO WONDER THAT MYSELF. THOUGHT IT WAS JUST A BUNCH OF *MUMBO JUMBO.*
MAGICAL POWER HOLDING TOGETHER GOOD AND EVIL? THE DARK SIDE AND THE LIGHT?
CRAZY THING IS, IT'S ALL TRUE. THE FORCE. THE JEDI.
ALL OF IT.
YOU WANT *MY* HELP? WELL, YOU'RE GETTING IT.
GONNA SEE AN OLD FRIEND. SHE'LL GET YOUR DROID HOME.
LET'S GO.

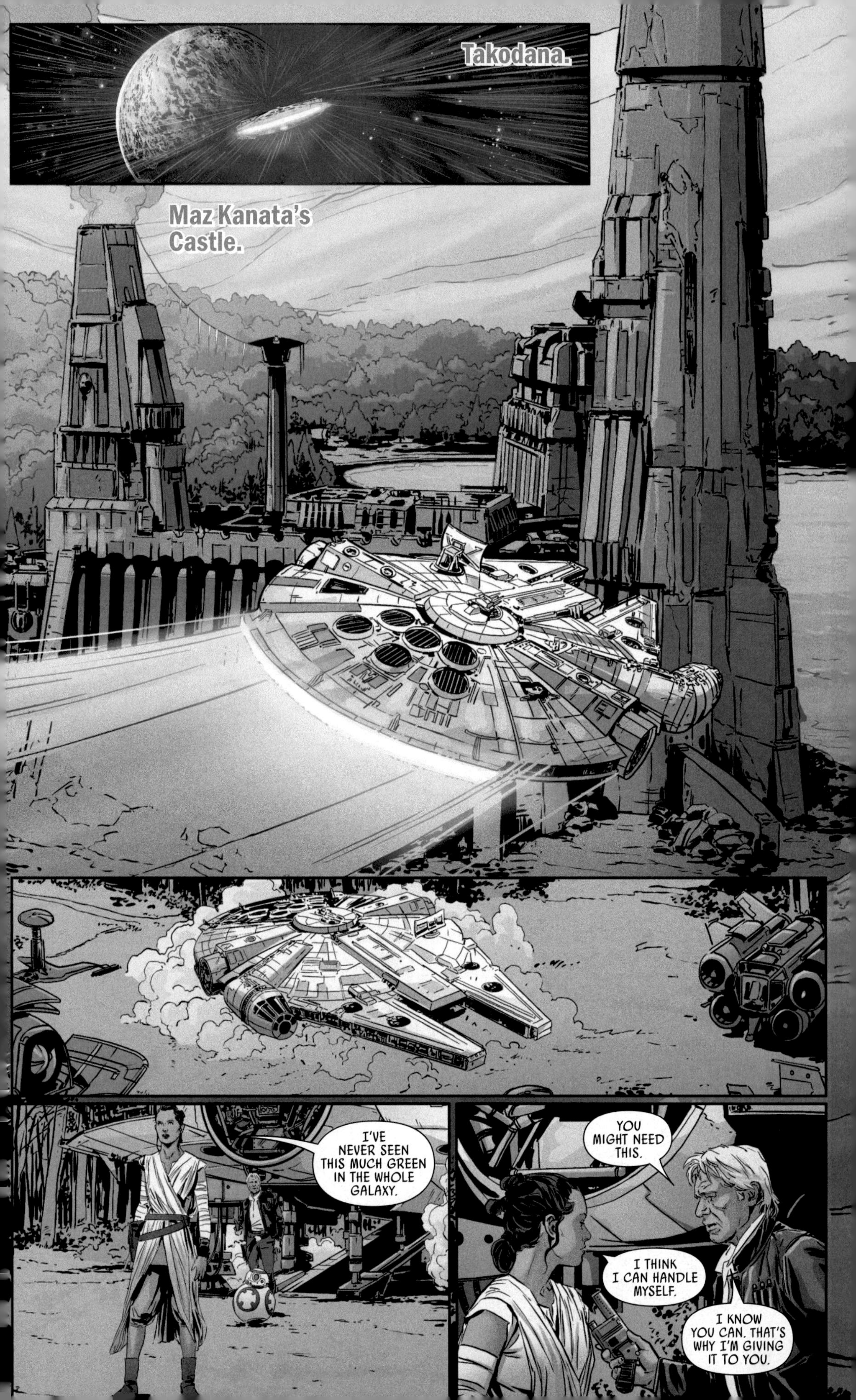
Takodana.
Maz Kanata's Castle.
I'VE NEVER SEEN THIS MUCH GREEN IN THE WHOLE GALAXY.
YOU MIGHT NEED THIS.
I THINK I CAN HANDLE MYSELF.
I KNOW YOU CAN. THAT'S WHY I'M GIVING IT TO YOU.

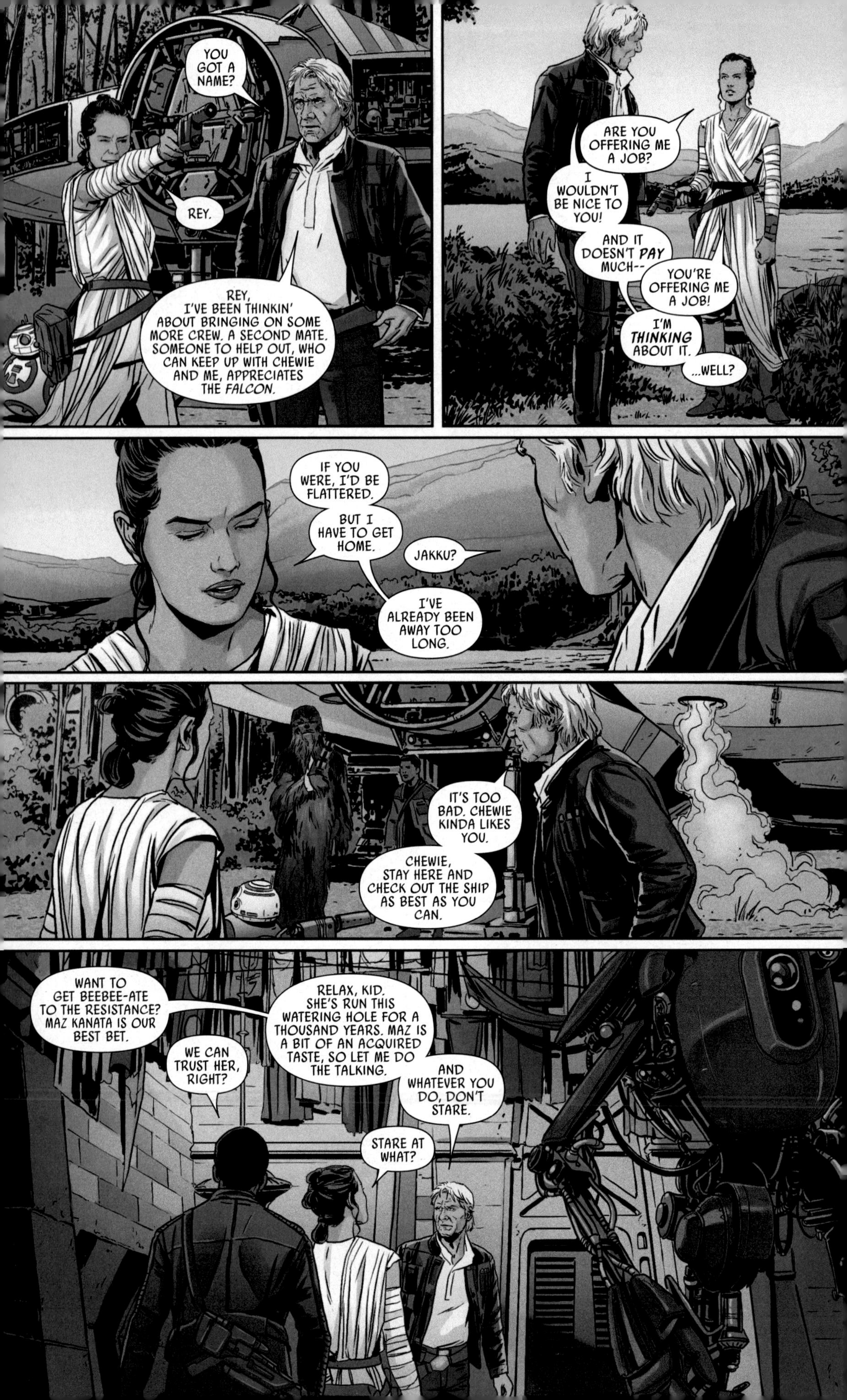
YOU GOT A NAME?
REY.
REY, I'VE BEEN THINKIN' ABOUT BRINGING ON SOME MORE CREW. A SECOND MATE. SOMEONE TO HELP OUT, WHO CAN KEEP UP WITH CHEWIE AND ME, APPRECIATES THE *FALCON.*
ARE YOU OFFERING ME A JOB?
I WOULDN'T BE NICE TO YOU!
AND IT DOESN'T *PAY* MUCH--
YOU'RE OFFERING ME A JOB!
I'M *THINKING* ABOUT IT.
...WELL?
IF YOU WERE, I'D BE FLATTERED.
BUT I HAVE TO GET HOME.
JAKKU?
I'VE ALREADY BEEN AWAY TOO LONG.
IT'S TOO BAD. CHEWIE KINDA LIKES YOU.
CHEWIE, STAY HERE AND CHECK OUT THE SHIP AS BEST AS YOU CAN.
WANT TO GET BEEBEE-ATE TO THE RESISTANCE? MAZ KANATA IS OUR BEST BET.
WE CAN TRUST HER, RIGHT?
RELAX, KID. SHE'S RUN THIS WATERING HOLE FOR A THOUSAND YEARS. MAZ IS A BIT OF AN ACQUIRED TASTE, SO LET ME DO THE TALKING.
AND WHATEVER YOU DO, DON'T STARE.
STARE AT WHAT?

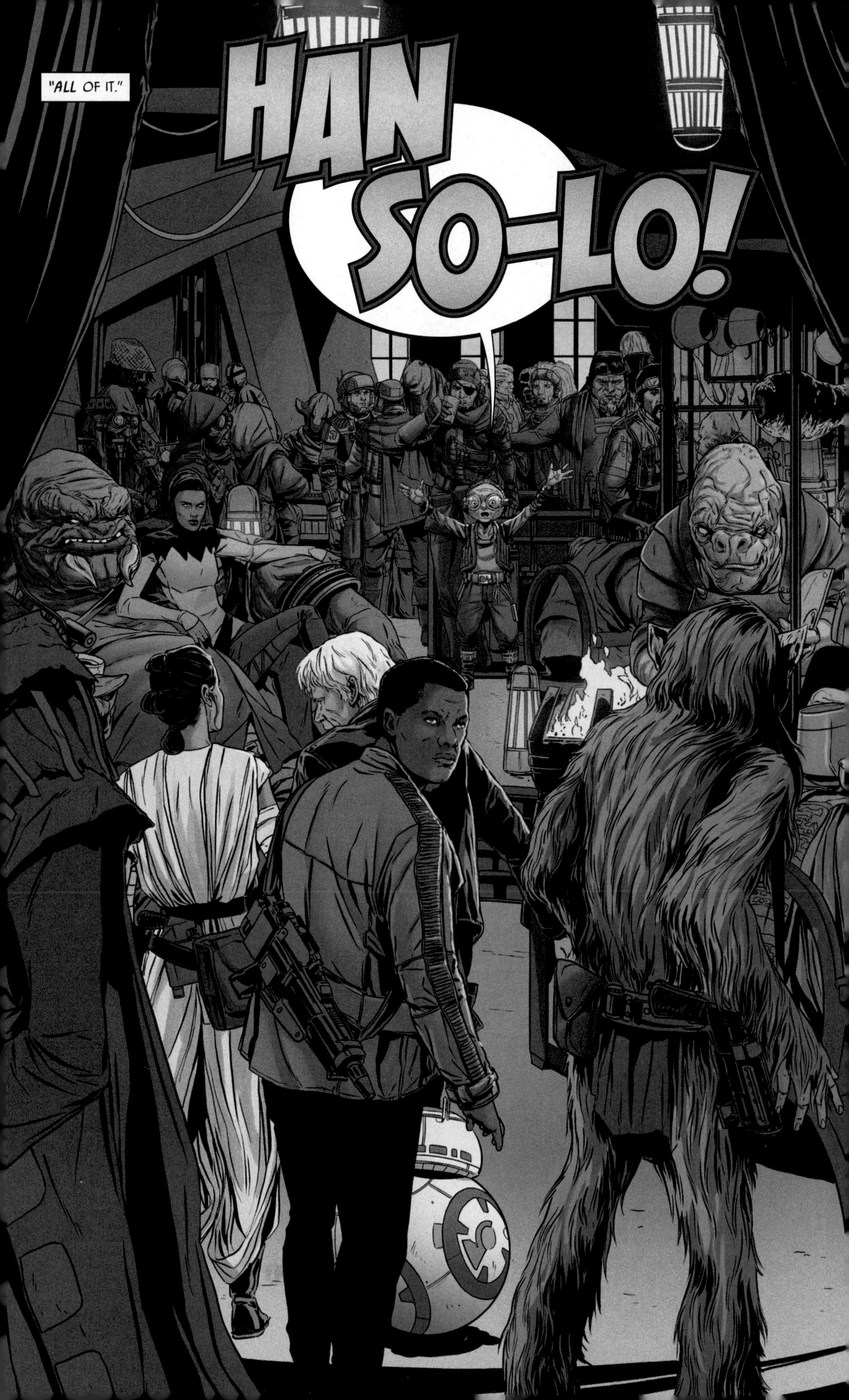
"ALL OF IT."
HAN SO-LO!

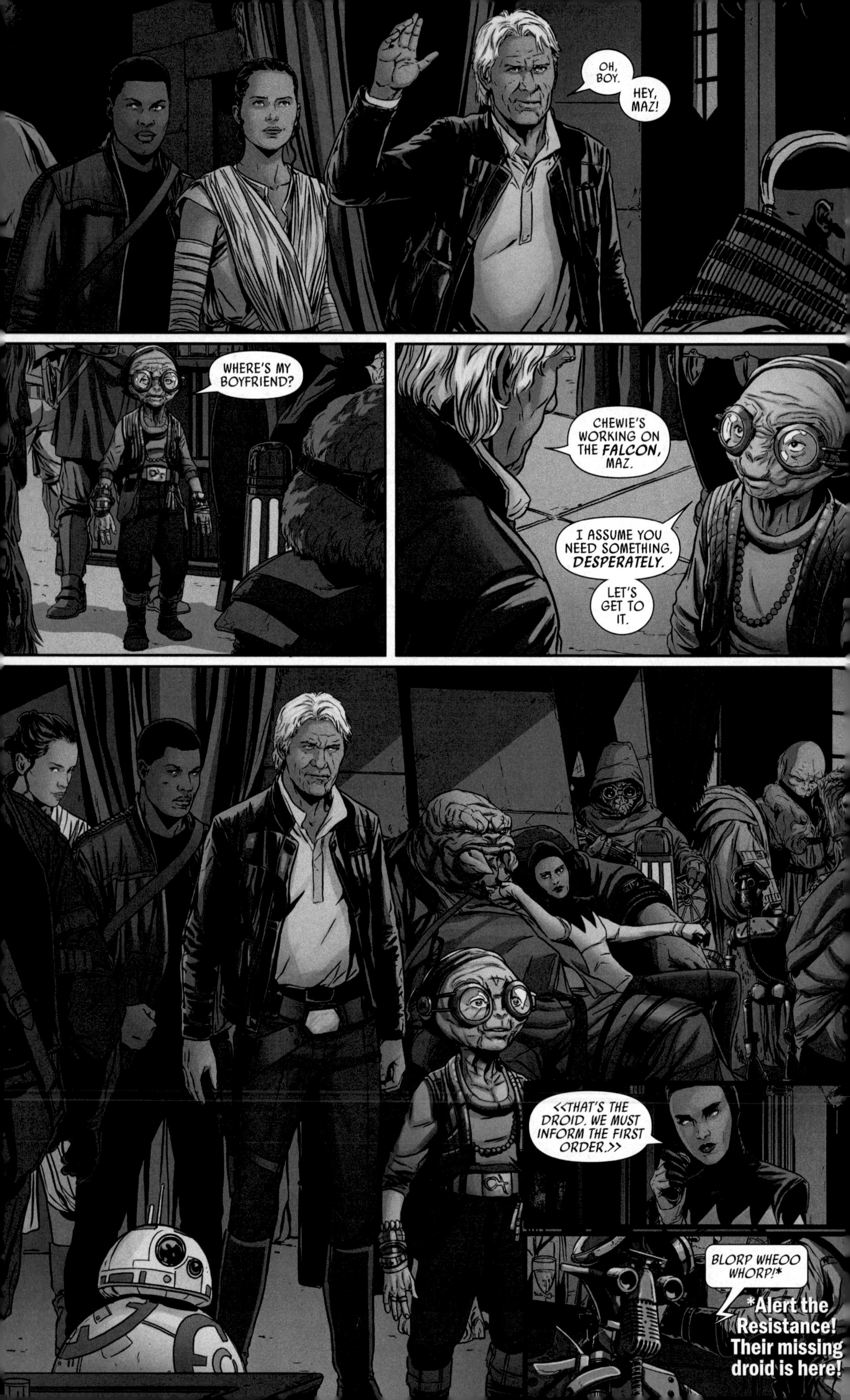
OH, BOY.
HEY, MAZ!
WHERE'S MY BOYFRIEND?
CHEWIE'S WORKING ON THE FALCON, MAZ.
I ASSUME YOU NEED SOMETHING. DESPERATELY.
LET'S GET TO IT.
<<THAT'S THE DROID. WE MUST INFORM THE FIRST ORDER.>>
BLORP WHEOO WHORP!*
*Alert the Resistance! Their missing droid is here!

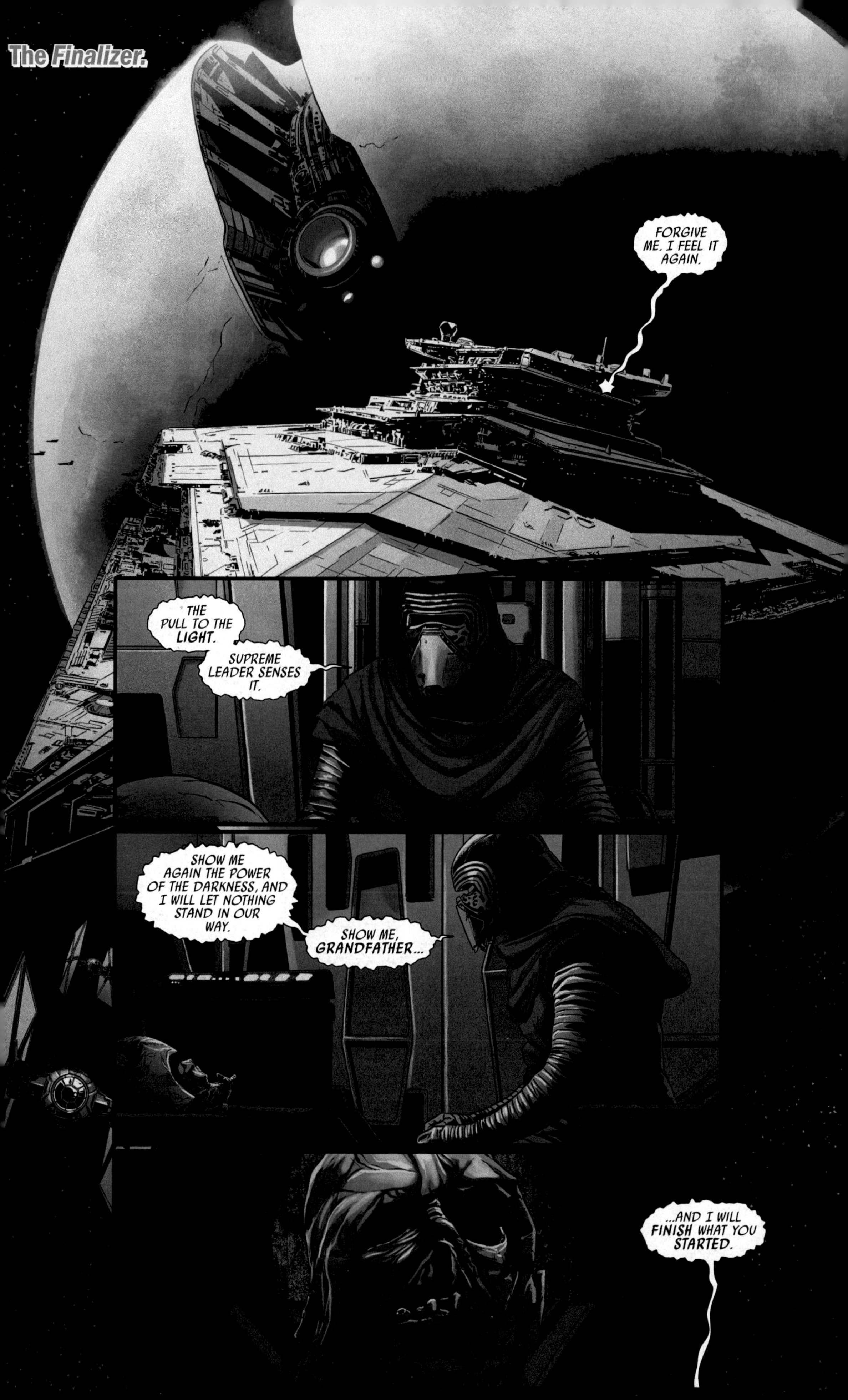
The Finalizer.
FORGIVE ME. I FEEL IT AGAIN.
THE PULL TO THE LIGHT.
SUPREME LEADER SENSES IT.
SHOW ME AGAIN THE POWER OF THE DARKNESS, AND I WILL LET NOTHING STAND IN OUR WAY.
SHOW ME, GRANDFATHER...
...AND I WILL FINISH WHAT YOU STARTED.

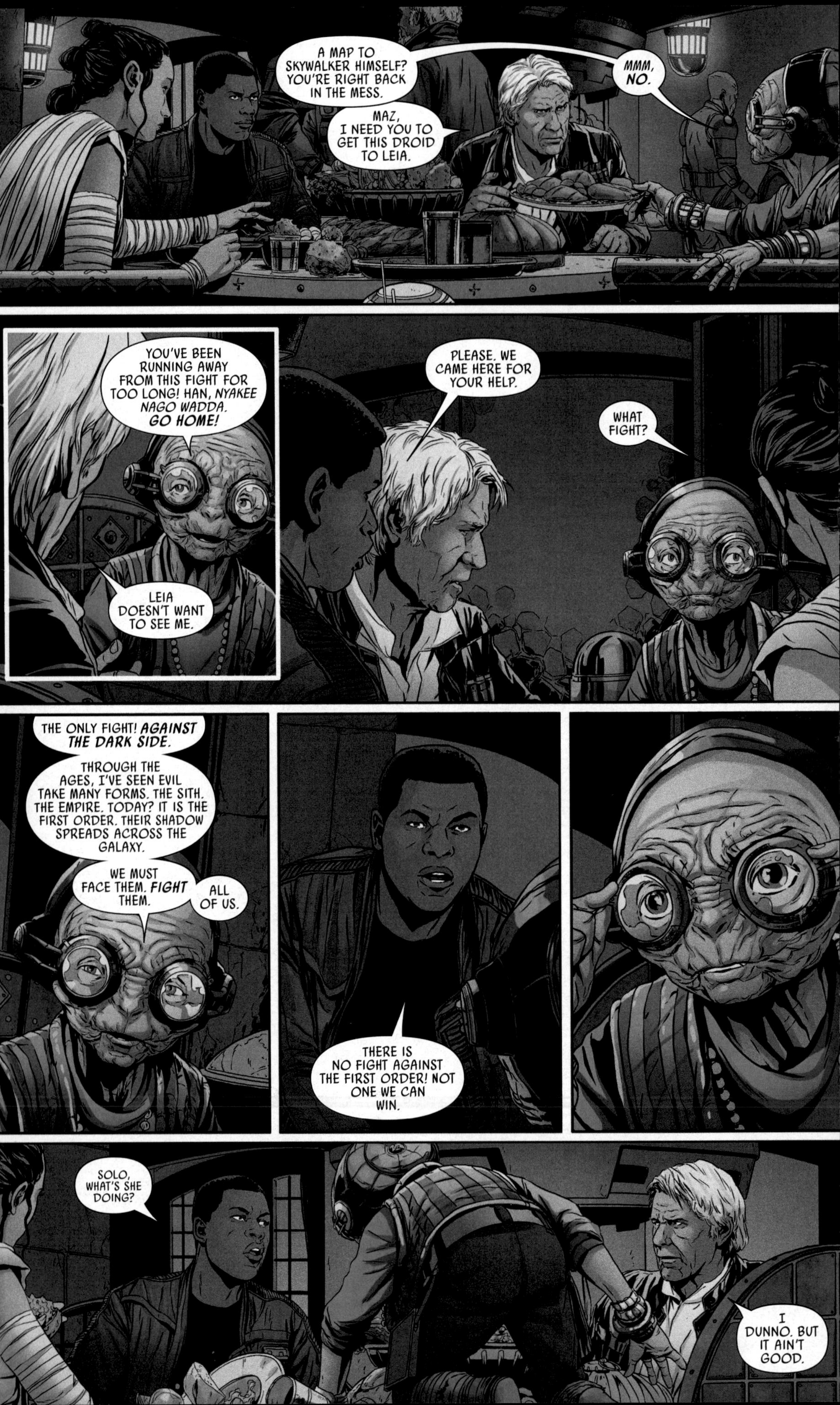
A MAP TO SKYWALKER HIMSELF? YOU'RE RIGHT BACK IN THE MESS.
MMM, *NO.*
MAZ, I NEED YOU TO GET THIS DROID TO LEIA.
YOU'VE BEEN RUNNING AWAY FROM THIS FIGHT FOR TOO LONG! HAN, *NYAKEE NAGO WADDA.* ***GO HOME!***
LEIA DOESN'T WANT TO SEE ME.
PLEASE. WE CAME HERE FOR YOUR HELP.
WHAT FIGHT?
THE ONLY FIGHT! ***AGAINST THE DARK SIDE.***
THROUGH THE AGES, I'VE SEEN EVIL TAKE MANY FORMS. THE SITH. THE EMPIRE. TODAY? IT IS THE FIRST ORDER. THEIR SHADOW SPREADS ACROSS THE GALAXY.
WE MUST FACE THEM. ***FIGHT*** THEM.
ALL OF US.
THERE IS NO FIGHT AGAINST THE FIRST ORDER! NOT ONE WE CAN WIN.
SOLO, WHAT'S SHE DOING?
I DUNNO. BUT IT AIN'T GOOD.

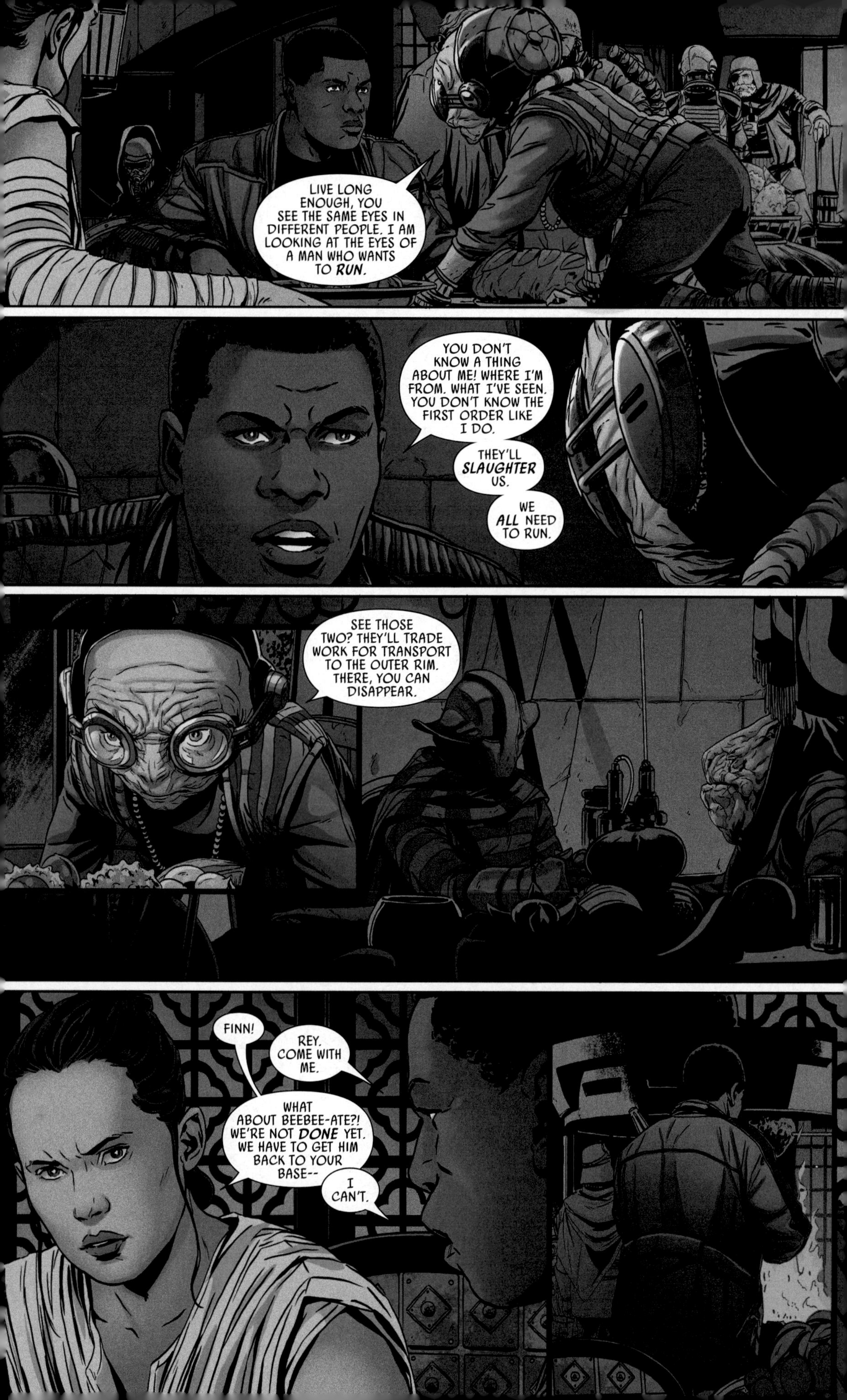
LIVE LONG ENOUGH, YOU SEE THE SAME EYES IN DIFFERENT PEOPLE. I AM LOOKING AT THE EYES OF A MAN WHO WANTS TO RUN.
YOU DON'T KNOW A THING ABOUT ME! WHERE I'M FROM. WHAT I'VE SEEN. YOU DON'T KNOW THE FIRST ORDER LIKE I DO.
THEY'LL SLAUGHTER US.
WE ALL NEED TO RUN.
SEE THOSE TWO? THEY'LL TRADE WORK FOR TRANSPORT TO THE OUTER RIM. THERE, YOU CAN DISAPPEAR.
FINN!
REY. COME WITH ME.
WHAT ABOUT BEEBEE-ATE?! WE'RE NOT DONE YET. WE HAVE TO GET HIM BACK TO YOUR BASE--
I CAN'T.

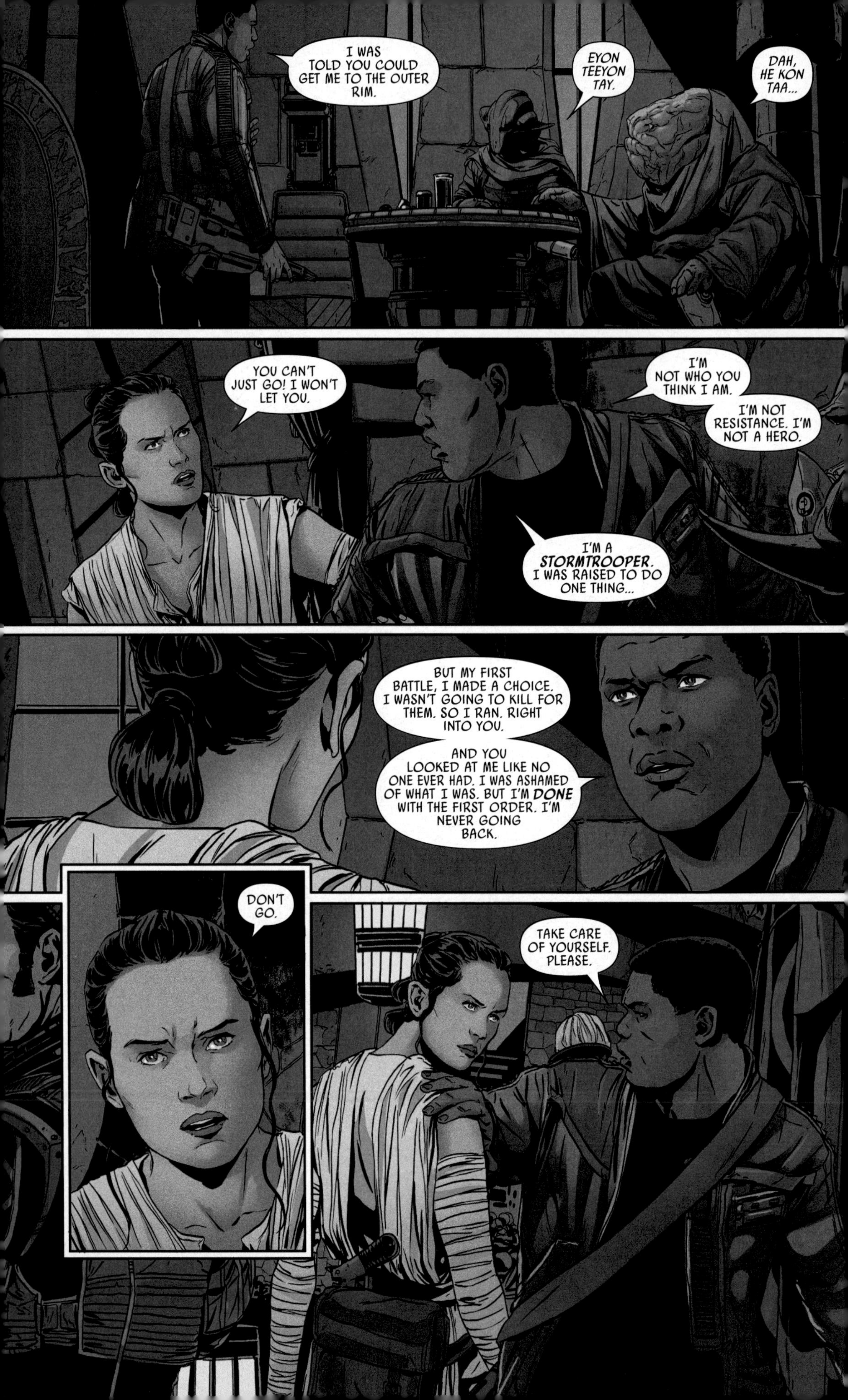
I WAS TOLD YOU COULD GET ME TO THE OUTER RIM.
EYON TEEYON TAY.
DAH, HE KON TAA...
YOU CAN'T JUST GO! I WON'T LET YOU.
I'M NOT WHO YOU THINK I AM.
I'M NOT RESISTANCE. I'M NOT A HERO.
I'M A STORMTROOPER. I WAS RAISED TO DO ONE THING...
BUT MY FIRST BATTLE, I MADE A CHOICE. I WASN'T GOING TO KILL FOR THEM. SO I RAN. RIGHT INTO YOU.
AND YOU LOOKED AT ME LIKE NO ONE EVER HAD. I WAS ASHAMED OF WHAT I WAS. BUT I'M DONE WITH THE FIRST ORDER. I'M NEVER GOING BACK.
DON'T GO.
TAKE CARE OF YOURSELF. PLEASE.

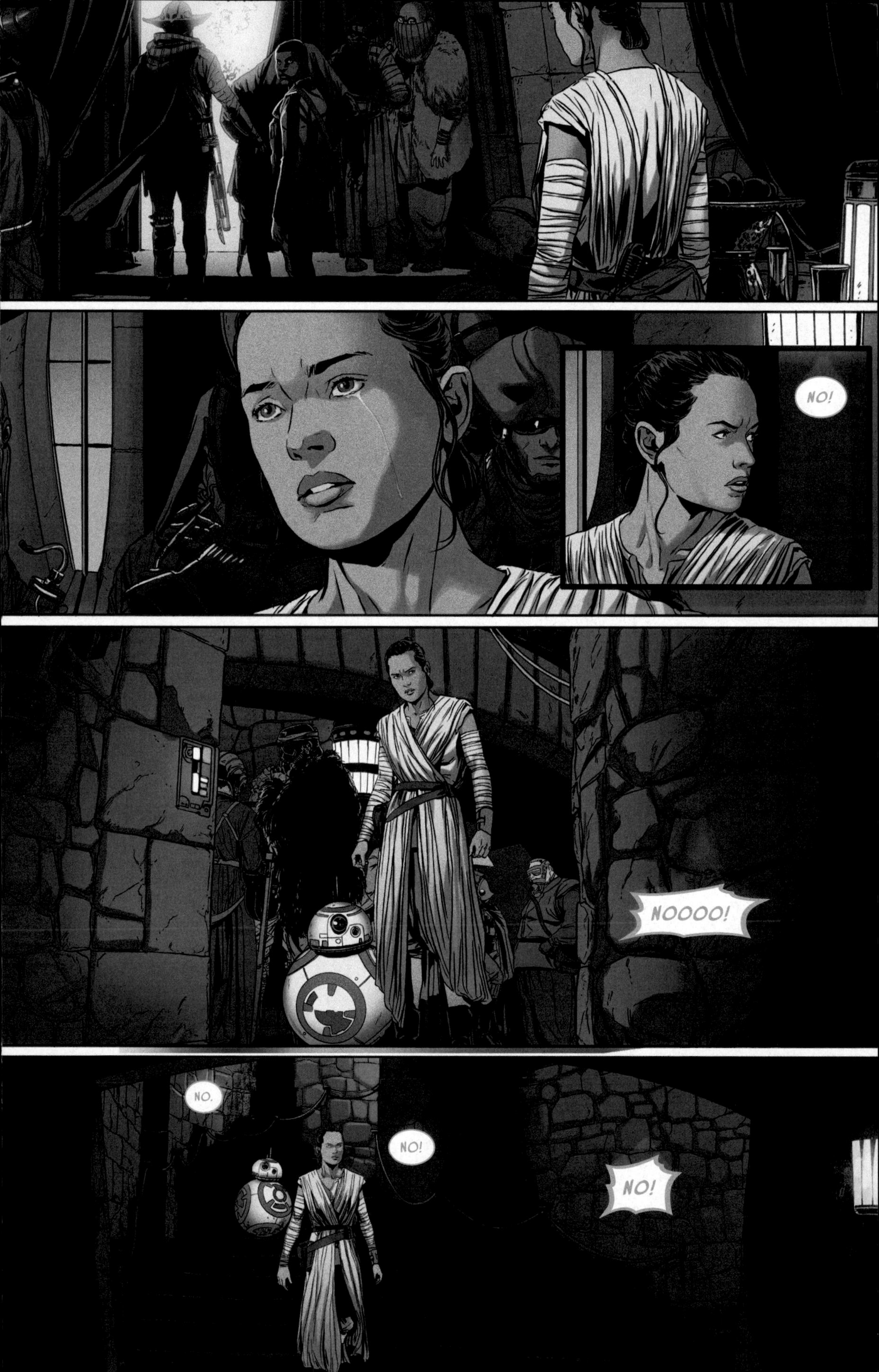
NO!
NOOOO!
NO.
NO!
NO!

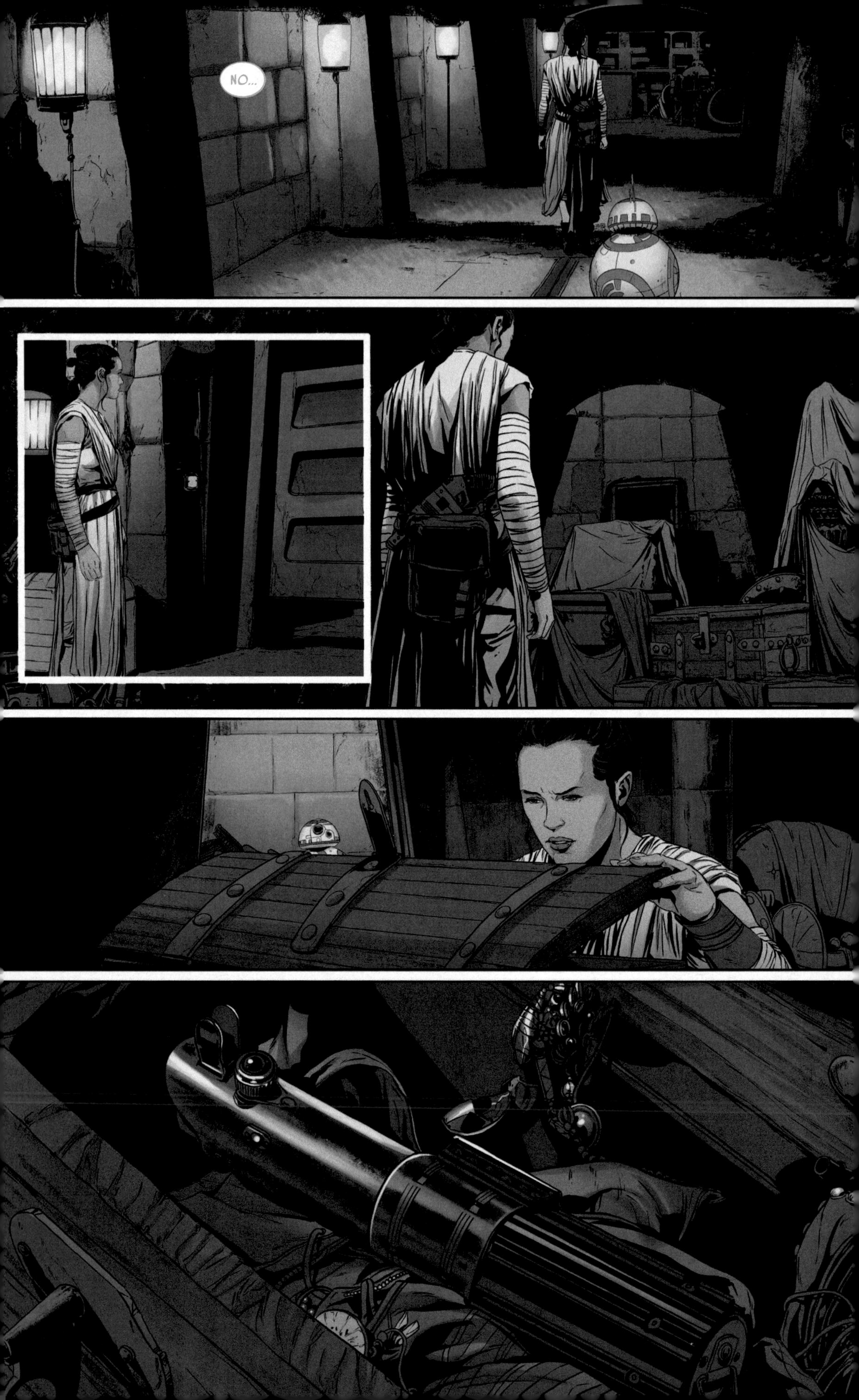
NO...

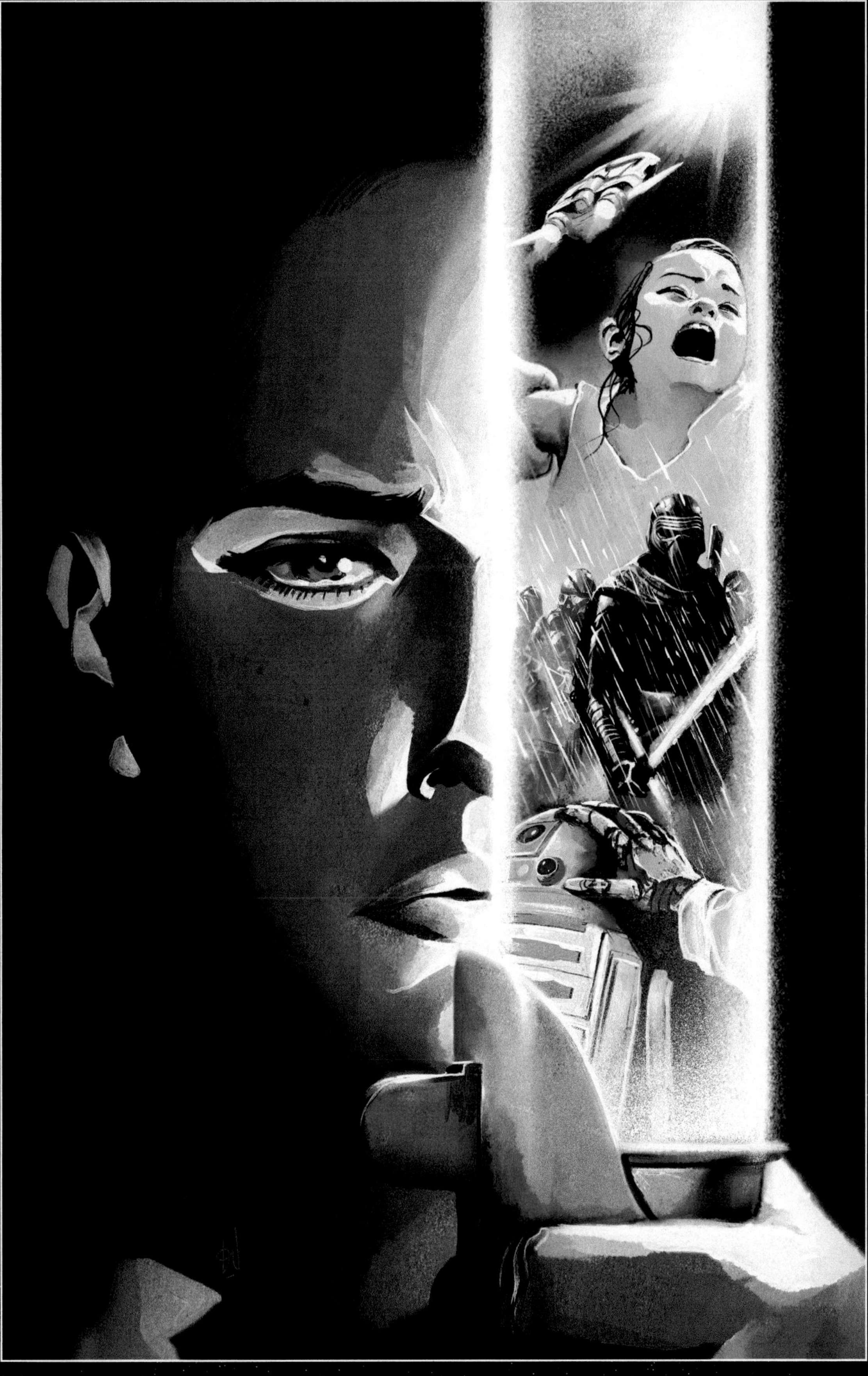

THE FORCE AWAKENS #4

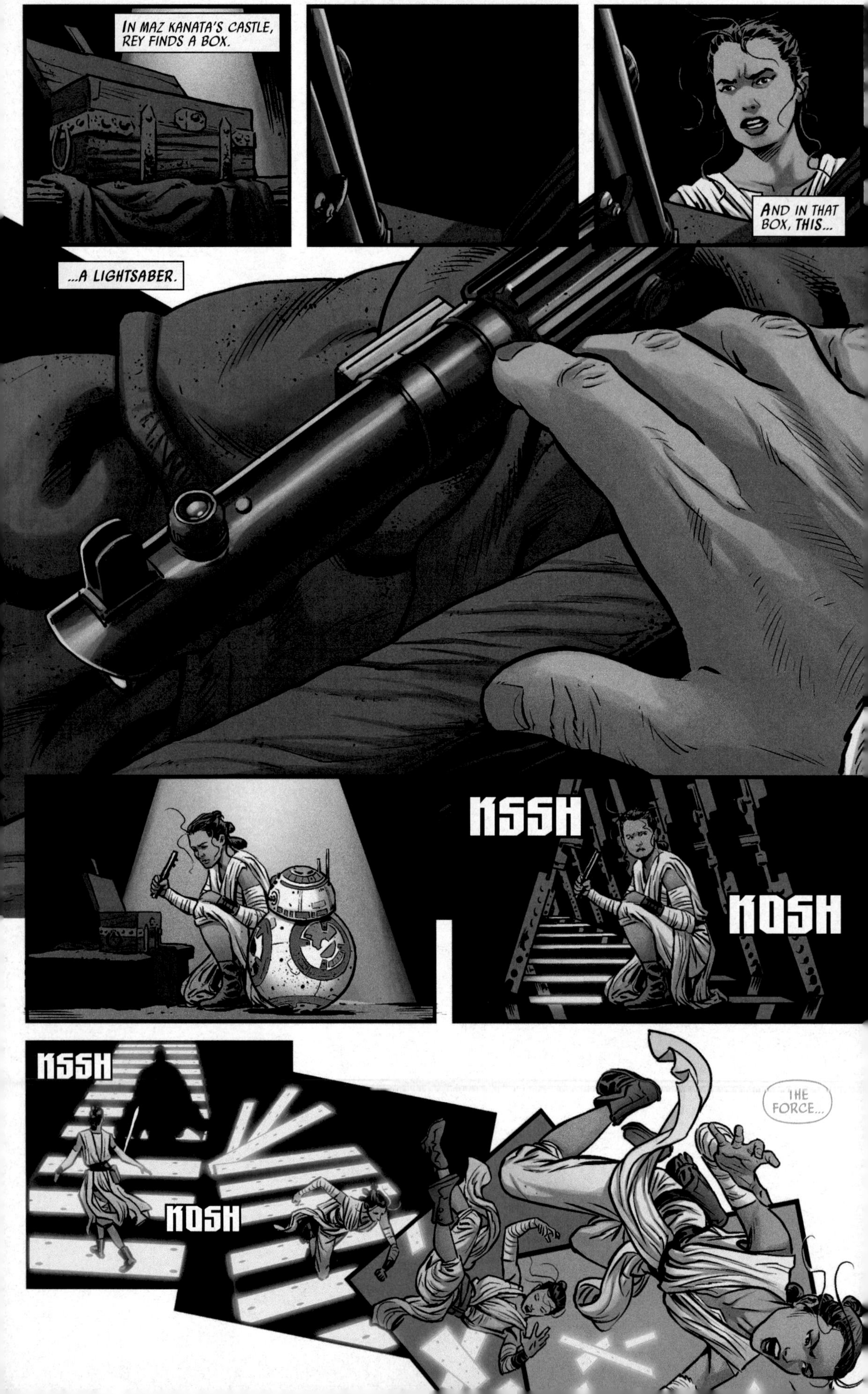
IN MAZ KANATA'S CASTLE, REY FINDS A BOX.
AND IN THAT BOX, THIS...
...A LIGHTSABER.
KSSH
KOSH
KSSH
KOSH
THE FORCE...

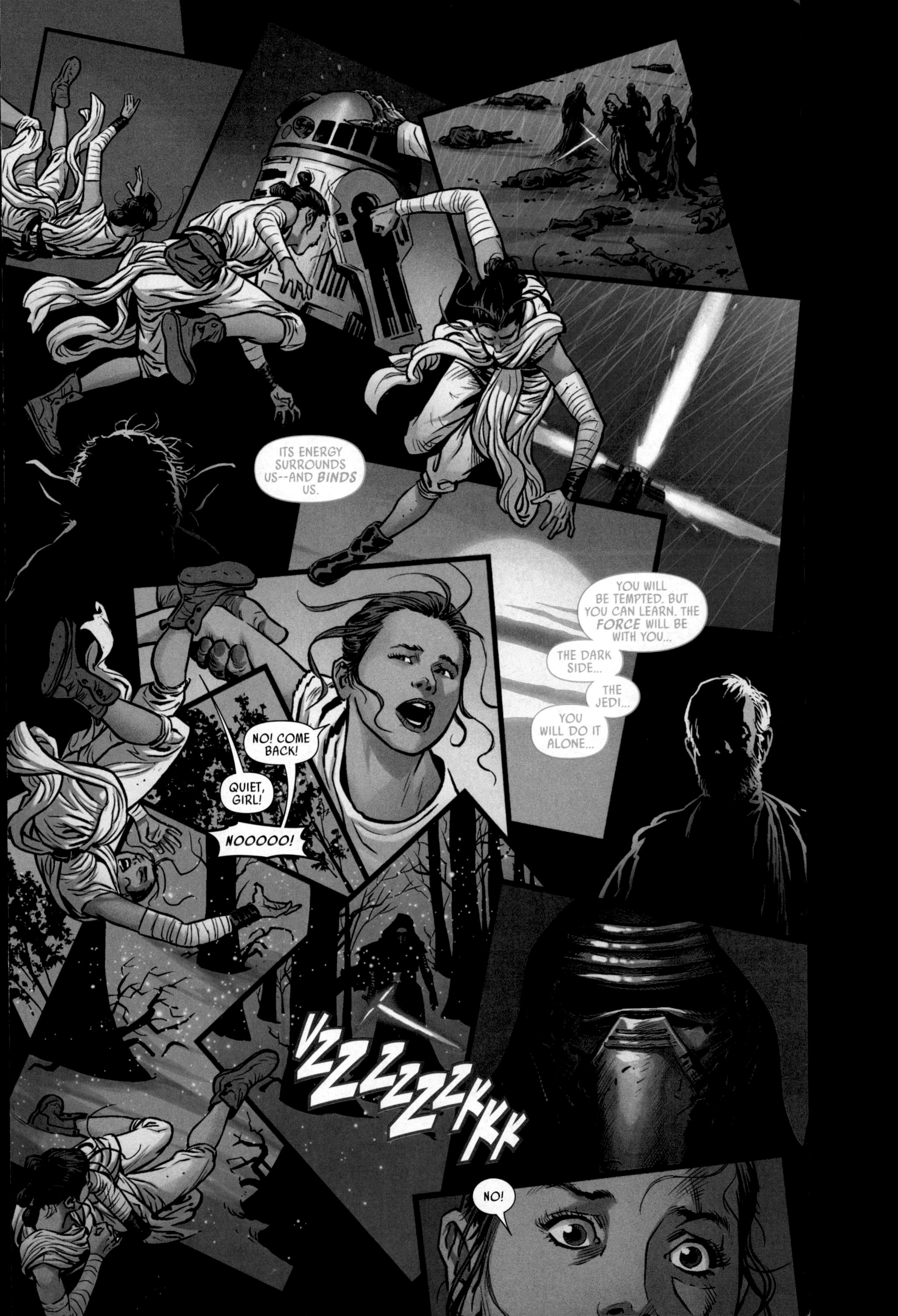
ITS ENERGY SURROUNDS US--AND BINDS US.
YOU WILL BE TEMPTED. BUT YOU CAN LEARN. THE FORCE WILL BE WITH YOU...
THE DARK SIDE...
THE JEDI...
YOU WILL DO IT ALONE...
NO! COME BACK!
QUIET, GIRL!
NOOOOO!
VZZZZZZKKK
NO!

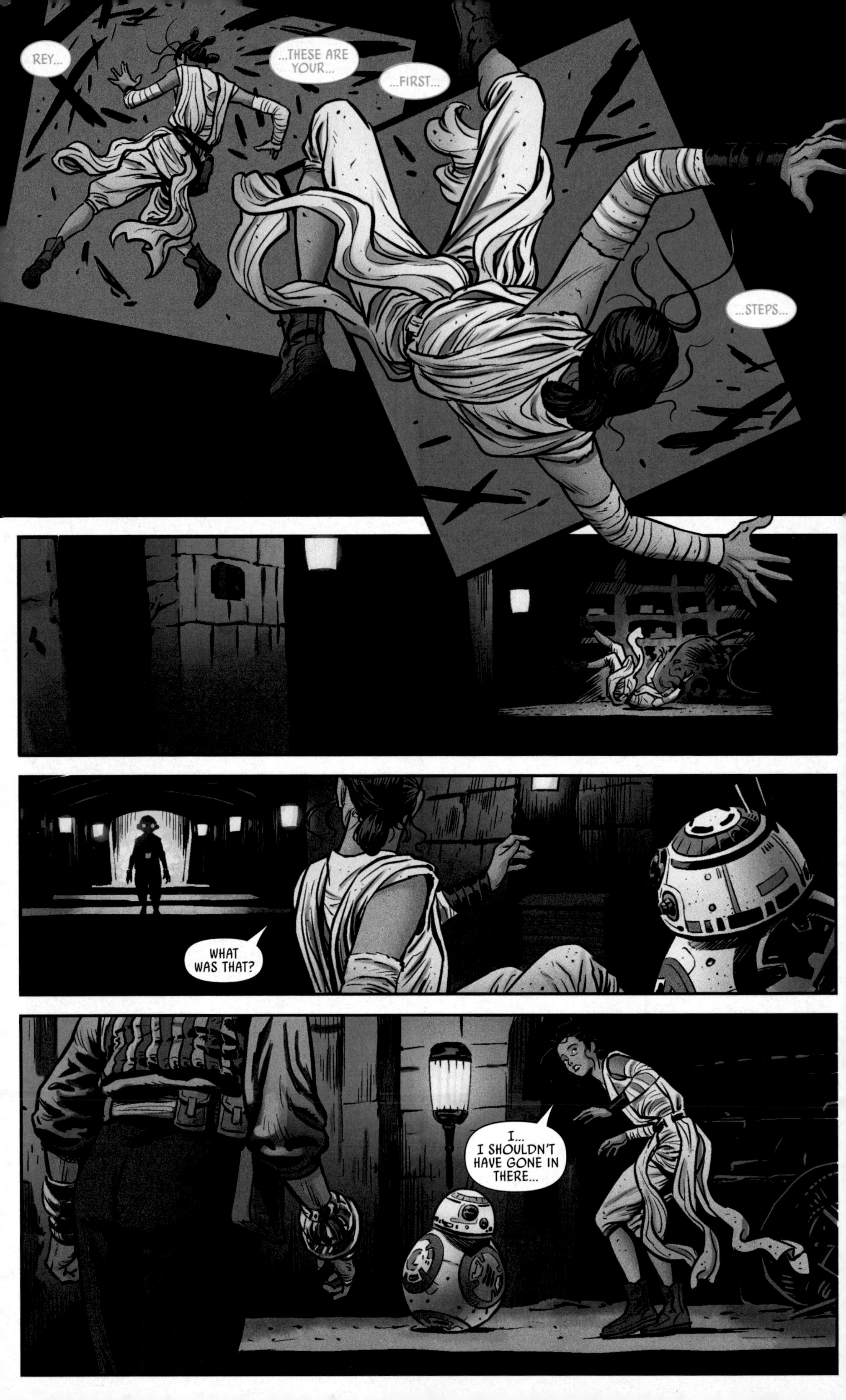
REY...
...THESE ARE YOUR...
...FIRST...
...STEPS...
WHAT WAS THAT?
I... I SHOULDN'T HAVE GONE IN THERE...

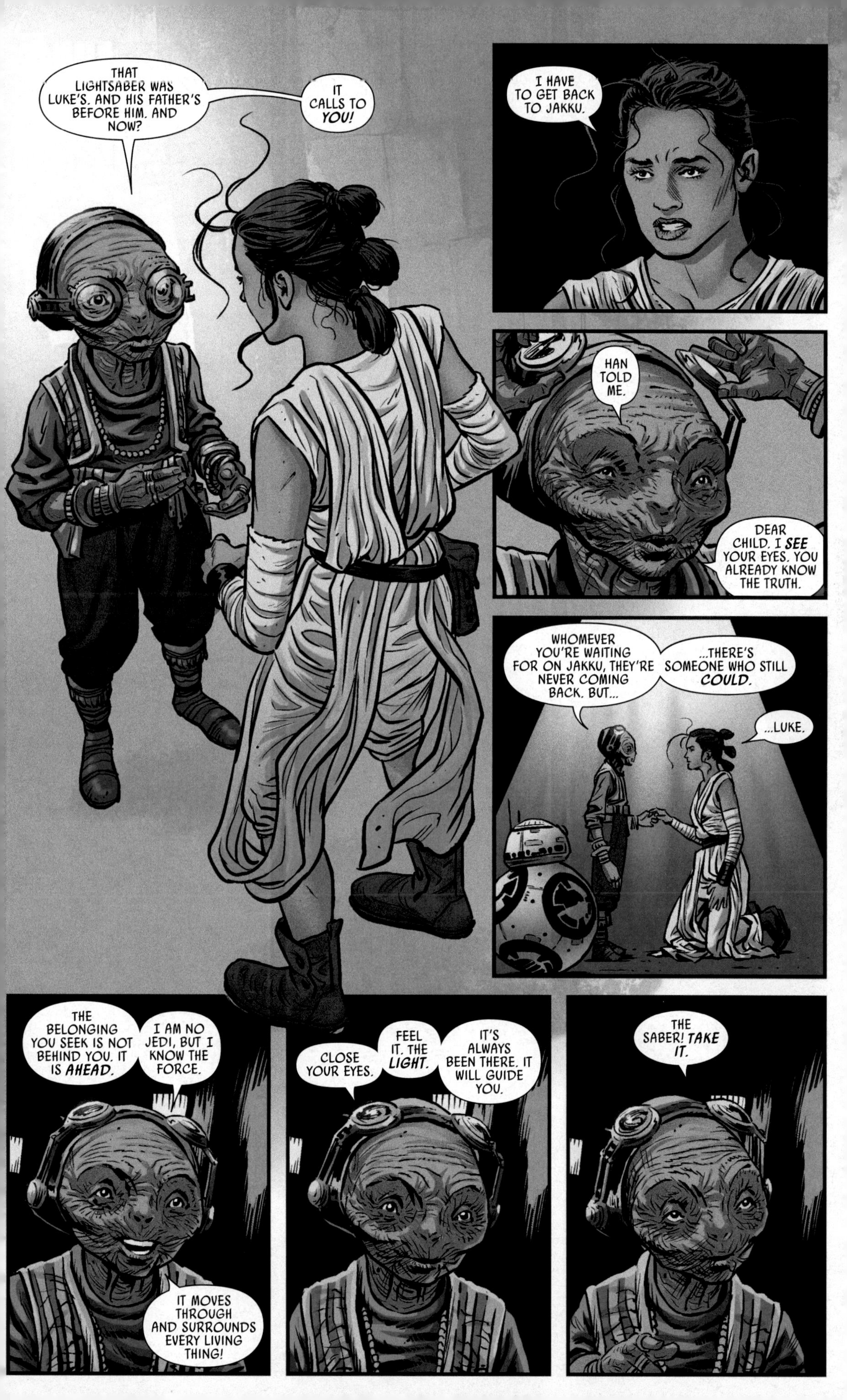
THAT LIGHTSABER WAS LUKE'S. AND HIS FATHER'S BEFORE HIM. AND NOW?
IT CALLS TO *YOU!*
I HAVE TO GET BACK TO JAKKU.
HAN TOLD ME.
DEAR CHILD. I **SEE** YOUR EYES. YOU ALREADY KNOW THE TRUTH.
WHOMEVER YOU'RE WAITING FOR ON JAKKU, THEY'RE NEVER COMING BACK. BUT...
...THERE'S SOMEONE WHO STILL ***COULD.***
...LUKE.
THE BELONGING YOU SEEK IS NOT BEHIND YOU. IT IS ***AHEAD.***
I AM NO JEDI, BUT I KNOW THE FORCE.
IT MOVES THROUGH AND SURROUNDS EVERY LIVING THING!
CLOSE YOUR EYES.
FEEL IT. THE ***LIGHT.***
IT'S ALWAYS BEEN THERE. IT WILL GUIDE YOU.
THE SABER! ***TAKE IT.***

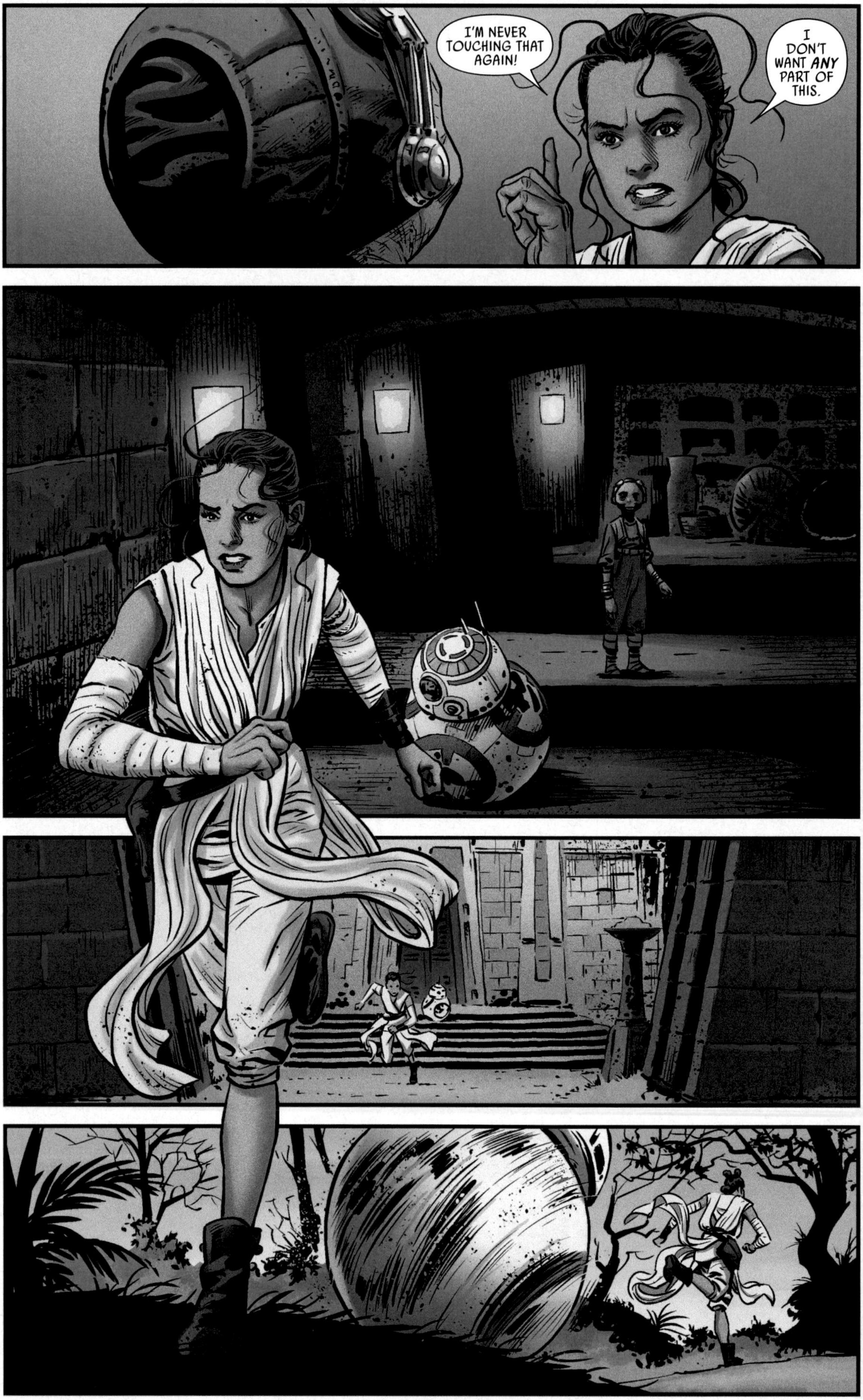
I'M NEVER TOUCHING THAT AGAIN!
I DON'T WANT ANY PART OF THIS.

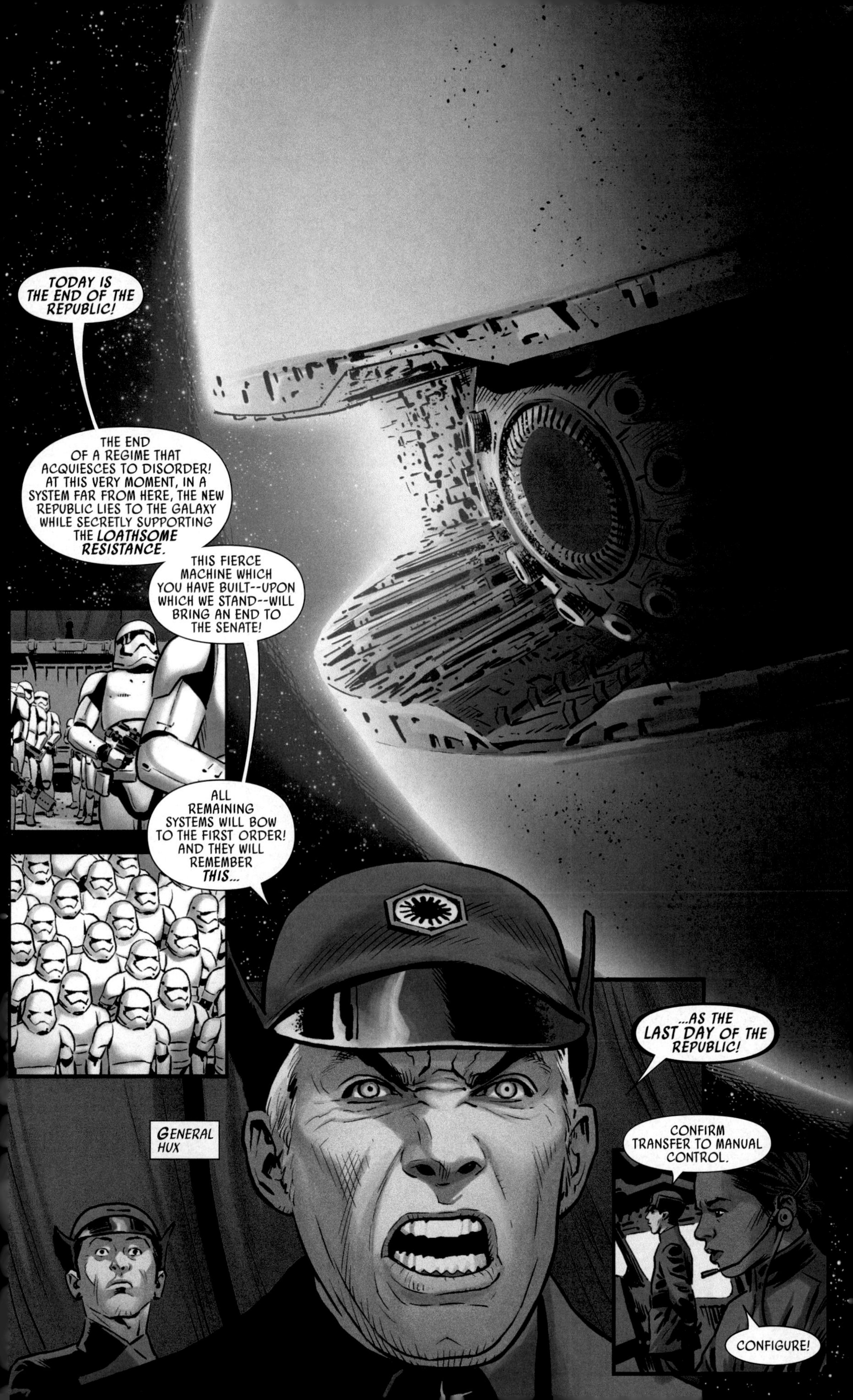
TODAY IS THE END OF THE REPUBLIC!
THE END OF A REGIME THAT ACQUIESCES TO DISORDER! AT THIS VERY MOMENT, IN A SYSTEM FAR FROM HERE, THE NEW REPUBLIC LIES TO THE GALAXY WHILE SECRETLY SUPPORTING THE LOATHSOME RESISTANCE.
THIS FIERCE MACHINE WHICH YOU HAVE BUILT--UPON WHICH WE STAND--WILL BRING AN END TO THE SENATE!
ALL REMAINING SYSTEMS WILL BOW TO THE FIRST ORDER! AND THEY WILL REMEMBER THIS...
...AS THE LAST DAY OF THE REPUBLIC!
GENERAL HUX
CONFIRM TRANSFER TO MANUAL CONTROL.
CONFIGURE!

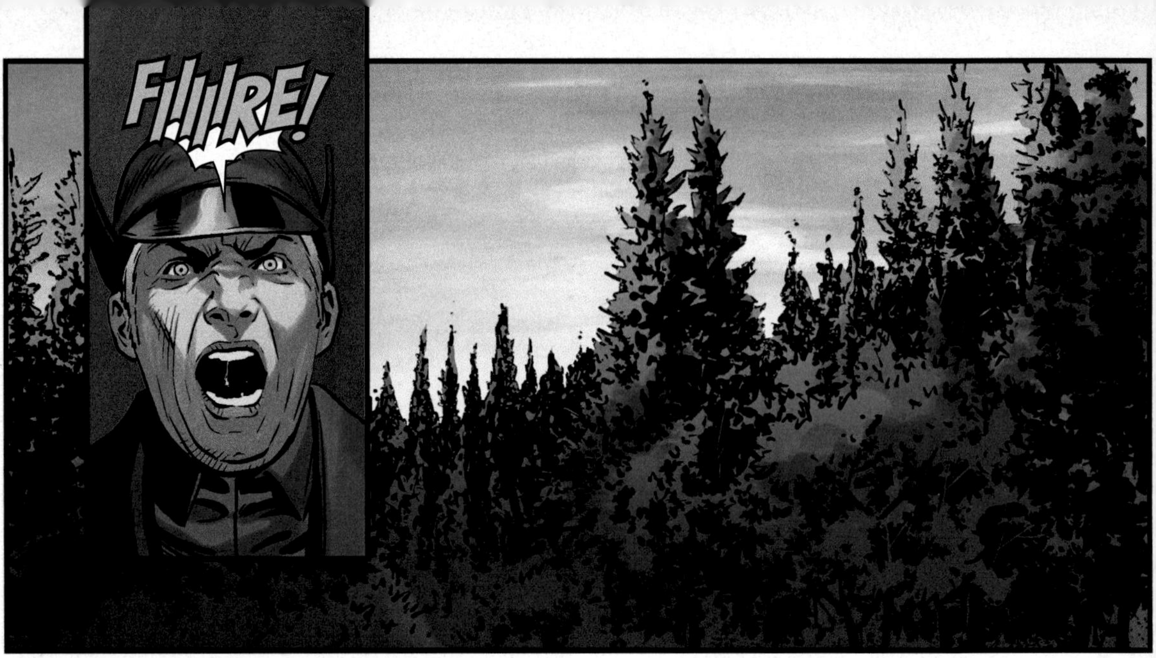
FIIIIRE!
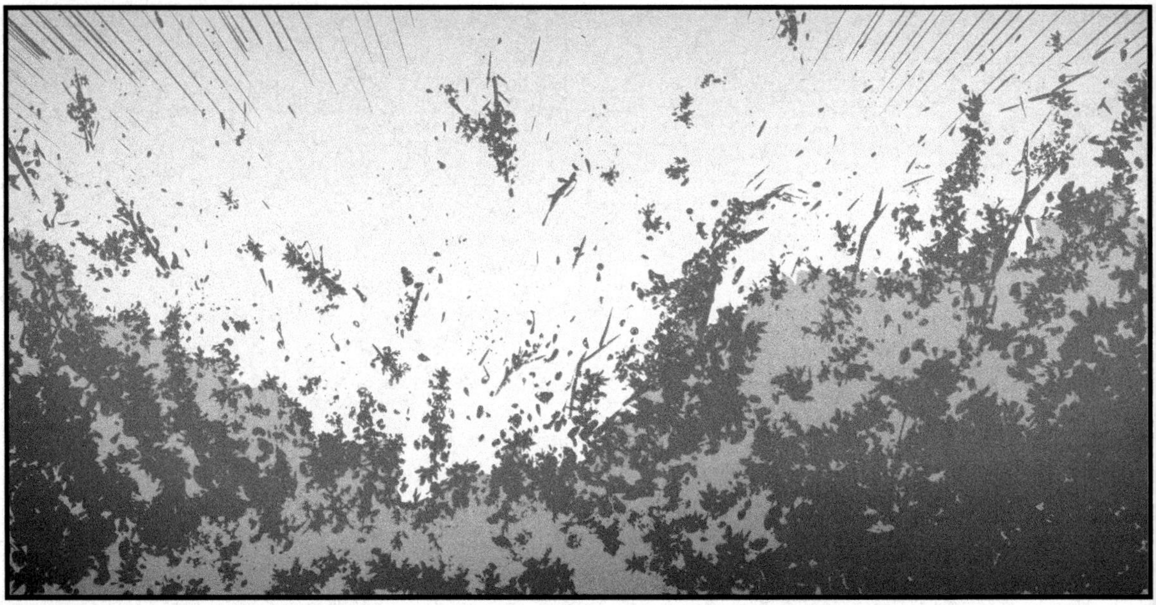
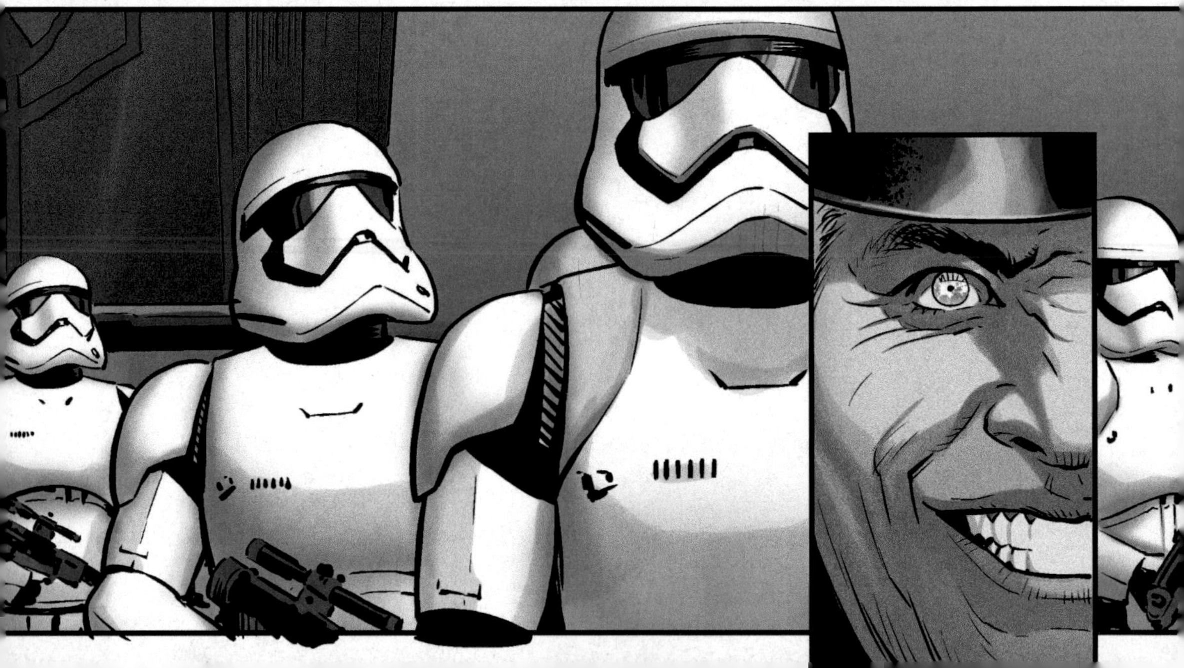

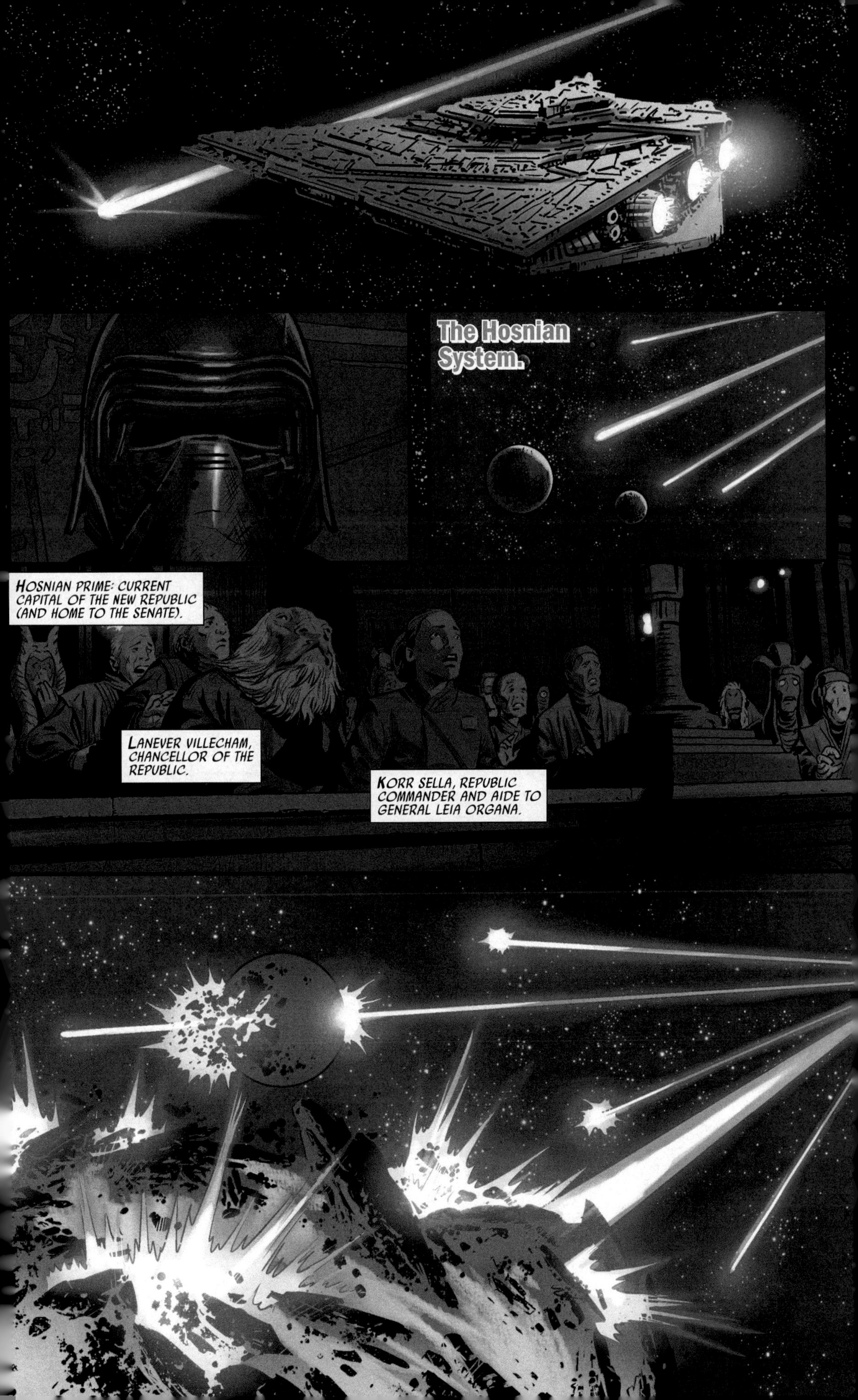
The Hosnian System.
HOSNIAN PRIME: CURRENT CAPITAL OF THE NEW REPUBLIC (AND HOME TO THE SENATE).
LANEVER VILLECHAM, CHANCELLOR OF THE REPUBLIC.
KORR SELLA, REPUBLIC COMMANDER AND AIDE TO GENERAL LEIA ORGANA.

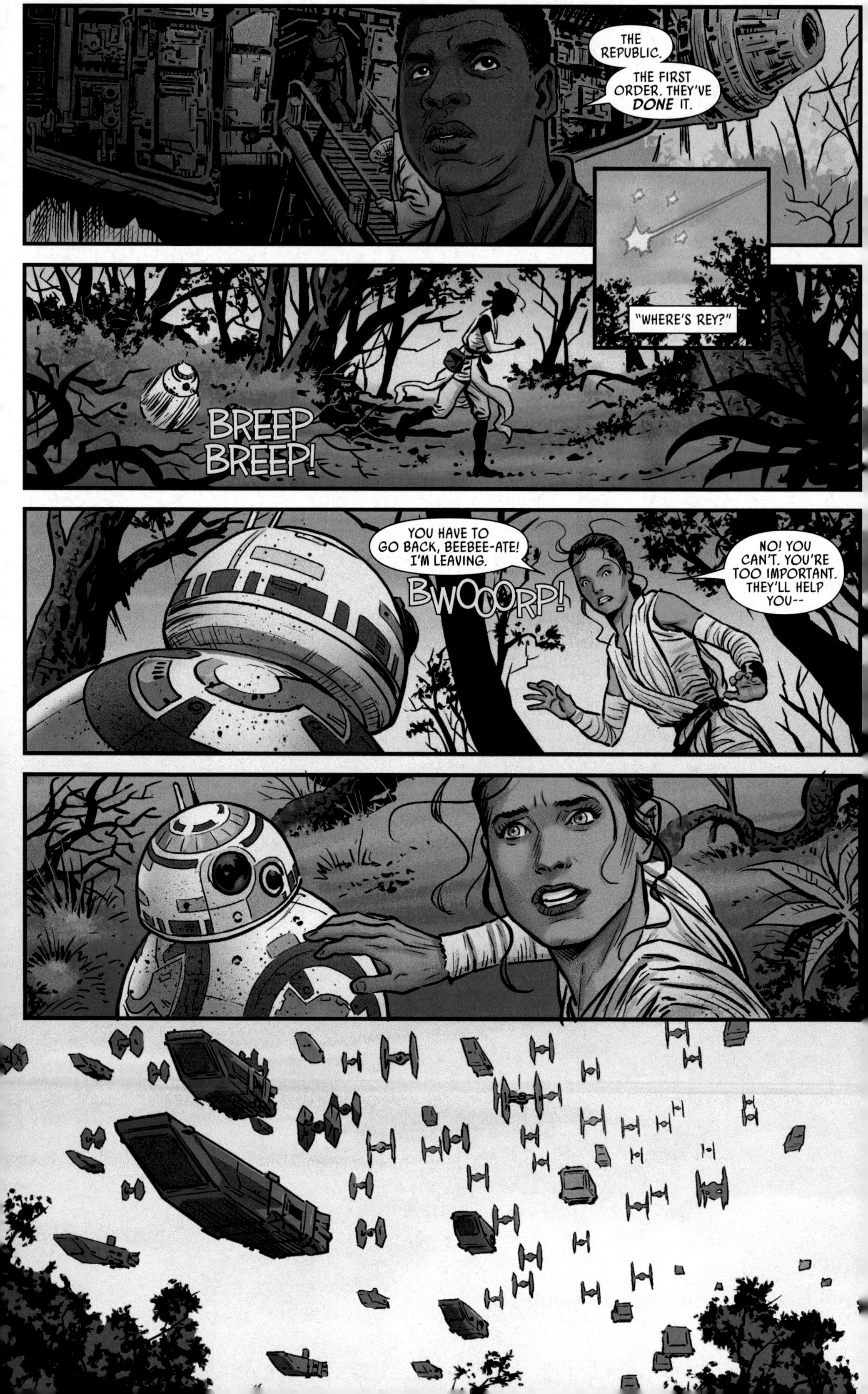
THE REPUBLIC.
THE FIRST ORDER. THEY'VE DONE IT.
"WHERE'S REY?"
BREEP BREEP!
YOU HAVE TO GO BACK, BEEBEE-ATE! I'M LEAVING.
BWOOORP!
NO! YOU CAN'T. YOU'RE TOO IMPORTANT. THEY'LL HELP YOU--

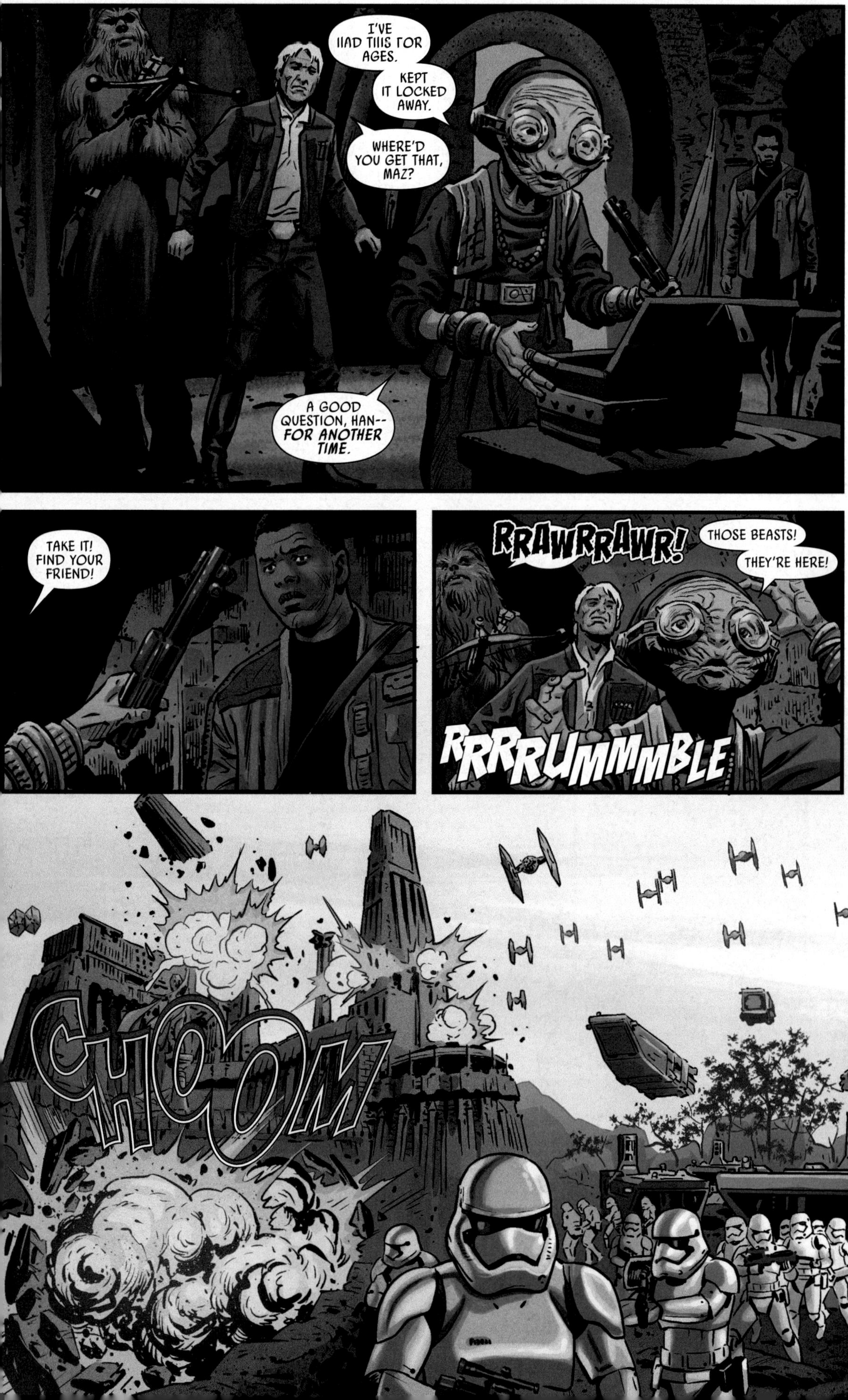
I'VE HAD THIS FOR AGES.
KEPT IT LOCKED AWAY.
WHERE'D YOU GET THAT, MAZ?
A GOOD QUESTION, HAN-- FOR ANOTHER TIME.
TAKE IT! FIND YOUR FRIEND!
RRAWRRAWR!
THOSE BEASTS!
THEY'RE HERE!
RRRRUMMMBLE
CHOOM

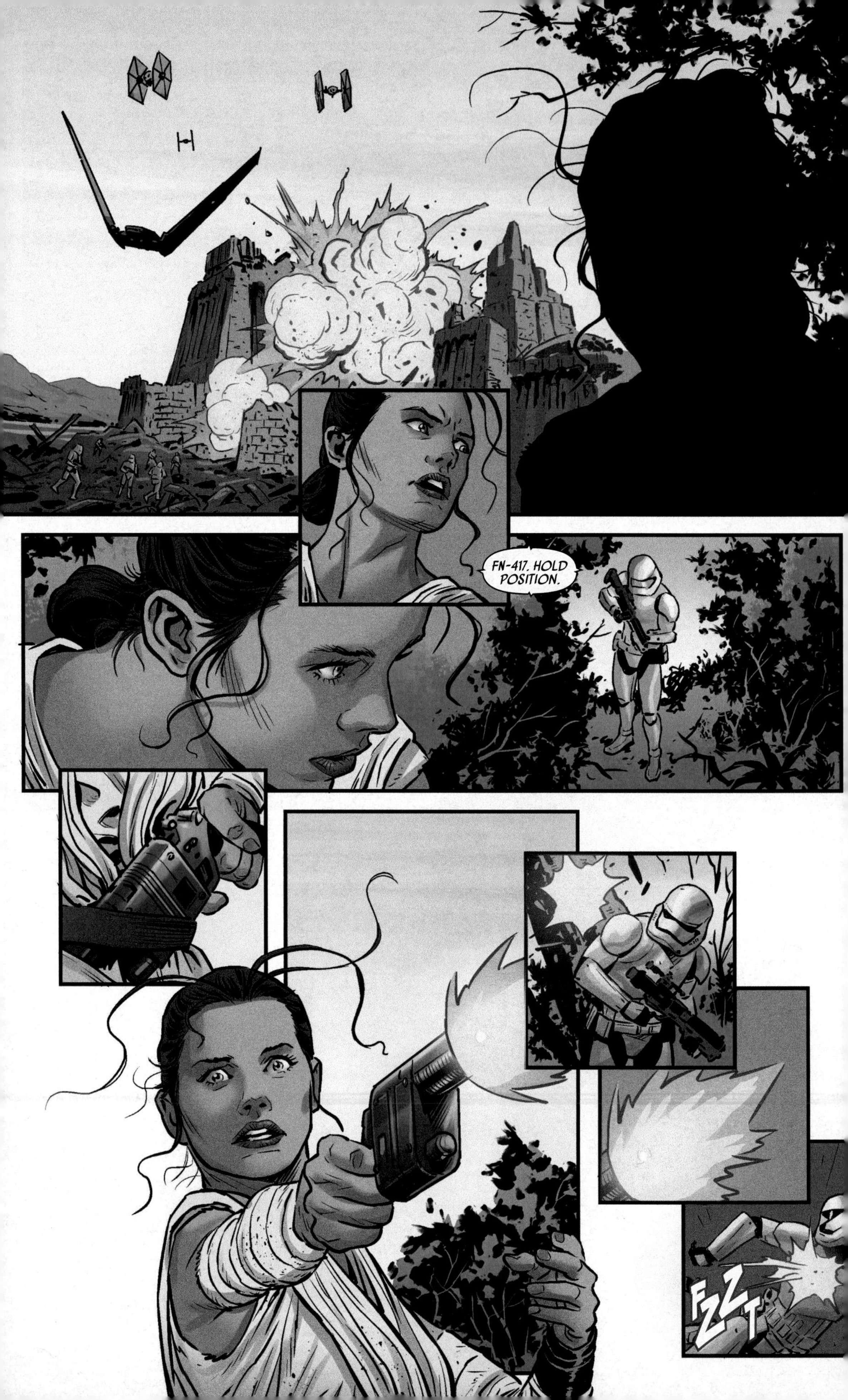
FN-417. HOLD POSITION.
FZZT

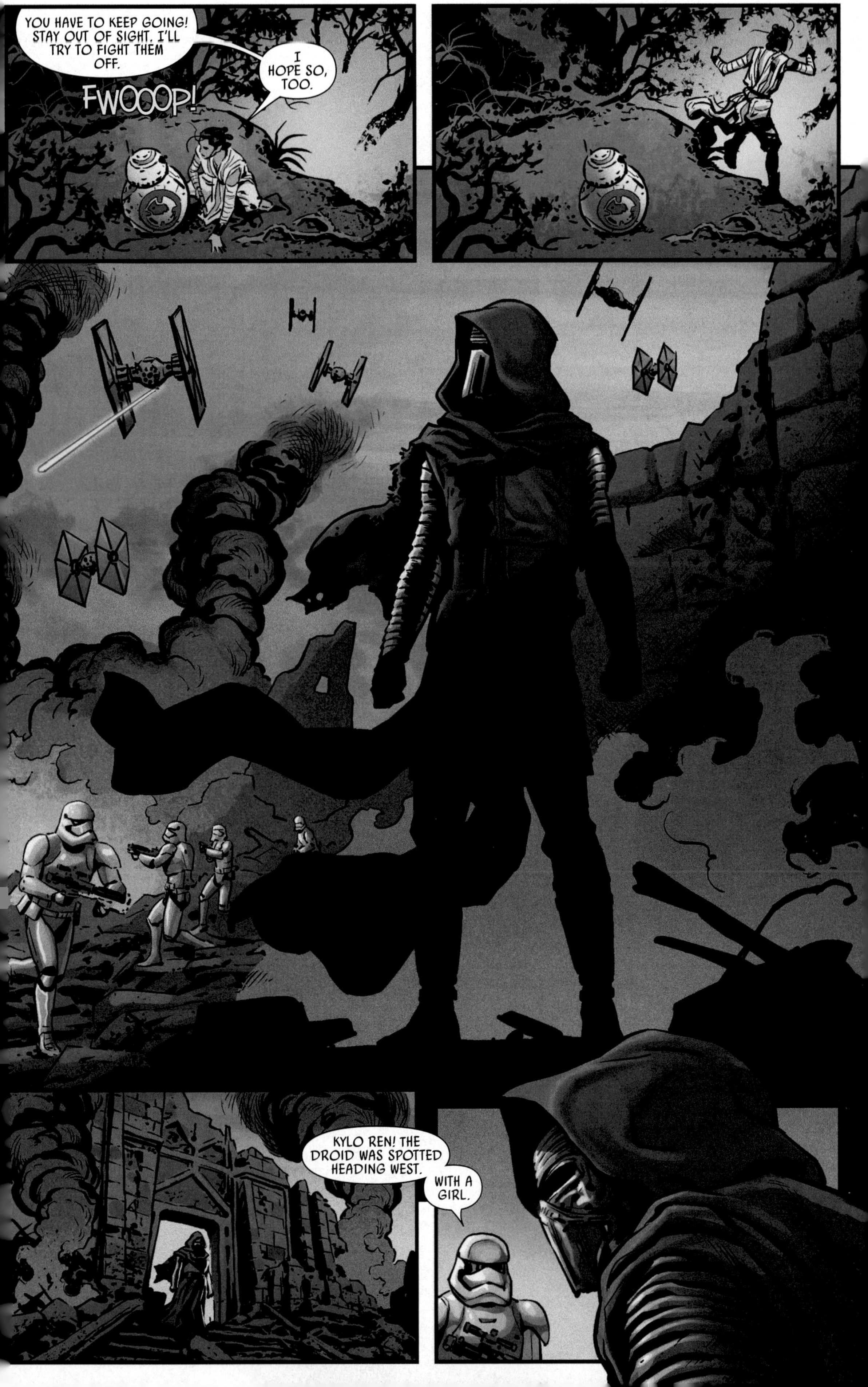
YOU HAVE TO KEEP GOING! STAY OUT OF SIGHT. I'LL TRY TO FIGHT THEM OFF.
I HOPE SO, TOO.
FWOOOP!
KYLO REN! THE DROID WAS SPOTTED HEADING WEST.
WITH A GIRL.

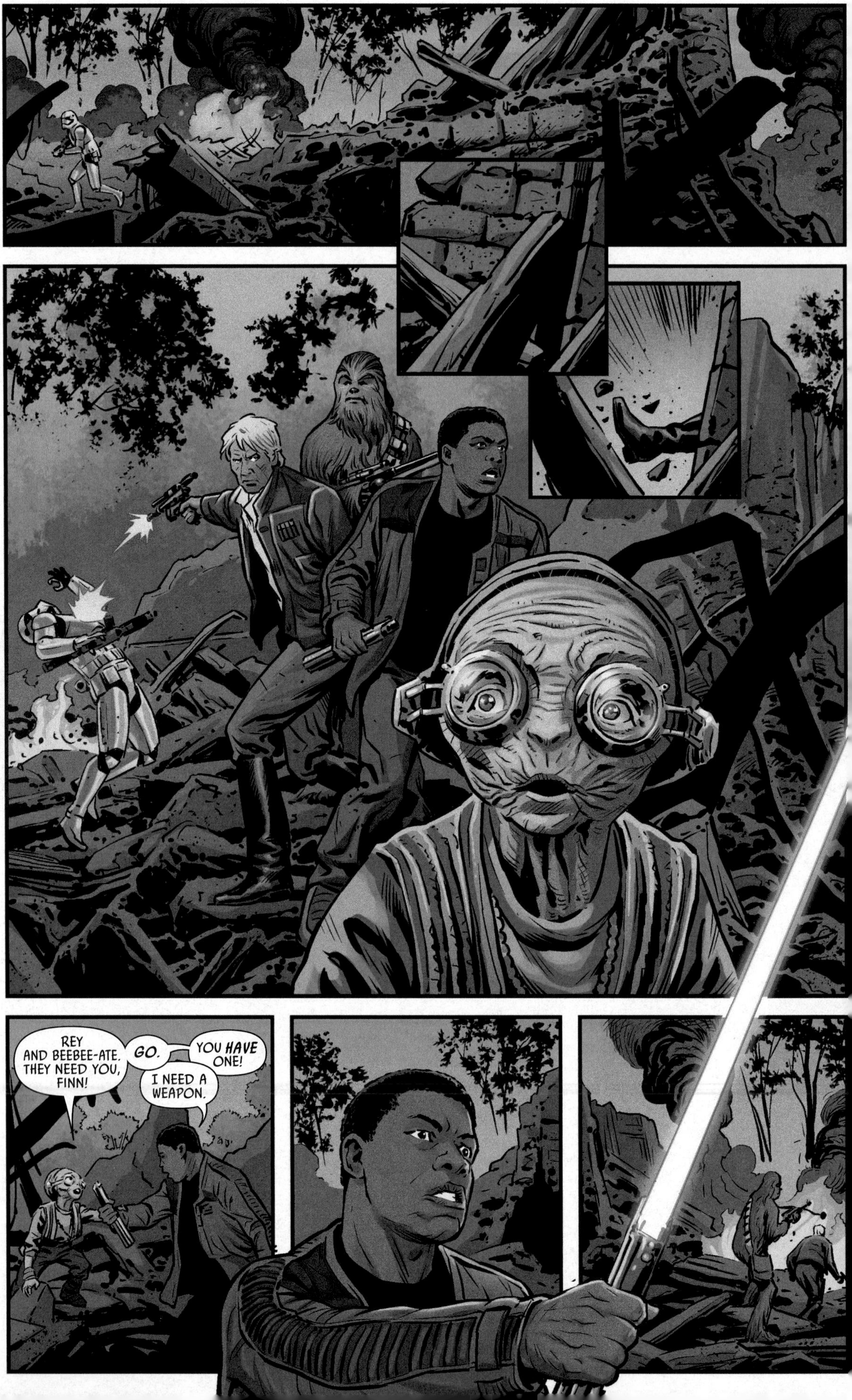
REY AND BEEBEE-ATE. THEY NEED YOU, FINN!
GO.
I NEED A WEAPON.
YOU HAVE ONE!

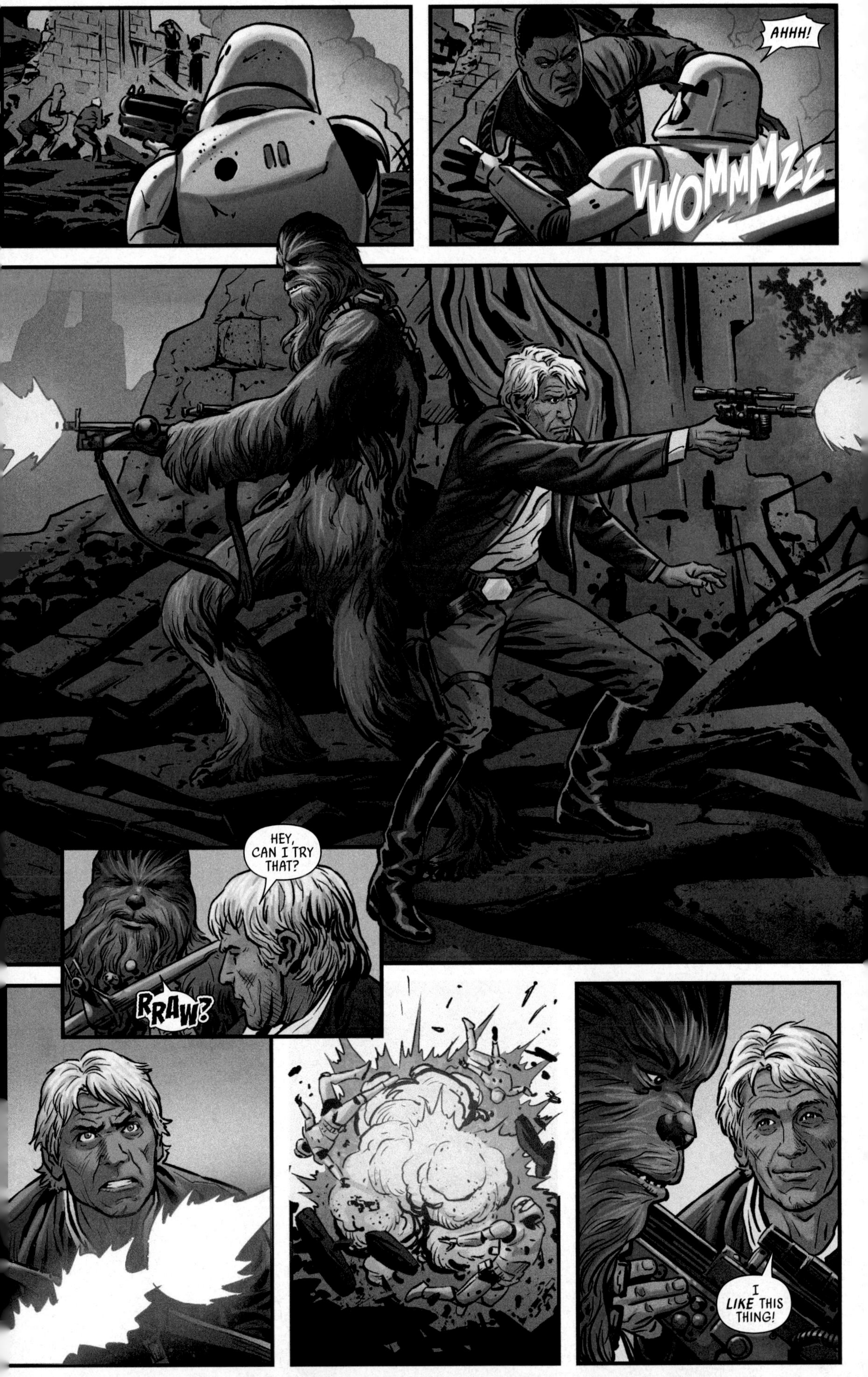
AHHH!
VWOMMMZZ
HEY, CAN I TRY THAT?
RRAW?
I LIKE THIS THING!

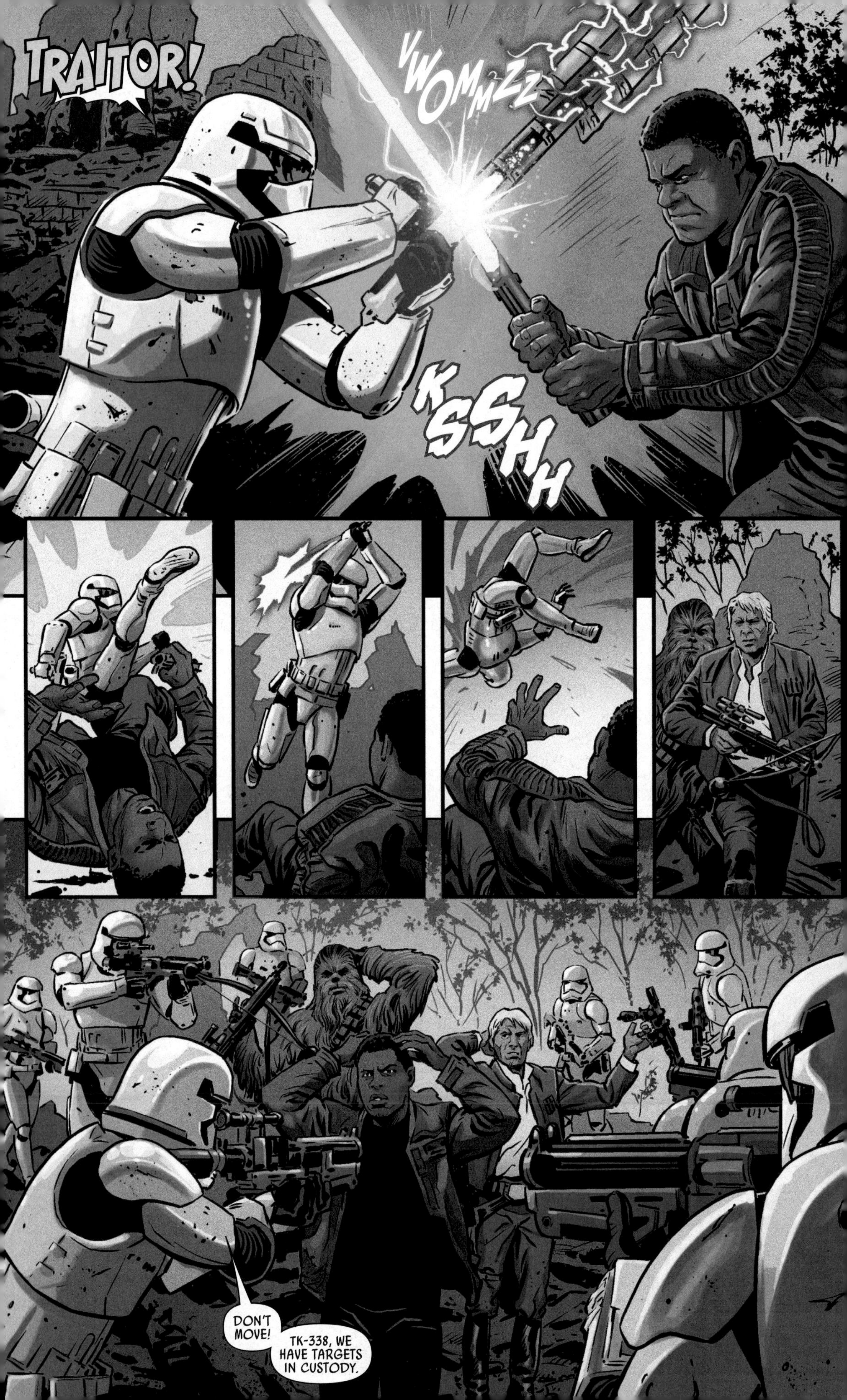
TRAITOR!
VWOMMZZ
KSSHH
DON'T MOVE!
TK-338, WE HAVE TARGETS IN CUSTODY.

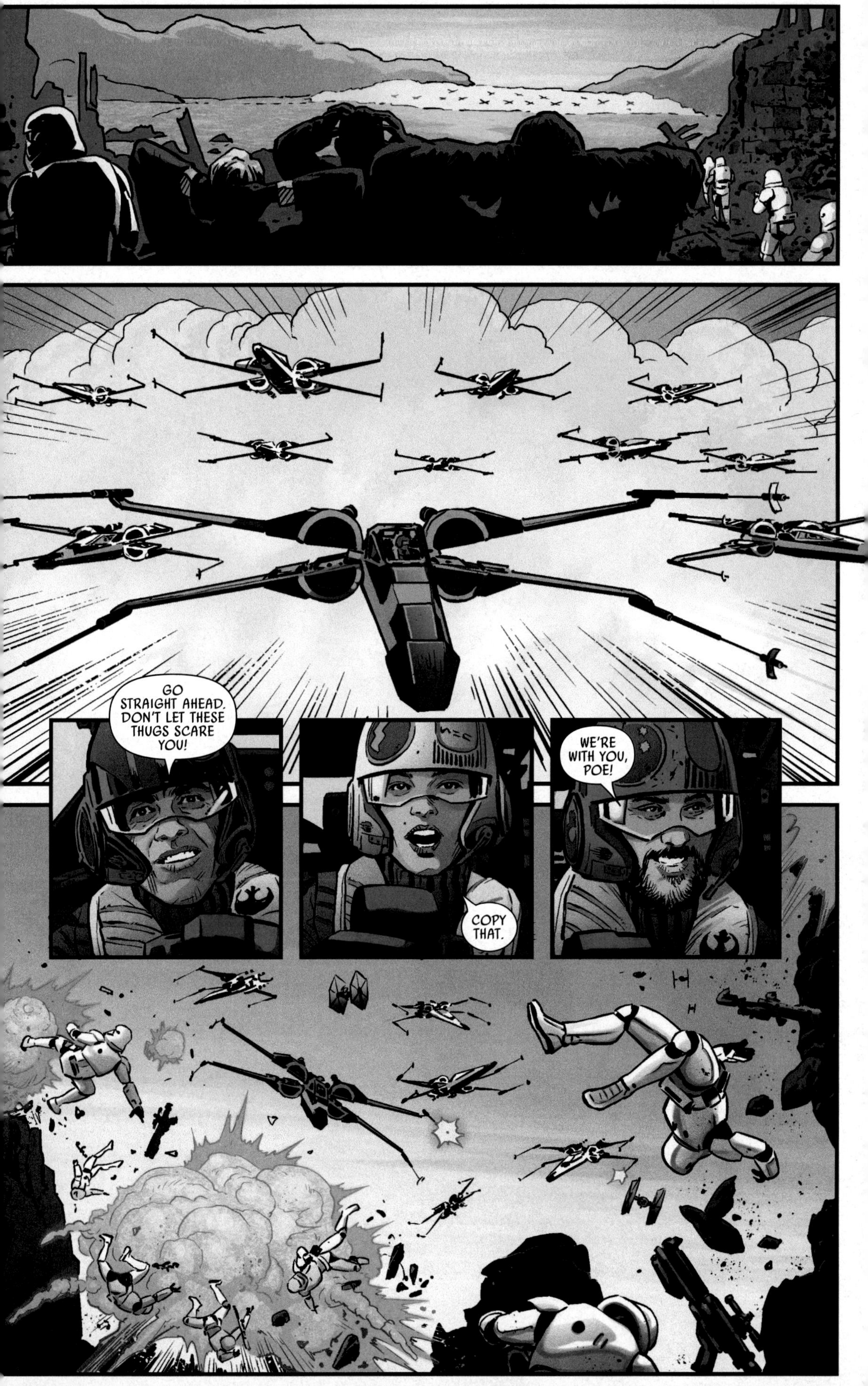
GO STRAIGHT AHEAD. DON'T LET THESE THUGS SCARE YOU!
COPY THAT.
WE'RE WITH YOU, POE!

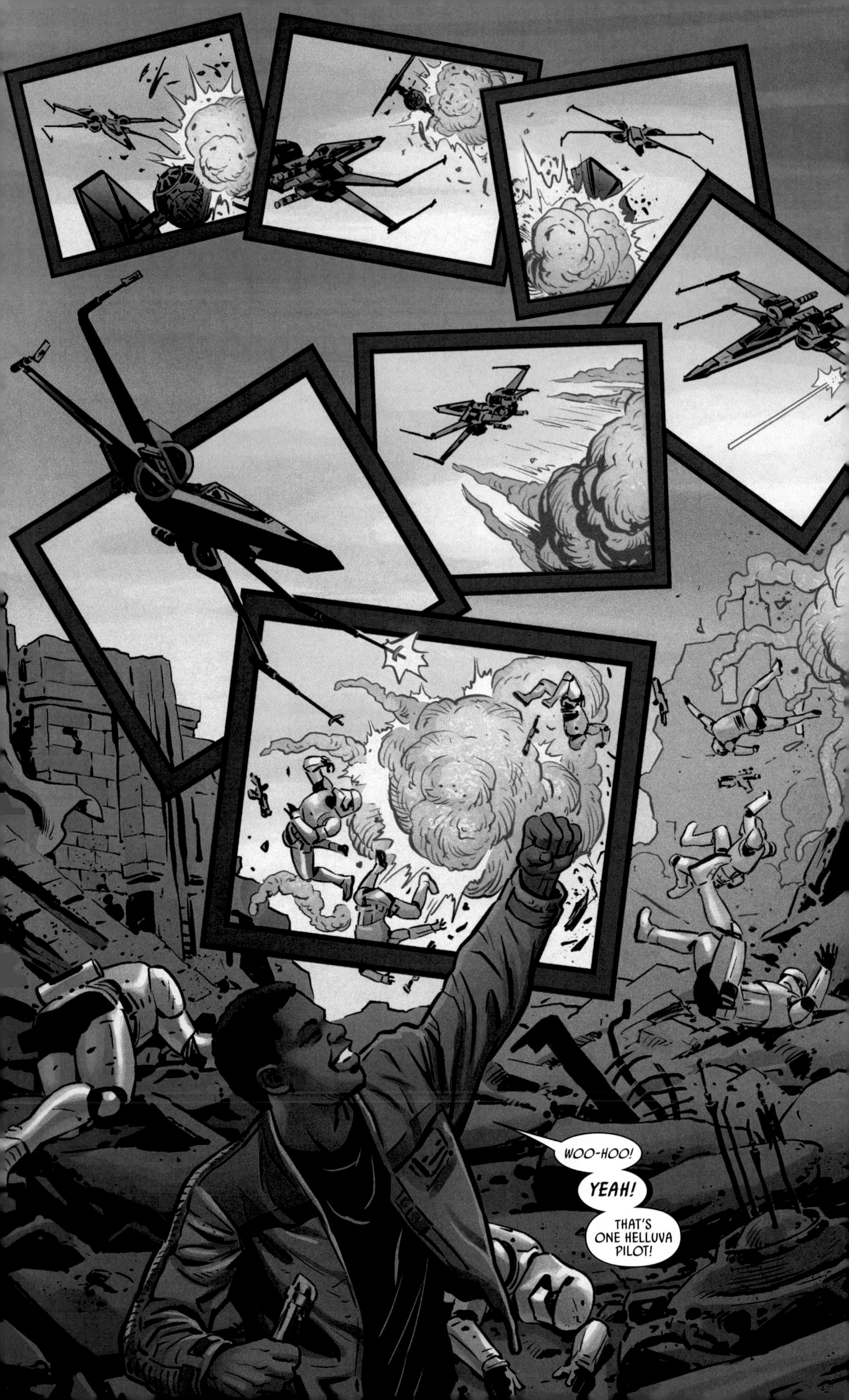
WOO-HOO!
YEAH!
THAT'S ONE HELLUVA PILOT!

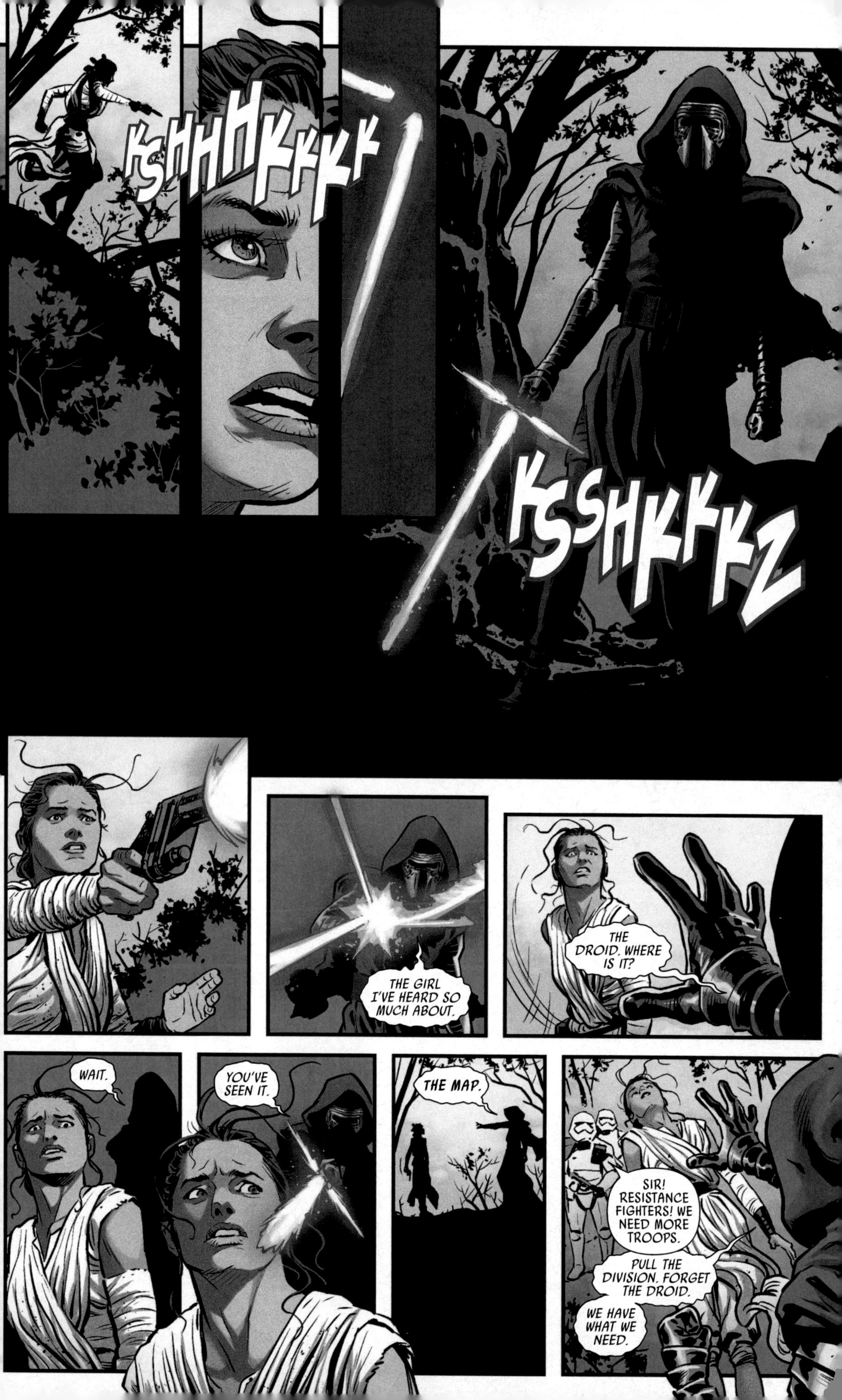
KSHHKKKK
KSSHKKKZ
THE GIRL I'VE HEARD SO MUCH ABOUT.
THE DROID. WHERE IS IT?
WAIT.
YOU'VE SEEN IT.
THE MAP.
SIR! RESISTANCE FIGHTERS! WE NEED MORE TROOPS.
PULL THE DIVISION. FORGET THE DROID.
WE HAVE WHAT WE NEED.

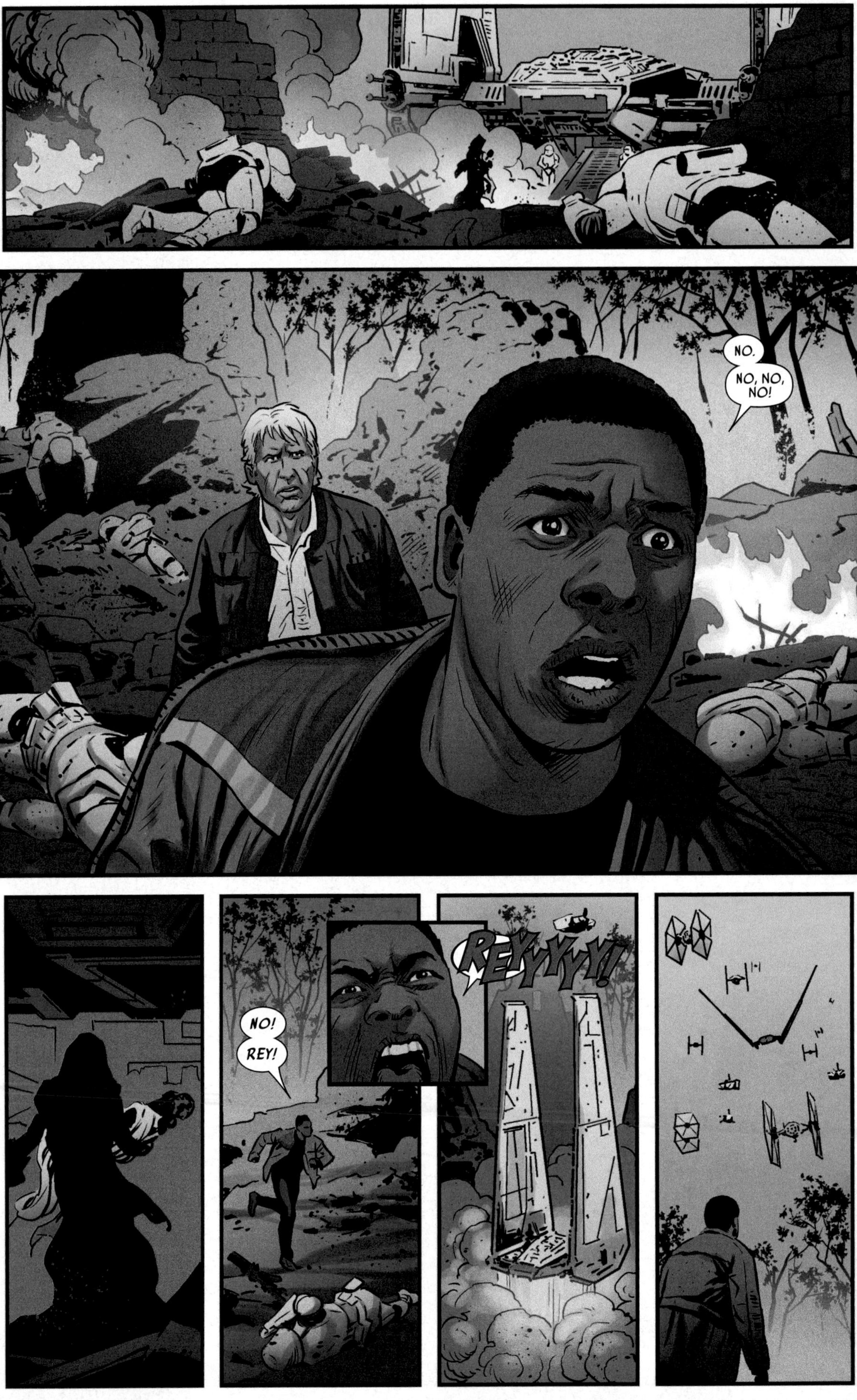
NO.
NO, NO, NO!
NO!
REY!
REYYYYY!

HE TOOK HER! SHE'S *GONE!*

YEAH. YEAH...I KNOW...

LOOK WHO IT IS! DID YOU SEE WHO--? OH.

EXCUSE ME, PRINC--

UH, *GENERAL.* SORRY.

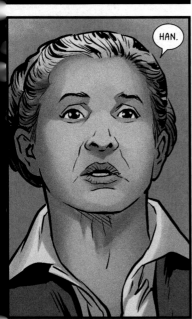

HAN.

I SAW HIM, LEIA.

I SAW OUR SON.

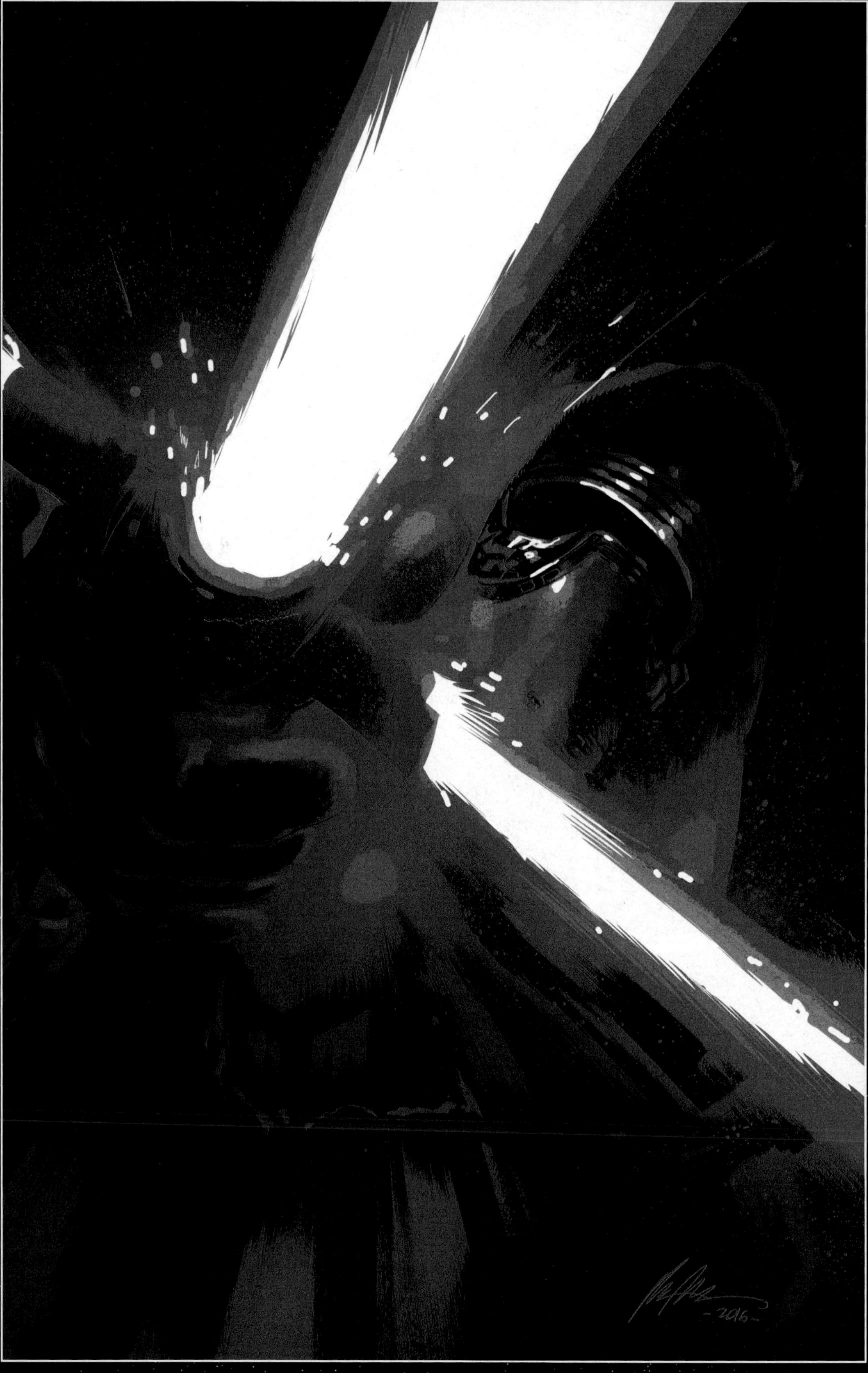

THE FORCE AWAKENS #5

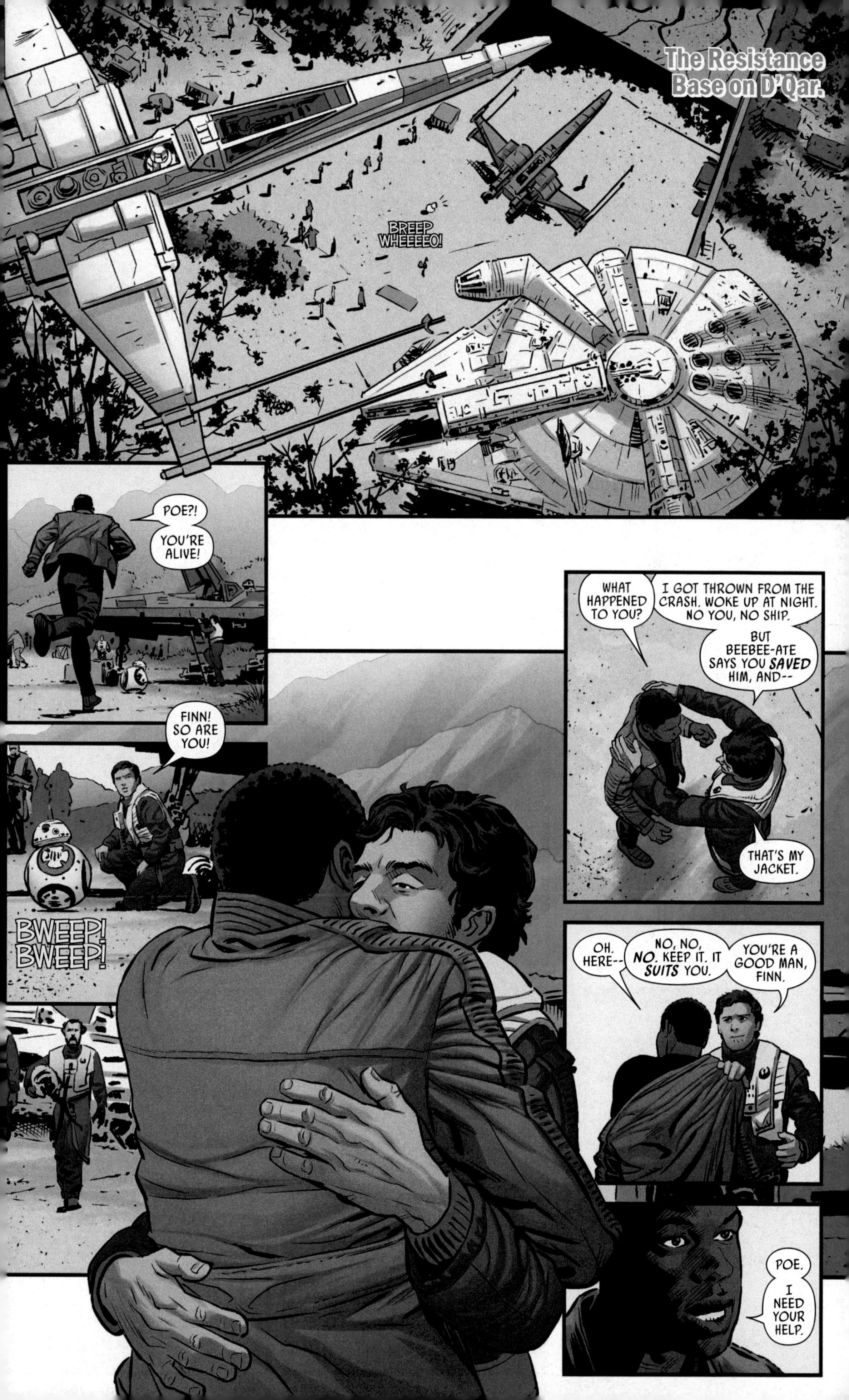
The Resistance Base on D'Qar.
BREEP WHEEEEO!
POE?!
YOU'RE ALIVE!
FINN! SO ARE YOU!
BWEEP! BWEEP!
WHAT HAPPENED TO YOU?
I GOT THROWN FROM THE CRASH. WOKE UP AT NIGHT. NO YOU, NO SHIP.
BUT BEEBEE-ATE SAYS YOU SAVED HIM, AND--
THAT'S MY JACKET.
OH. HERE--
NO, NO, NO. KEEP IT. IT SUITS YOU.
YOU'RE A GOOD MAN, FINN.
POE.
I NEED YOUR HELP.

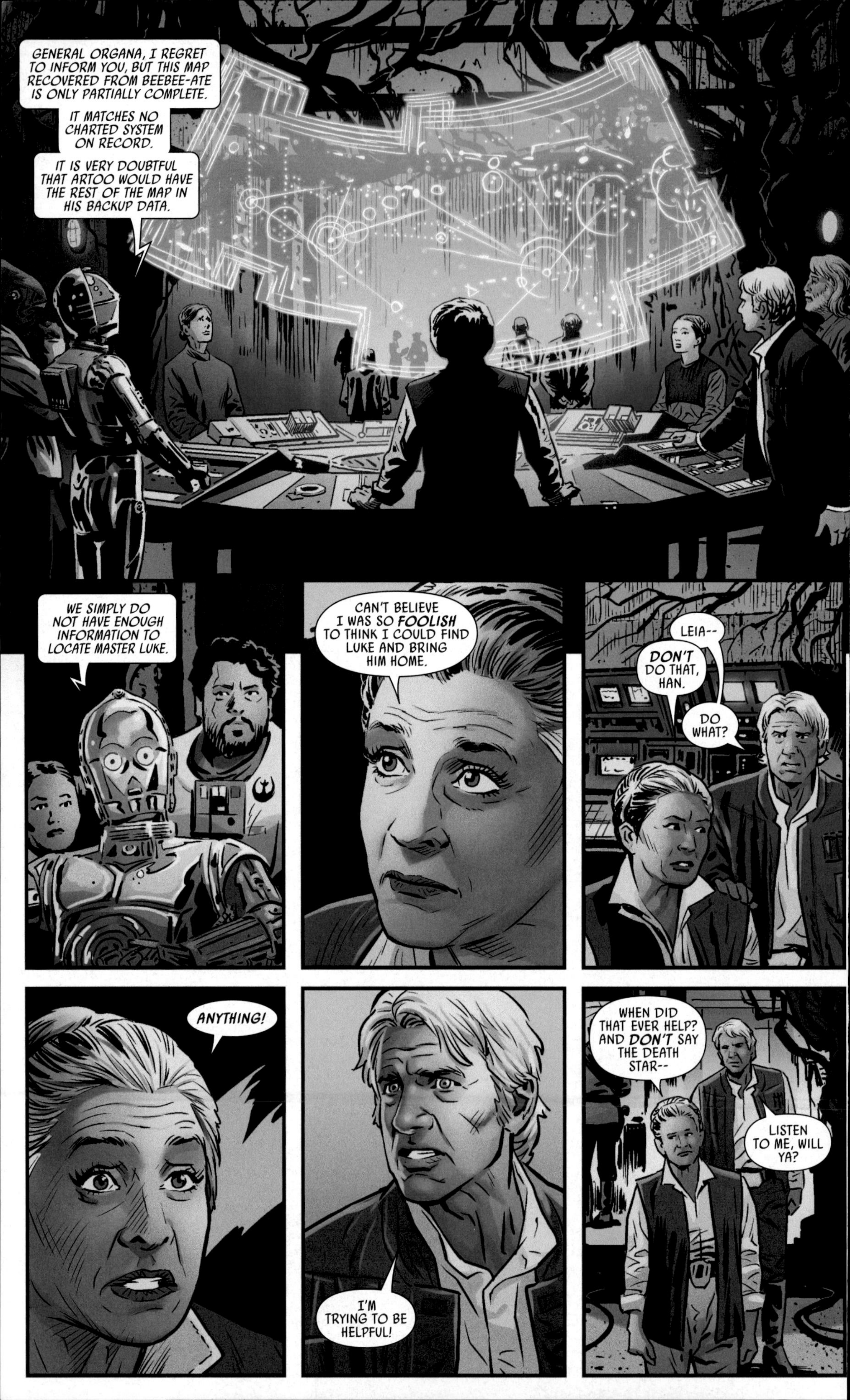
GENERAL ORGANA, I REGRET TO INFORM YOU, BUT THIS MAP RECOVERED FROM BEEBEE-ATE IS ONLY PARTIALLY COMPLETE.
IT MATCHES NO CHARTED SYSTEM ON RECORD.
IT IS VERY DOUBTFUL THAT ARTOO WOULD HAVE THE REST OF THE MAP IN HIS BACKUP DATA.
WE SIMPLY DO NOT HAVE ENOUGH INFORMATION TO LOCATE MASTER LUKE.
CAN'T BELIEVE I WAS SO FOOLISH TO THINK I COULD FIND LUKE AND BRING HIM HOME.
LEIA--
DON'T DO THAT, HAN.
DO WHAT?
ANYTHING!
I'M TRYING TO BE HELPFUL!
WHEN DID THAT EVER HELP? AND DON'T SAY THE DEATH STAR--
LISTEN TO ME, WILL YA?

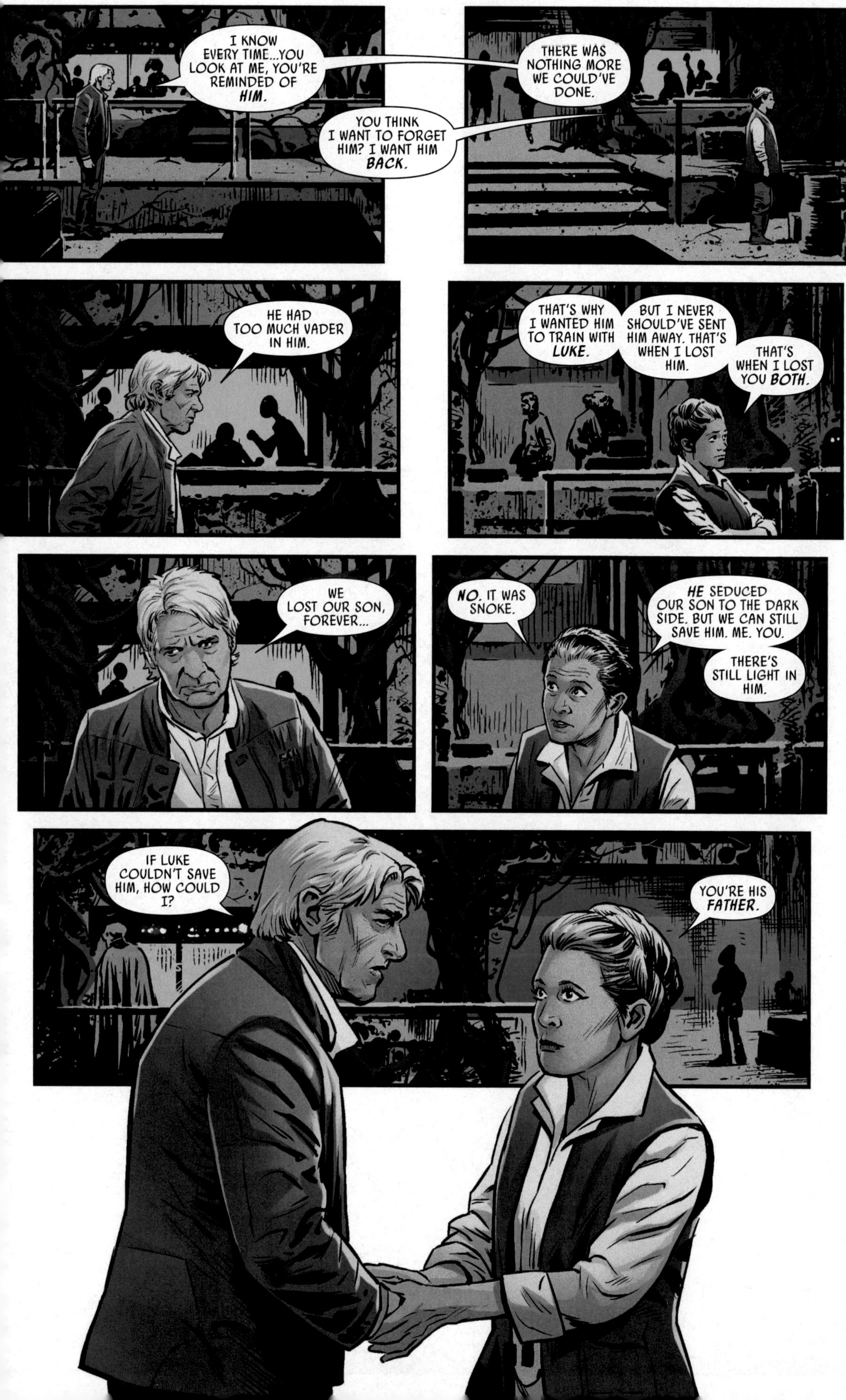

I KNOW EVERY TIME...YOU LOOK AT ME, YOU'RE REMINDED OF HIM.
THERE WAS NOTHING MORE WE COULD'VE DONE.
YOU THINK I WANT TO FORGET HIM? I WANT HIM BACK.
HE HAD TOO MUCH VADER IN HIM.
THAT'S WHY I WANTED HIM TO TRAIN WITH LUKE.
BUT I NEVER SHOULD'VE SENT HIM AWAY. THAT'S WHEN I LOST HIM.
THAT'S WHEN I LOST YOU BOTH.
WE LOST OUR SON, FOREVER...
NO. IT WAS SNOKE.
HE SEDUCED OUR SON TO THE DARK SIDE. BUT WE CAN STILL SAVE HIM. ME. YOU.
THERE'S STILL LIGHT IN HIM.
IF LUKE COULDN'T SAVE HIM, HOW COULD I?
YOU'RE HIS FATHER.

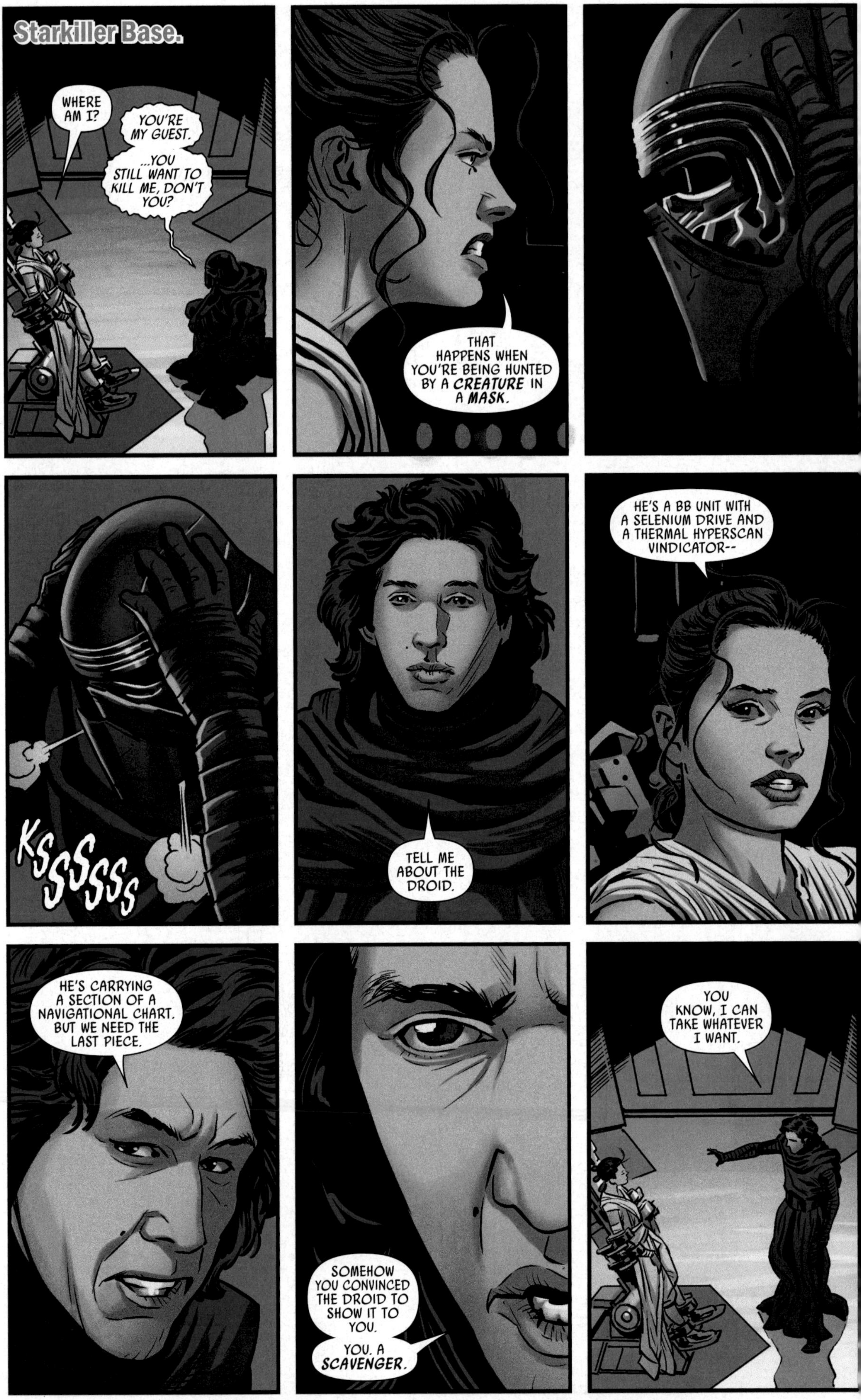
Starkiller Base.
WHERE AM I?
YOU'RE MY GUEST.
...YOU STILL WANT TO KILL ME, DON'T YOU?
THAT HAPPENS WHEN YOU'RE BEING HUNTED BY A CREATURE IN A MASK.
KSSSSSS
TELL ME ABOUT THE DROID.
HE'S A BB UNIT WITH A SELENIUM DRIVE AND A THERMAL HYPERSCAN VINDICATOR--
HE'S CARRYING A SECTION OF A NAVIGATIONAL CHART. BUT WE NEED THE LAST PIECE.
SOMEHOW YOU CONVINCED THE DROID TO SHOW IT TO YOU.
YOU. A SCAVENGER.
YOU KNOW, I CAN TAKE WHATEVER I WANT.

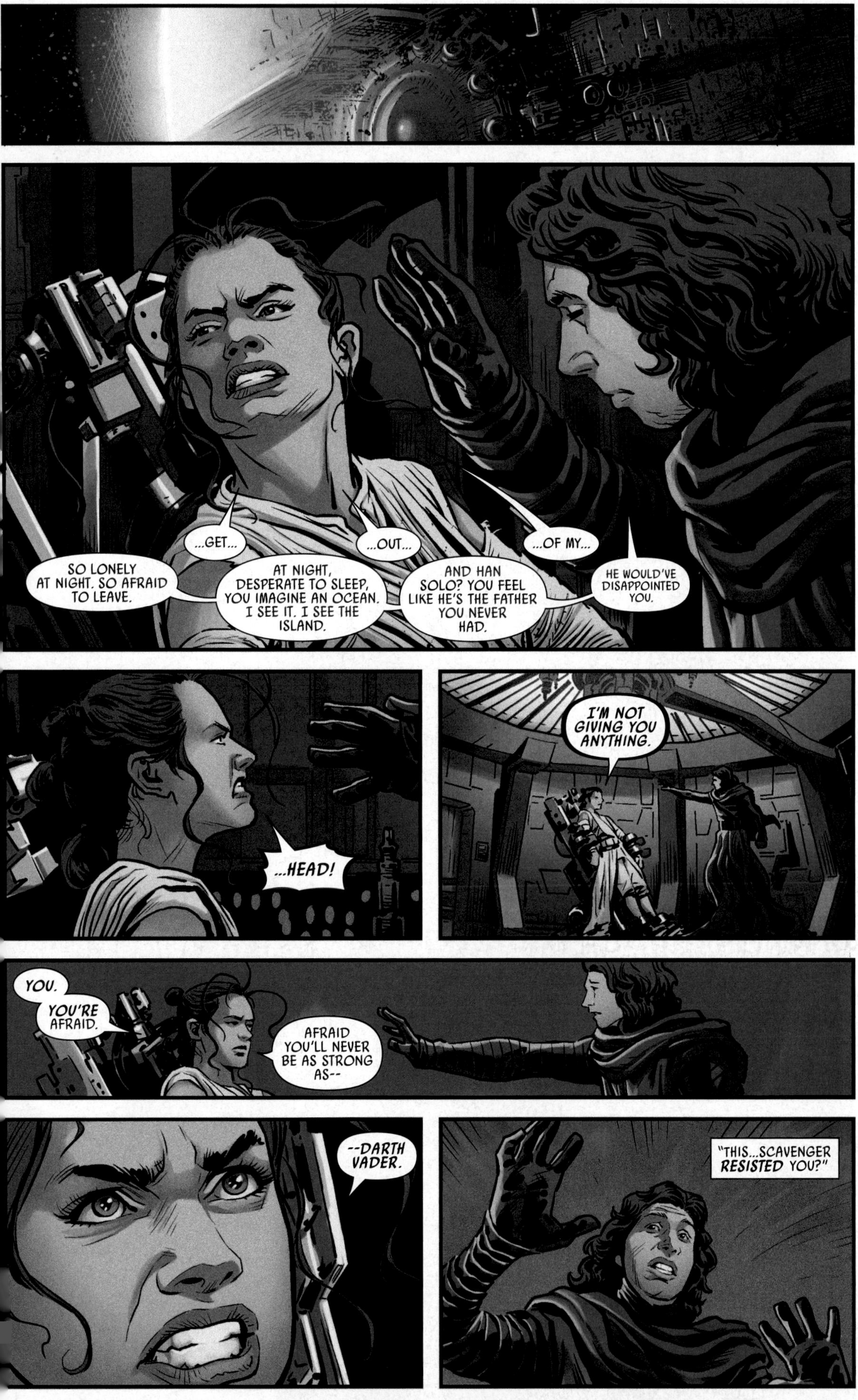

...GET...
...OUT...
...OF MY...
SO LONELY AT NIGHT. SO AFRAID TO LEAVE.
AT NIGHT, DESPERATE TO SLEEP, YOU IMAGINE AN OCEAN. I SEE IT. I SEE THE ISLAND.
AND HAN SOLO? YOU FEEL LIKE HE'S THE FATHER YOU NEVER HAD.
HE WOULD'VE DISAPPOINTED YOU.
...HEAD!
I'M NOT GIVING YOU ANYTHING.
YOU.
YOU'RE AFRAID.
AFRAID YOU'LL NEVER BE AS STRONG AS--
--DARTH VADER.
"THIS...SCAVENGER RESISTED YOU?"

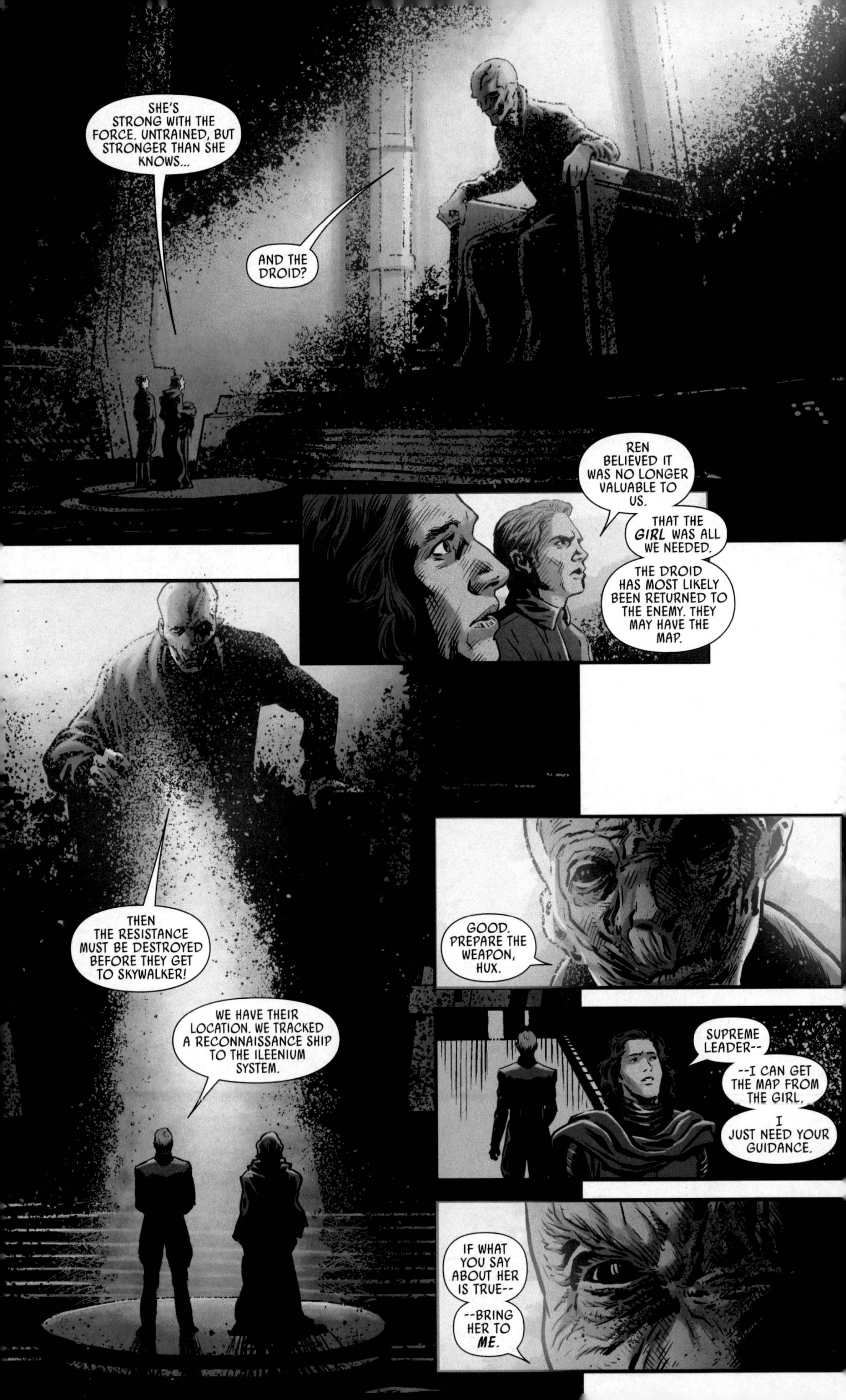
SHE'S STRONG WITH THE FORCE. UNTRAINED, BUT STRONGER THAN SHE KNOWS...
AND THE DROID?
REN BELIEVED IT WAS NO LONGER VALUABLE TO US.
THAT THE *GIRL* WAS ALL WE NEEDED.
THE DROID HAS MOST LIKELY BEEN RETURNED TO THE ENEMY. THEY MAY HAVE THE MAP.
THEN THE RESISTANCE MUST BE DESTROYED BEFORE THEY GET TO SKYWALKER!
WE HAVE THEIR LOCATION. WE TRACKED A RECONNAISSANCE SHIP TO THE ILEENIUM SYSTEM.
GOOD. PREPARE THE WEAPON, HUX.
SUPREME LEADER--
--I CAN GET THE MAP FROM THE GIRL.
I JUST NEED YOUR GUIDANCE.
IF WHAT YOU SAY ABOUT HER IS TRUE--
--BRING HER TO *ME.*

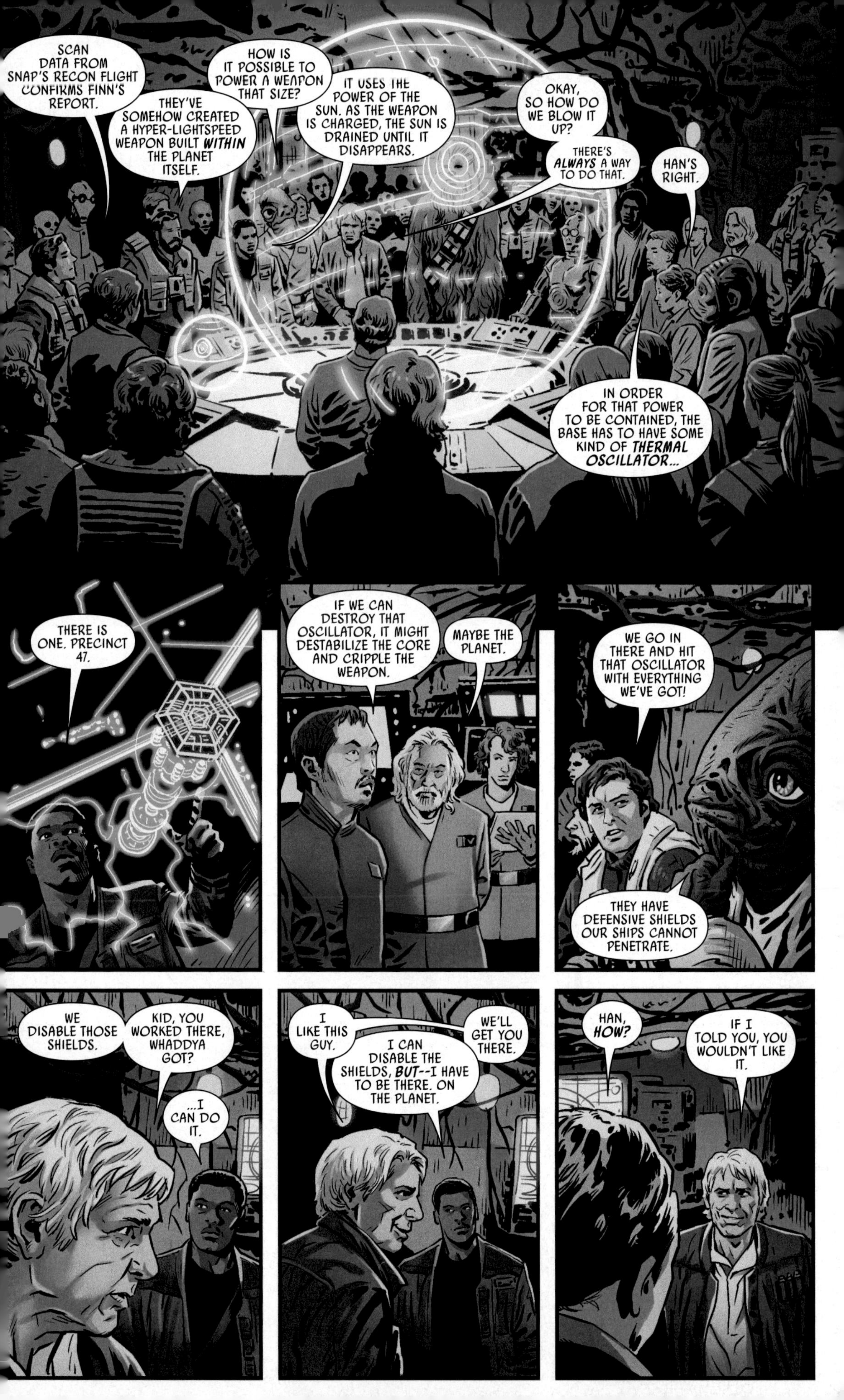
SCAN DATA FROM SNAP'S RECON FLIGHT CONFIRMS FINN'S REPORT.
THEY'VE SOMEHOW CREATED A HYPER-LIGHTSPEED WEAPON BUILT *WITHIN* THE PLANET ITSELF.
HOW IS IT POSSIBLE TO POWER A WEAPON THAT SIZE?
IT USES THE POWER OF THE SUN. AS THE WEAPON IS CHARGED, THE SUN IS DRAINED UNTIL IT DISAPPEARS.
OKAY, SO HOW DO WE BLOW IT UP?
THERE'S *ALWAYS* A WAY TO DO THAT.
HAN'S RIGHT.
IN ORDER FOR THAT POWER TO BE CONTAINED, THE BASE HAS TO HAVE SOME KIND OF *THERMAL OSCILLATOR*...
THERE IS ONE. PRECINCT 47.
IF WE CAN DESTROY THAT OSCILLATOR, IT MIGHT DESTABILIZE THE CORE AND CRIPPLE THE WEAPON.
MAYBE THE PLANET.
WE GO IN THERE AND HIT THAT OSCILLATOR WITH EVERYTHING WE'VE GOT!
THEY HAVE DEFENSIVE SHIELDS OUR SHIPS CANNOT PENETRATE.
WE DISABLE THOSE SHIELDS.
KID, YOU WORKED THERE, WHADDYA GOT?
...I CAN DO IT.
I LIKE THIS GUY.
WE'LL GET YOU THERE.
I CAN DISABLE THE SHIELDS, *BUT*--I HAVE TO BE THERE. ON THE PLANET.
HAN, *HOW?*
IF I TOLD YOU, YOU WOULDN'T LIKE IT.

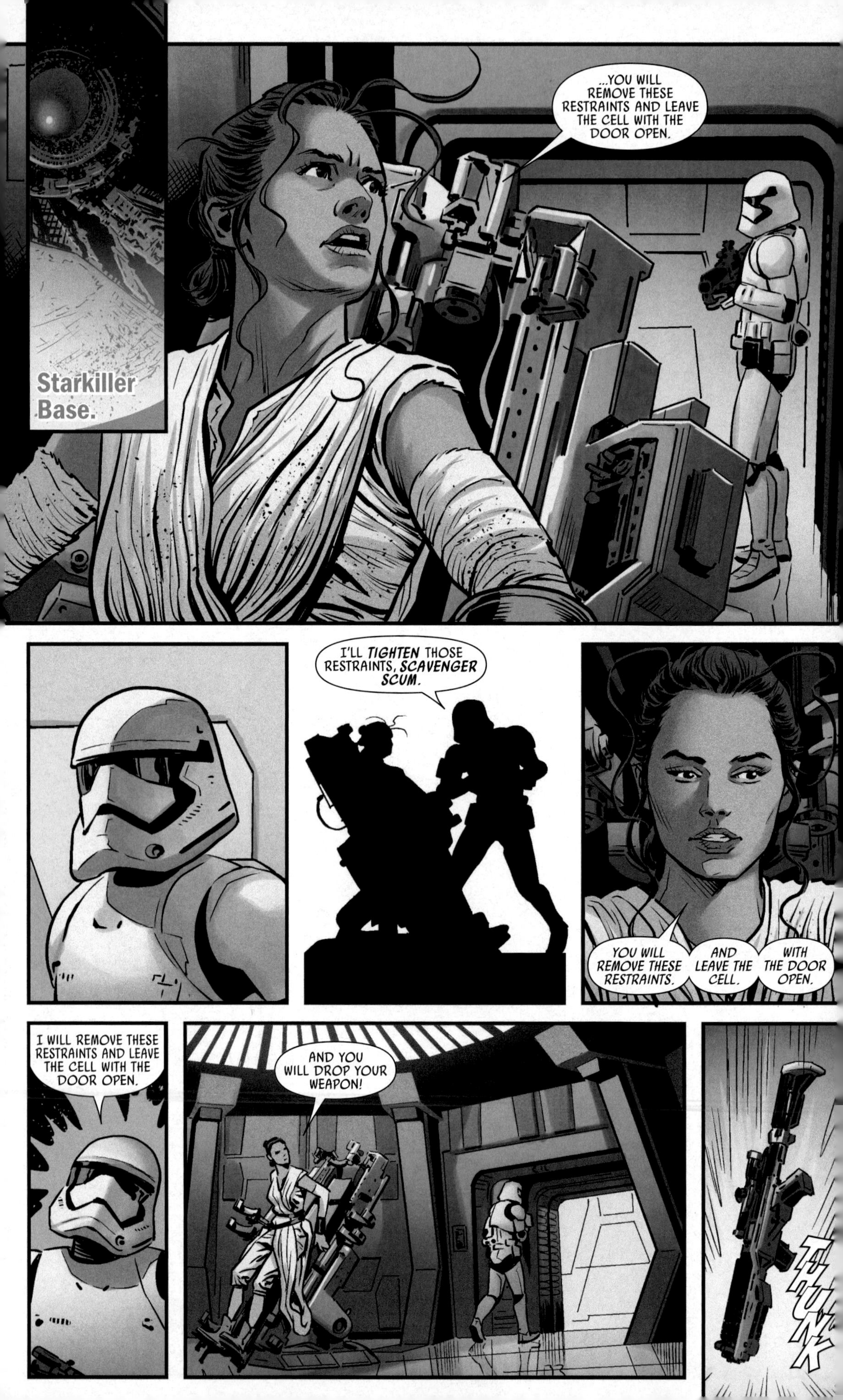
Starkiller Base.
...YOU WILL REMOVE THESE RESTRAINTS AND LEAVE THE CELL WITH THE DOOR OPEN.
I'LL TIGHTEN THOSE RESTRAINTS, SCAVENGER SCUM.
YOU WILL REMOVE THESE RESTRAINTS.
AND LEAVE THE CELL.
WITH THE DOOR OPEN.
I WILL REMOVE THESE RESTRAINTS AND LEAVE THE CELL WITH THE DOOR OPEN.
AND YOU WILL DROP YOUR WEAPON!
THUNK

NO.
KZZZSH
BEGIN CHARGING THE WEAPON!
YES, SIR. WEAPON CHARGING.

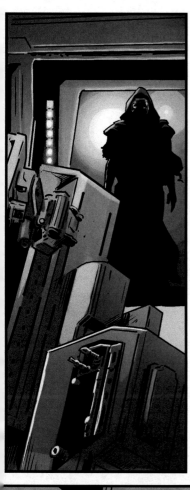

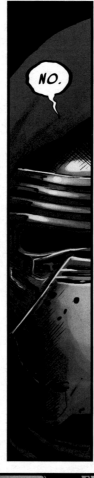

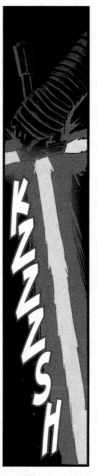

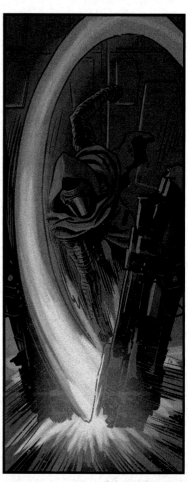

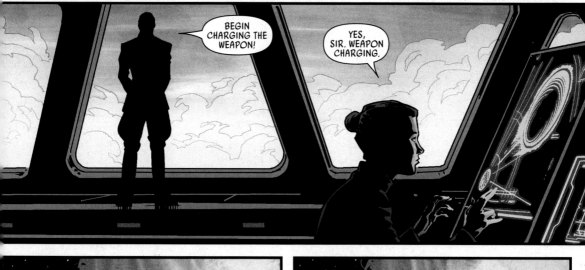

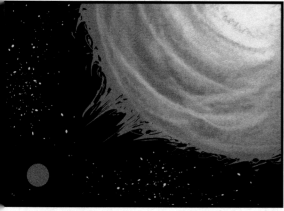

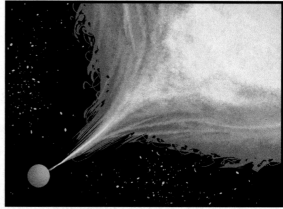

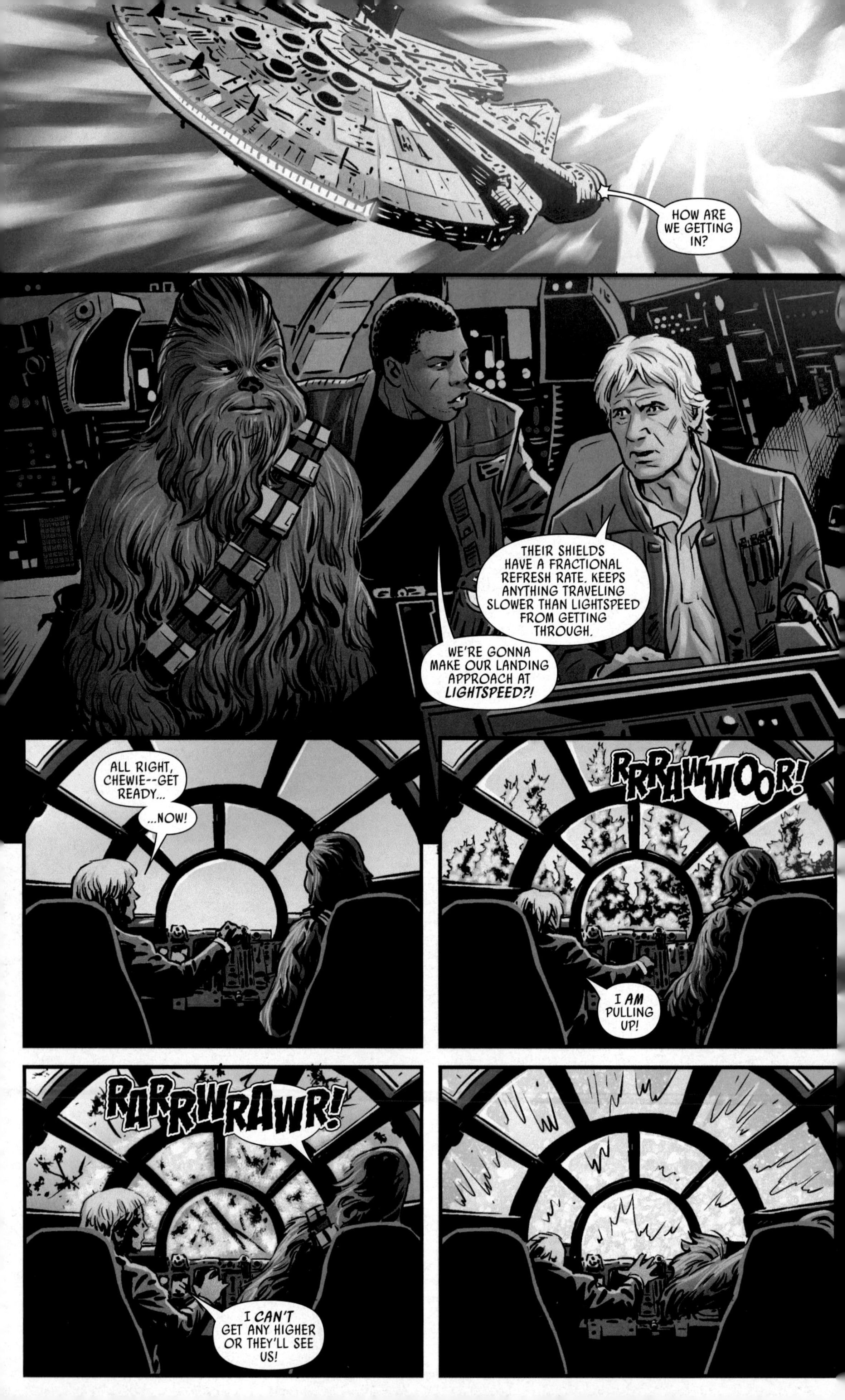
HOW ARE WE GETTING IN?
THEIR SHIELDS HAVE A FRACTIONAL REFRESH RATE. KEEPS ANYTHING TRAVELING SLOWER THAN LIGHTSPEED FROM GETTING THROUGH.
WE'RE GONNA MAKE OUR LANDING APPROACH AT *LIGHTSPEED?!*
ALL RIGHT, CHEWIE--GET READY...
...NOW!
RRRAWWOOR!
I AM PULLING UP!
RARRRWRAWR!
I *CAN'T* GET ANY HIGHER OR THEY'LL SEE US!

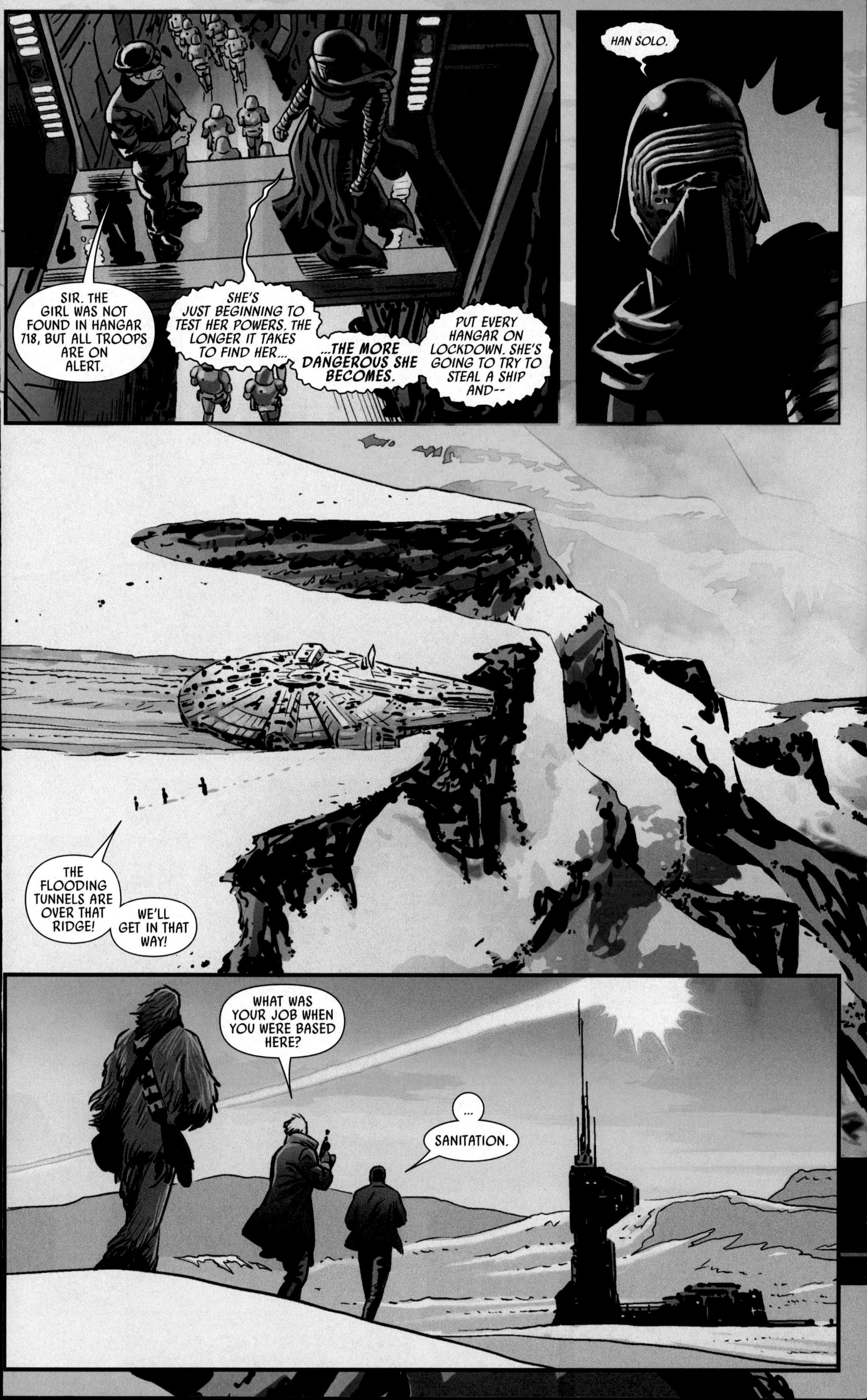
SIR. THE GIRL WAS NOT FOUND IN HANGAR 718, BUT ALL TROOPS ARE ON ALERT.
SHE'S JUST BEGINNING TO TEST HER POWERS. THE LONGER IT TAKES TO FIND HER...
...THE MORE DANGEROUS SHE BECOMES.
PUT EVERY HANGAR ON LOCKDOWN. SHE'S GOING TO TRY TO STEAL A SHIP AND--
HAN SOLO.
THE FLOODING TUNNELS ARE OVER THAT RIDGE!
WE'LL GET IN THAT WAY!
WHAT WAS YOUR JOB WHEN YOU WERE BASED HERE?
...
SANITATION.

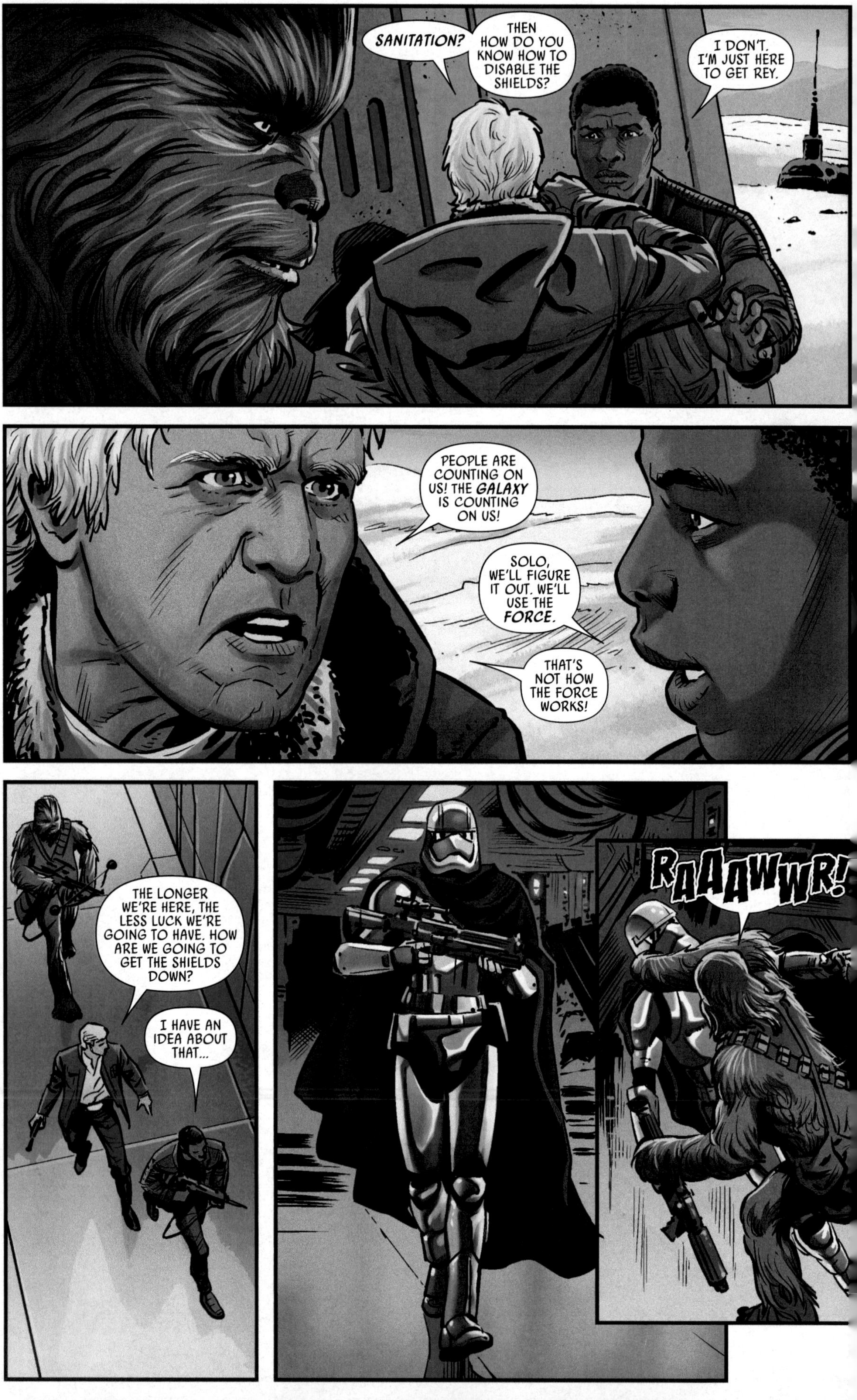
SANITATION?
THEN HOW DO YOU KNOW HOW TO DISABLE THE SHIELDS?
I DON'T. I'M JUST HERE TO GET REY.
PEOPLE ARE COUNTING ON US! THE GALAXY IS COUNTING ON US!
SOLO, WE'LL FIGURE IT OUT. WE'LL USE THE FORCE.
THAT'S NOT HOW THE FORCE WORKS!
THE LONGER WE'RE HERE, THE LESS LUCK WE'RE GOING TO HAVE. HOW ARE WE GOING TO GET THE SHIELDS DOWN?
I HAVE AN IDEA ABOUT THAT...
RAAAWWR!

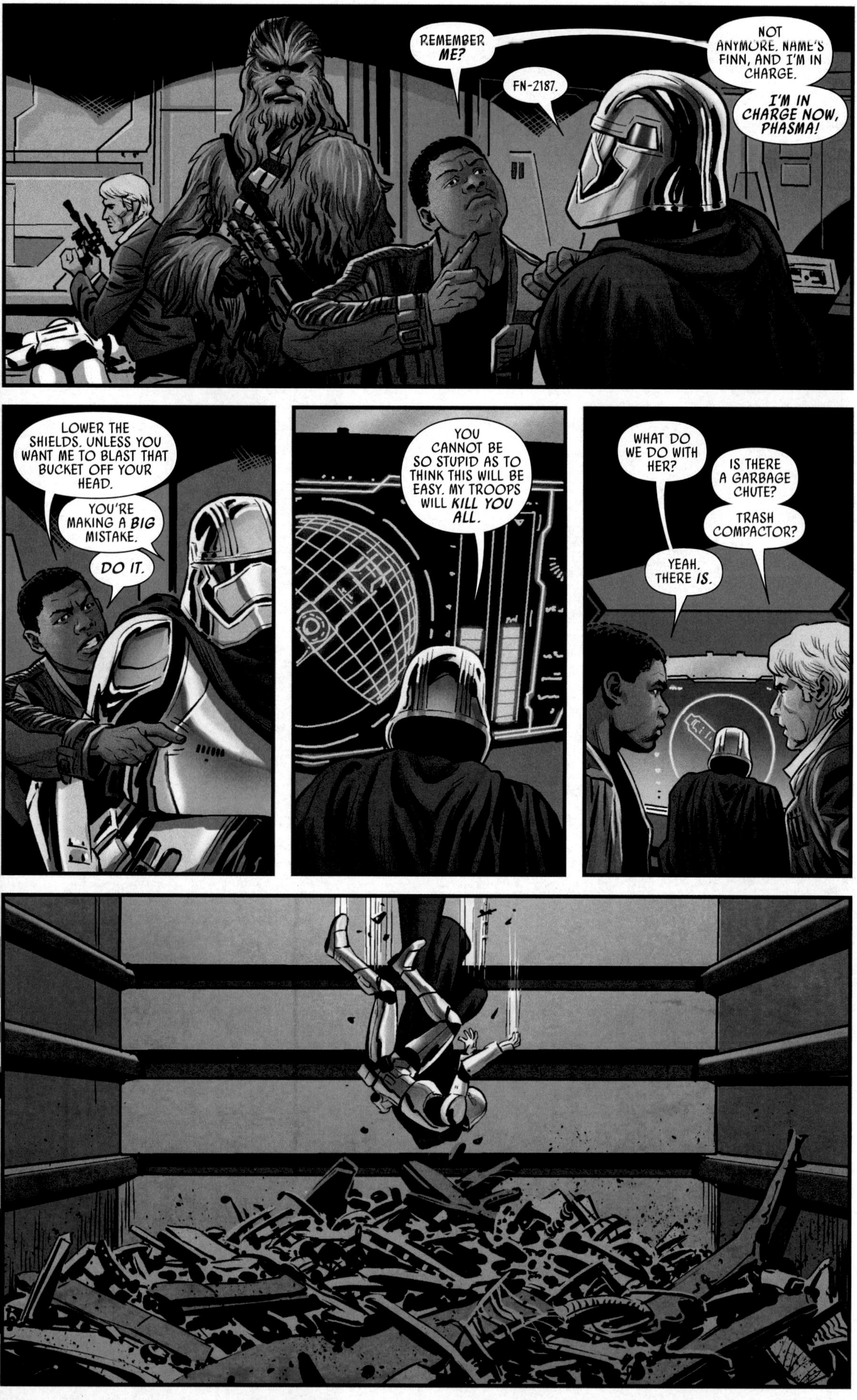
REMEMBER ME?
FN-2187.
NOT ANYMORE. NAME'S FINN, AND I'M IN CHARGE.
I'M IN CHARGE NOW, PHASMA!
LOWER THE SHIELDS. UNLESS YOU WANT ME TO BLAST THAT BUCKET OFF YOUR HEAD.
YOU'RE MAKING A BIG MISTAKE.
DO IT.
YOU CANNOT BE SO STUPID AS TO THINK THIS WILL BE EASY. MY TROOPS WILL KILL YOU ALL.
WHAT DO WE DO WITH HER?
IS THERE A GARBAGE CHUTE?
TRASH COMPACTOR?
YEAH. THERE IS.

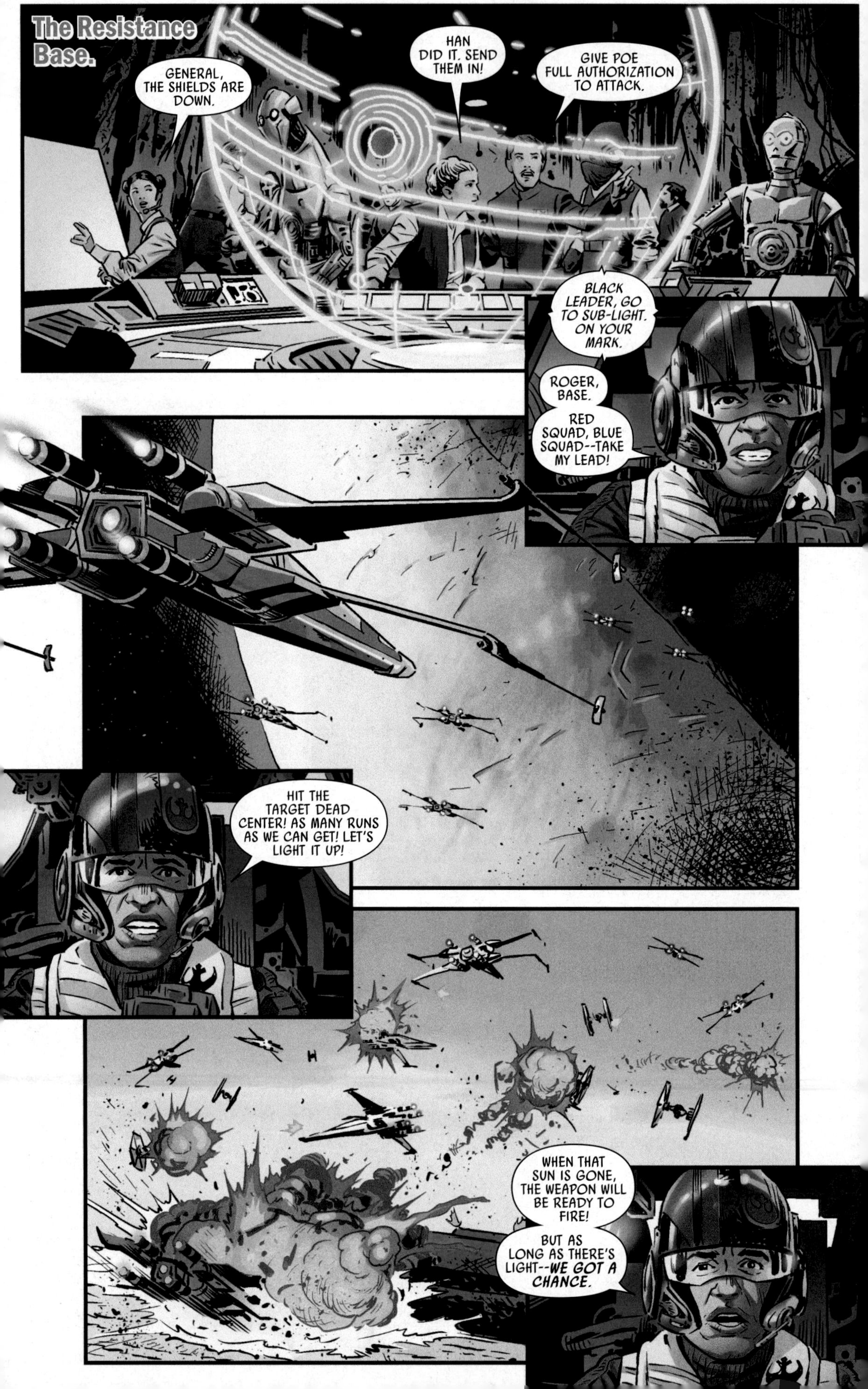
The Resistance Base.
GENERAL, THE SHIELDS ARE DOWN.
HAN DID IT. SEND THEM IN!
GIVE POE FULL AUTHORIZATION TO ATTACK.
BLACK LEADER, GO TO SUB-LIGHT. ON YOUR MARK.
ROGER, BASE.
RED SQUAD, BLUE SQUAD--TAKE MY LEAD!
HIT THE TARGET DEAD CENTER! AS MANY RUNS AS WE CAN GET! LET'S LIGHT IT UP!
WHEN THAT SUN IS GONE, THE WEAPON WILL BE READY TO FIRE!
BUT AS LONG AS THERE'S LIGHT--WE GOT A CHANCE.

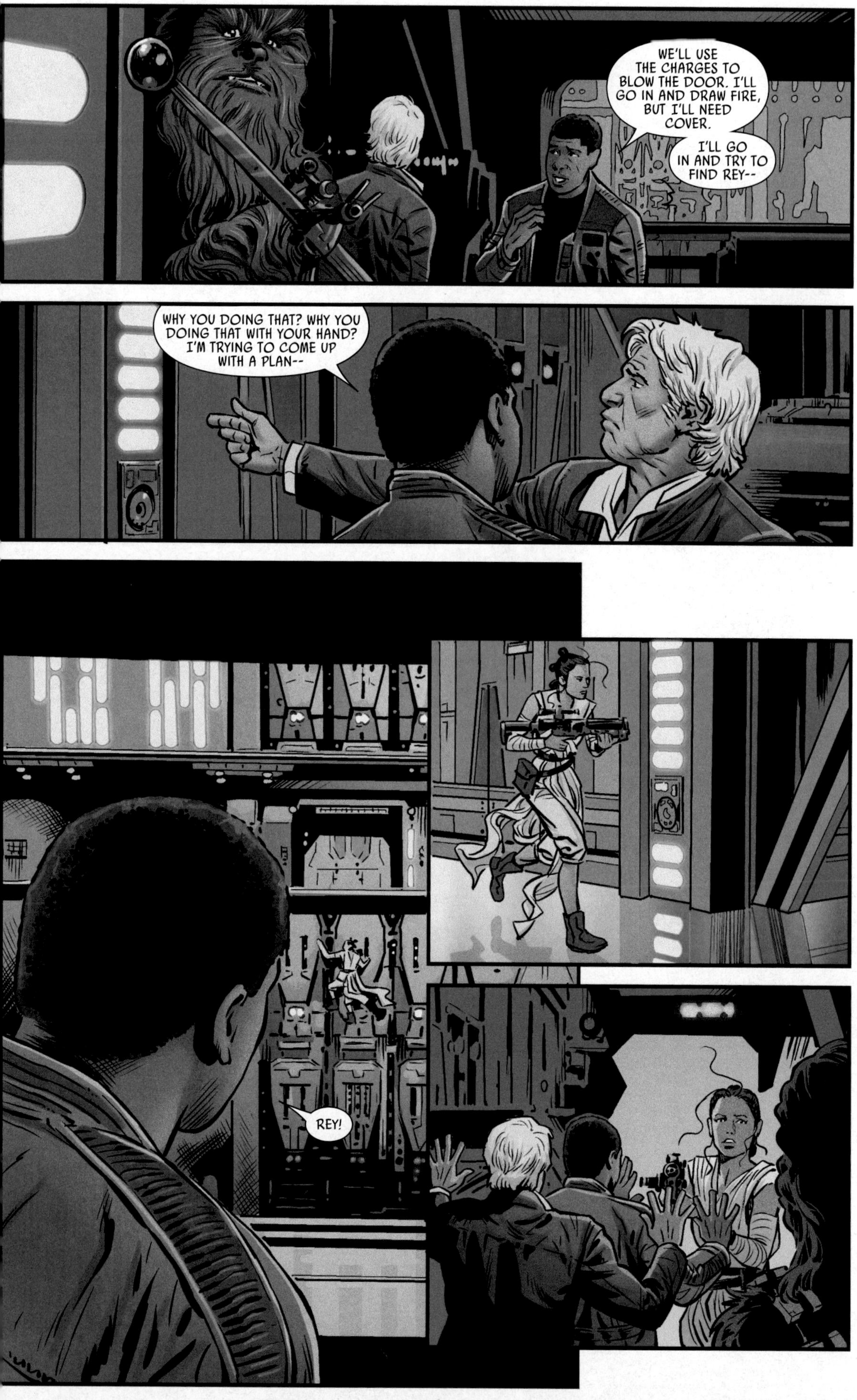
WE'LL USE THE CHARGES TO BLOW THE DOOR. I'LL GO IN AND DRAW FIRE, BUT I'LL NEED COVER.
I'LL GO IN AND TRY TO FIND REY--
WHY YOU DOING THAT? WHY YOU DOING THAT WITH YOUR HAND? I'M TRYING TO COME UP WITH A PLAN--
REY!

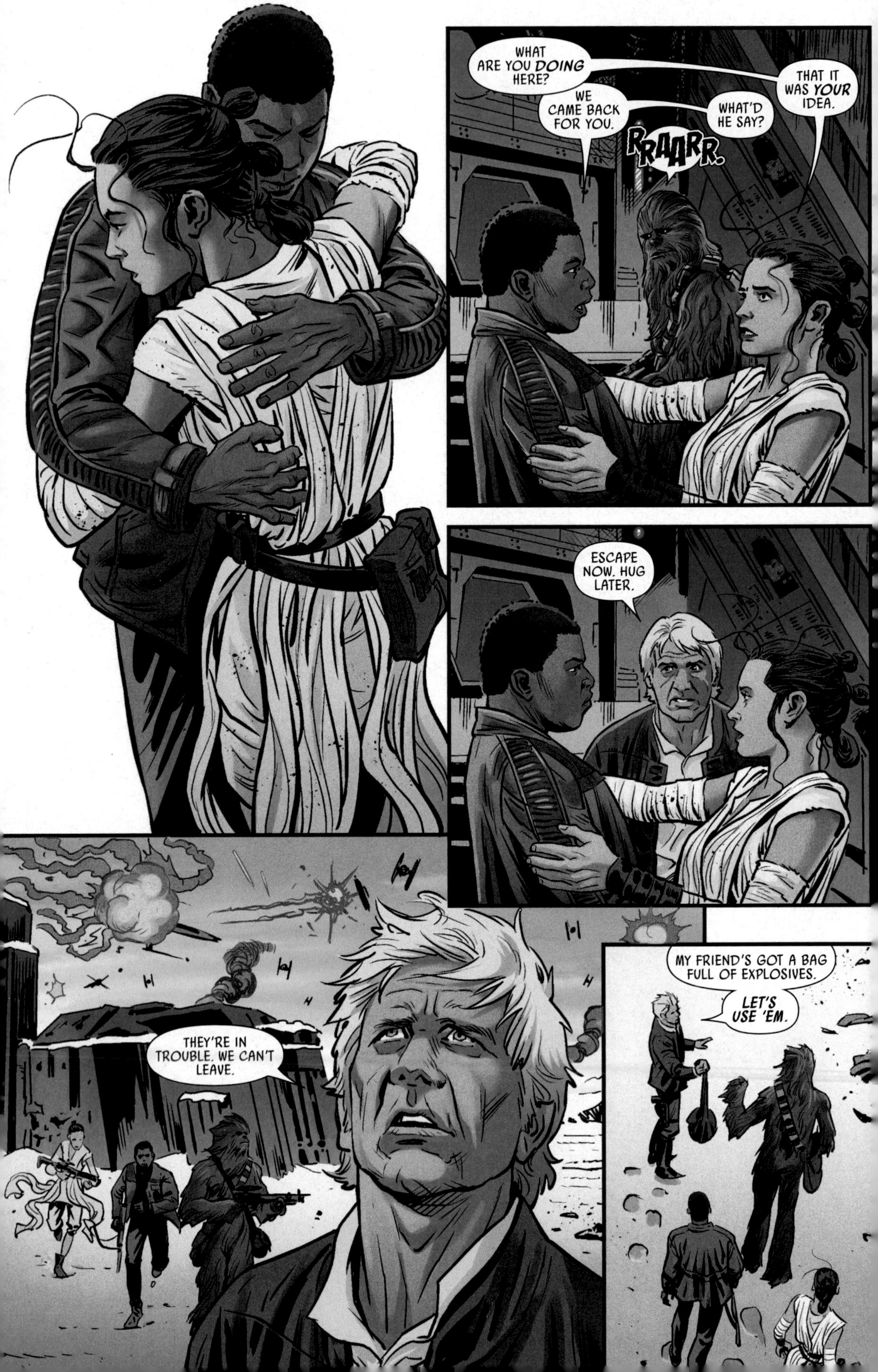
WHAT ARE YOU DOING HERE?
WE CAME BACK FOR YOU.
WHAT'D HE SAY?
RRAARR.
THAT IT WAS YOUR IDEA.
ESCAPE NOW. HUG LATER.
THEY'RE IN TROUBLE. WE CAN'T LEAVE.
MY FRIEND'S GOT A BAG FULL OF EXPLOSIVES.
LET'S USE 'EM.

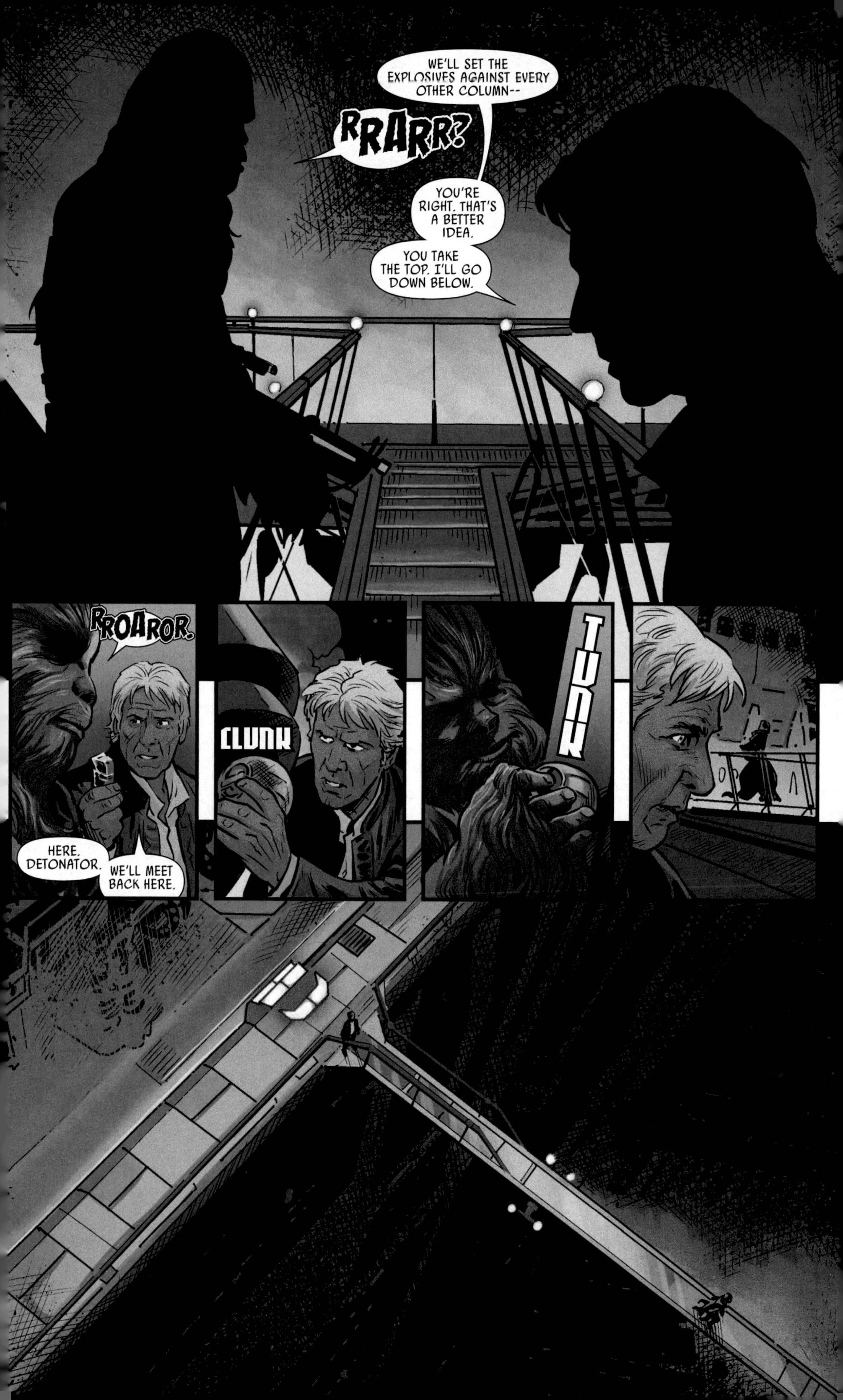
WE'LL SET THE EXPLOSIVES AGAINST EVERY OTHER COLUMN--
RRARR?
YOU'RE RIGHT. THAT'S A BETTER IDEA.
YOU TAKE THE TOP. I'LL GO DOWN BELOW.
RROAROR.
HERE. DETONATOR.
WE'LL MEET BACK HERE.
CLUNK
TUNK

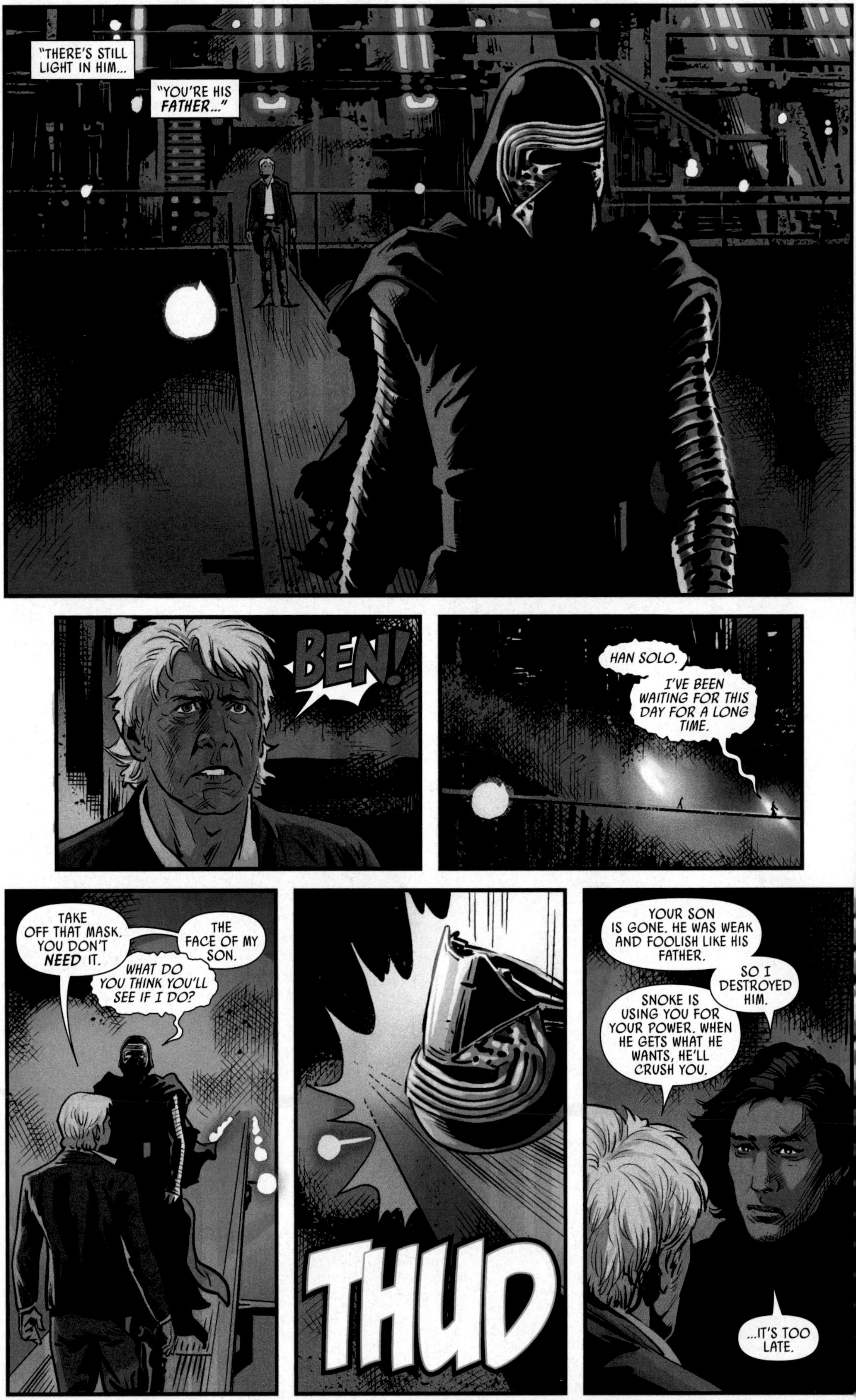
"THERE'S STILL LIGHT IN HIM...
"YOU'RE HIS FATHER..."
BEN!
HAN SOLO.
I'VE BEEN WAITING FOR THIS DAY FOR A LONG TIME.
TAKE OFF THAT MASK. YOU DON'T NEED IT.
WHAT DO YOU THINK YOU'LL SEE IF I DO?
THE FACE OF MY SON.
THUD
YOUR SON IS GONE. HE WAS WEAK AND FOOLISH LIKE HIS FATHER.
SO I DESTROYED HIM.
SNOKE IS USING YOU FOR YOUR POWER. WHEN HE GETS WHAT HE WANTS, HE'LL CRUSH YOU.
...IT'S TOO LATE.

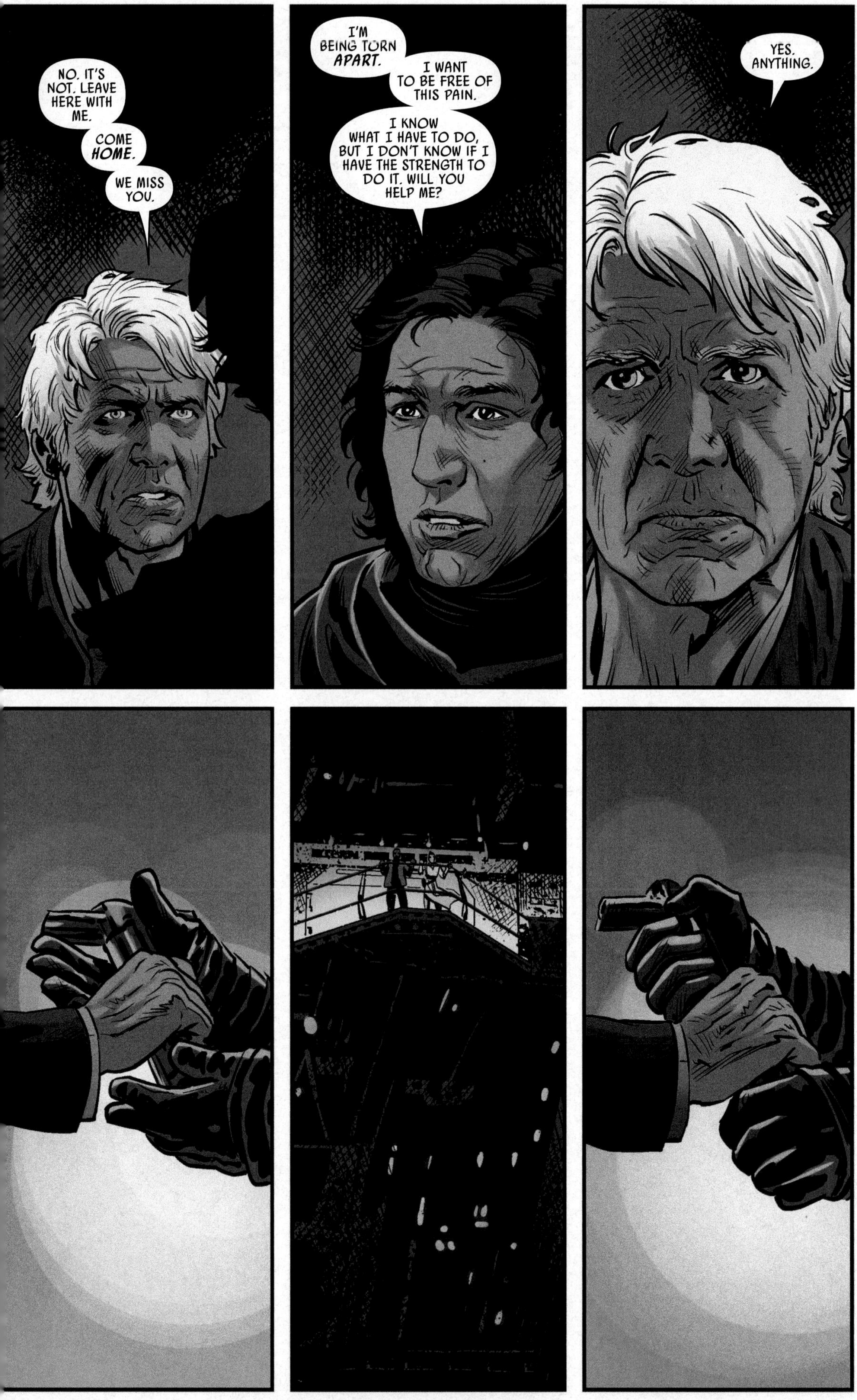

NO. IT'S NOT. LEAVE HERE WITH ME.
COME HOME.
WE MISS YOU.
I'M BEING TORN APART.
I WANT TO BE FREE OF THIS PAIN.
I KNOW WHAT I HAVE TO DO, BUT I DON'T KNOW IF I HAVE THE STRENGTH TO DO IT. WILL YOU HELP ME?
YES. ANYTHING.

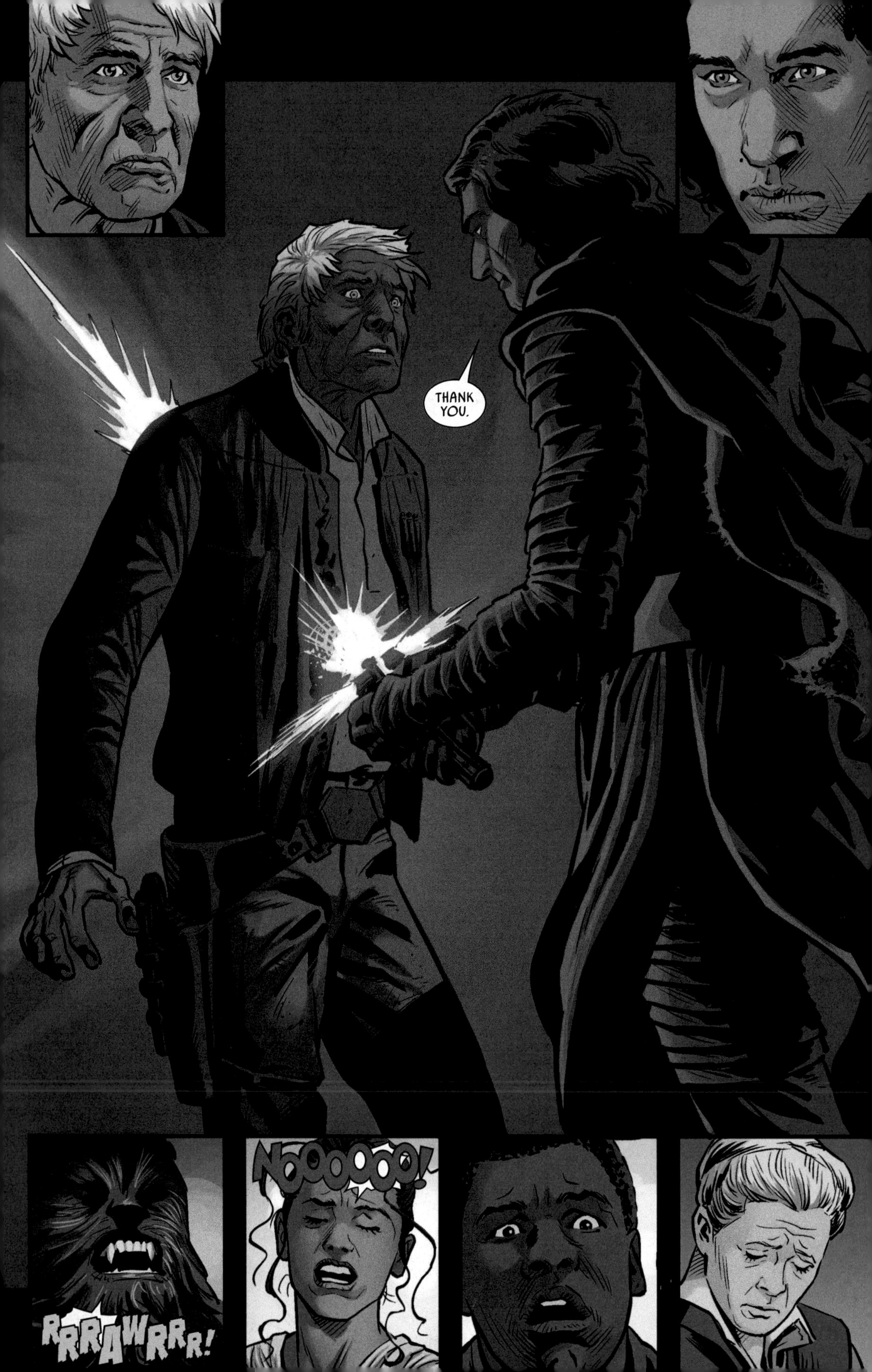
THANK YOU.
RRRAWRRRR!
NOOOOOO!

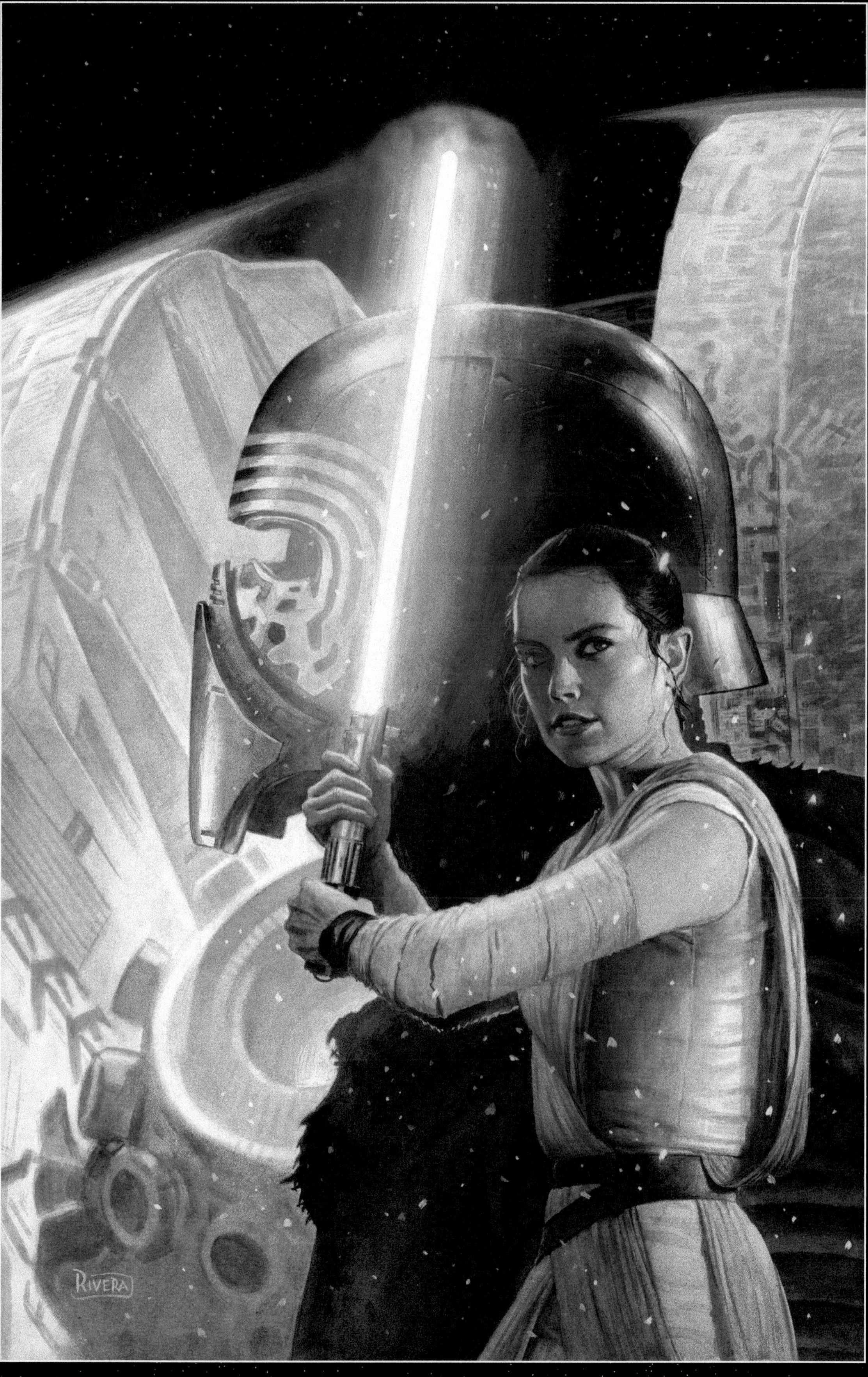
RIVERA

THE FORCE AWAKENS #6

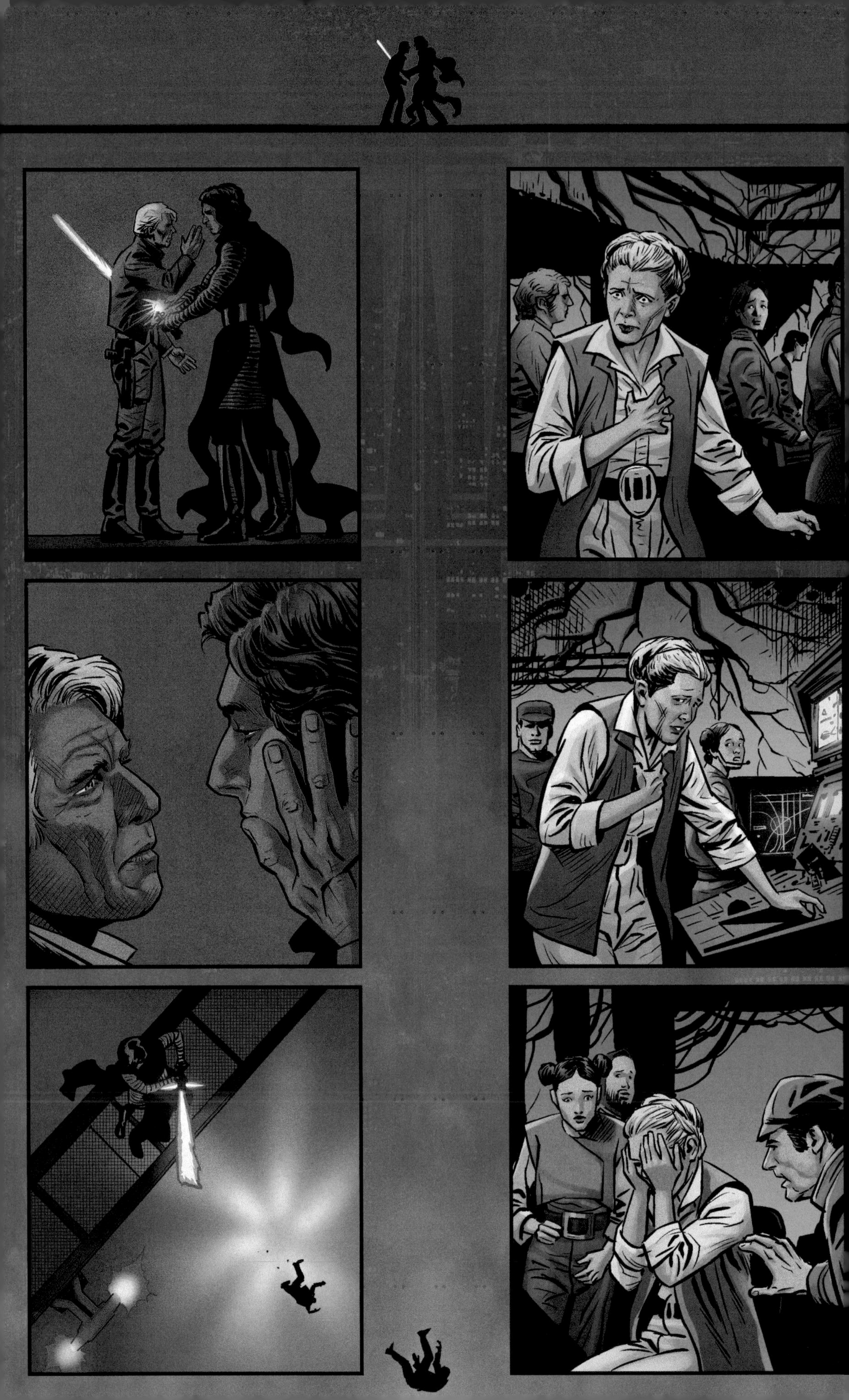

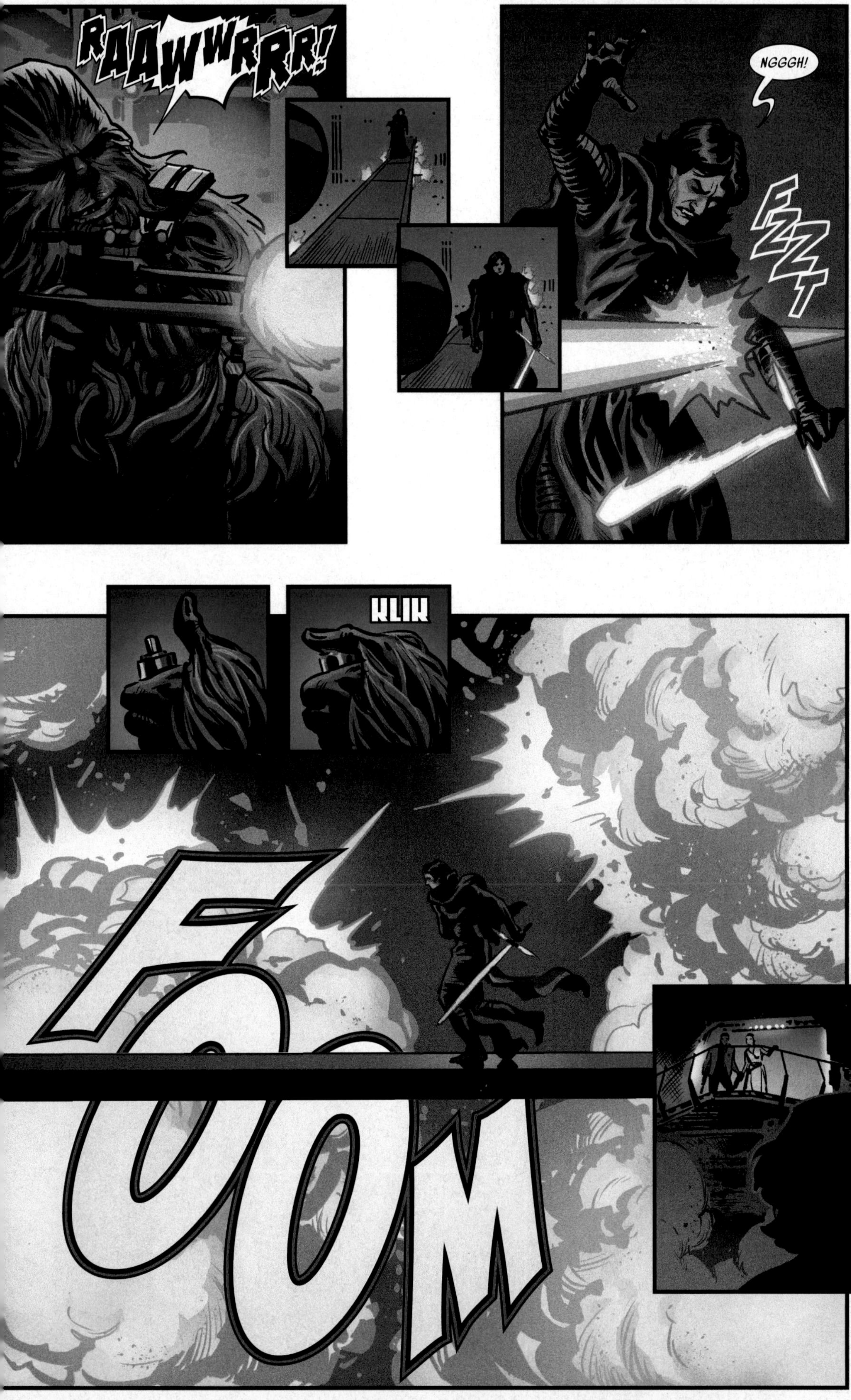
RAAWWRRR!
NGGGH!
FZZT
KLIK
FOOM

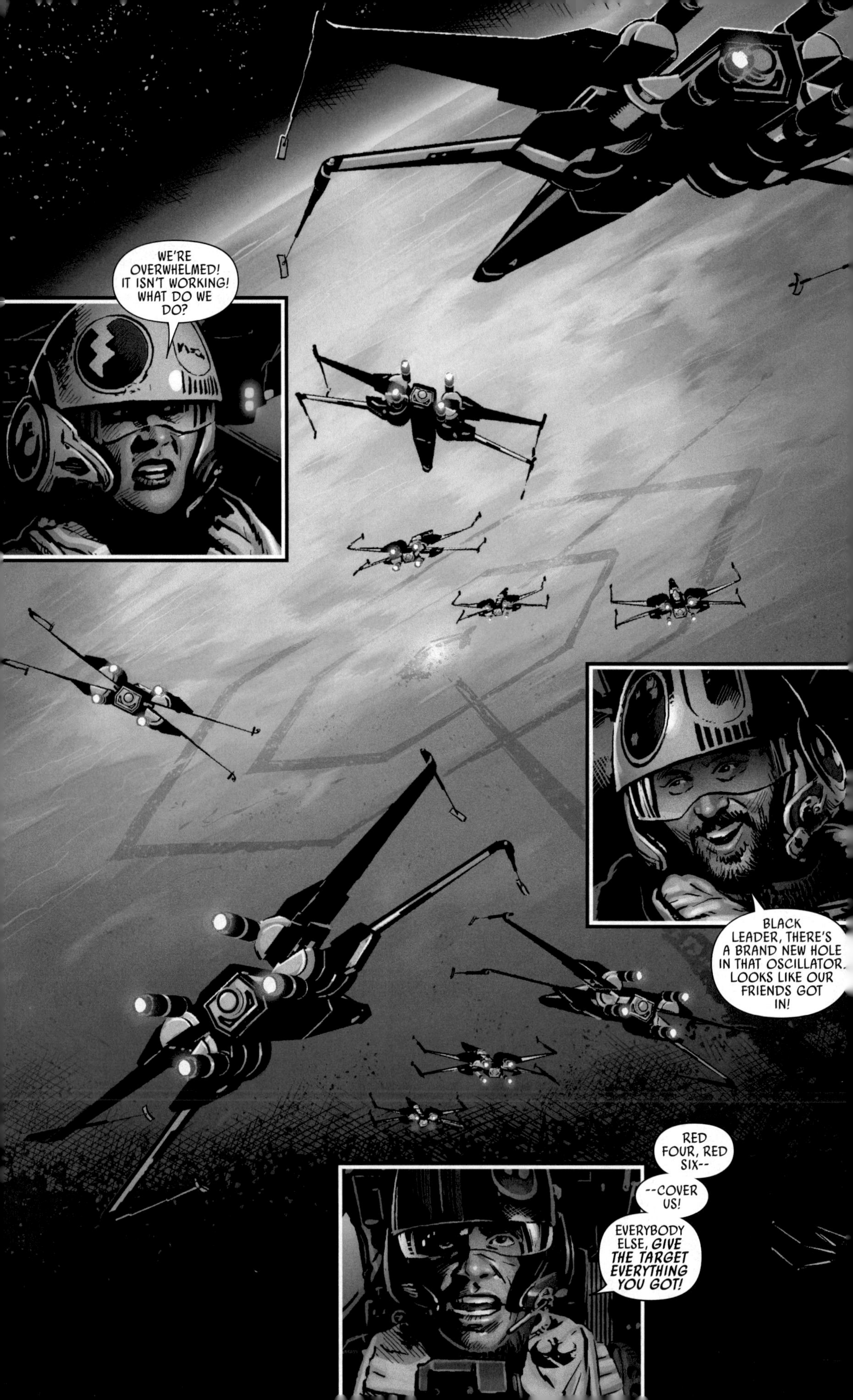
WE'RE OVERWHELMED! IT ISN'T WORKING! WHAT DO WE DO?
BLACK LEADER, THERE'S A BRAND NEW HOLE IN THAT OSCILLATOR. LOOKS LIKE OUR FRIENDS GOT IN!
RED FOUR, RED SIX--
--COVER US!
EVERYBODY ELSE, *GIVE THE TARGET EVERYTHING YOU GOT!*

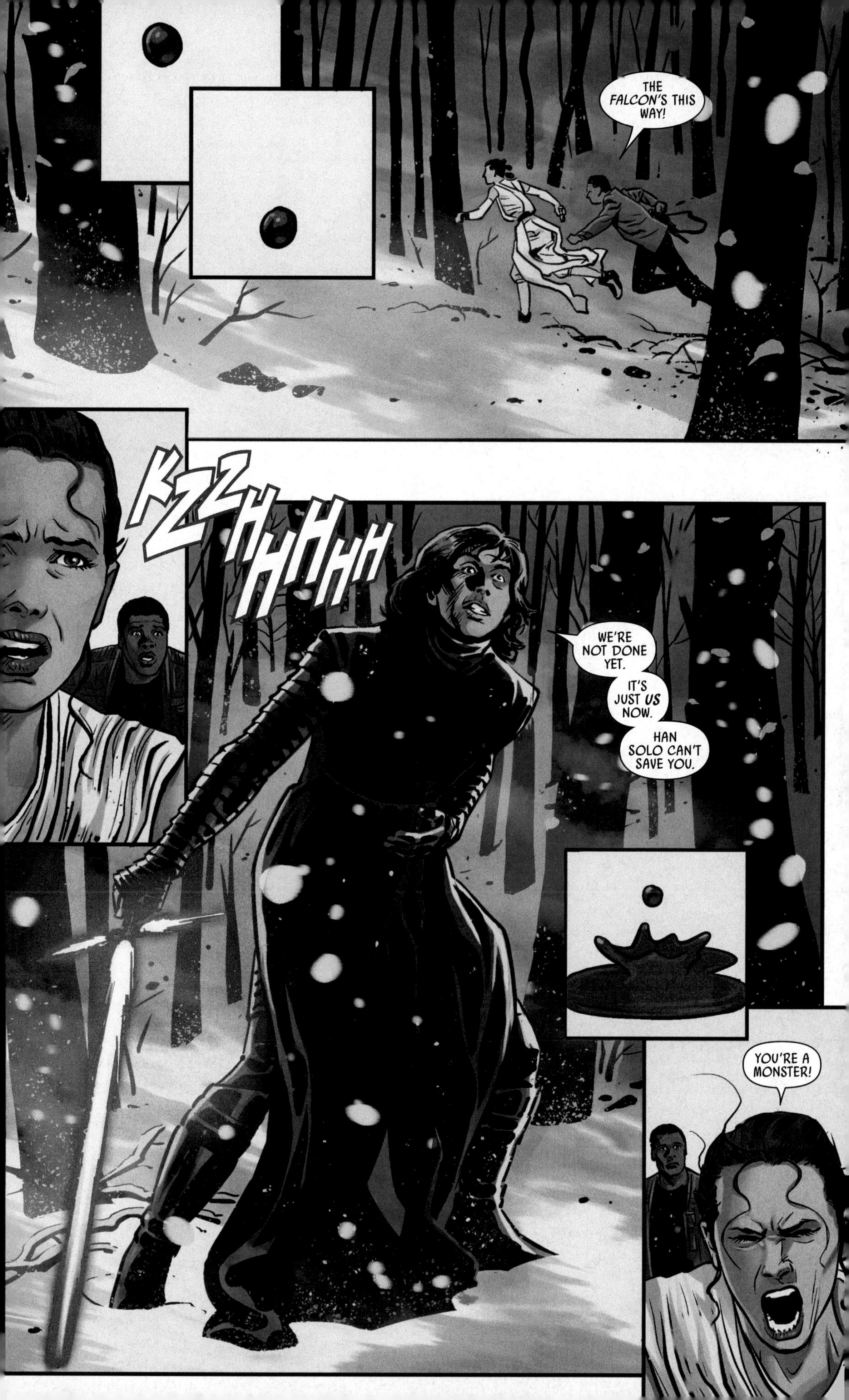
THE FALCON'S THIS WAY!
KZZHHHHHH
WE'RE NOT DONE YET.
IT'S JUST US NOW.
HAN SOLO CAN'T SAVE YOU.
YOU'RE A MONSTER!

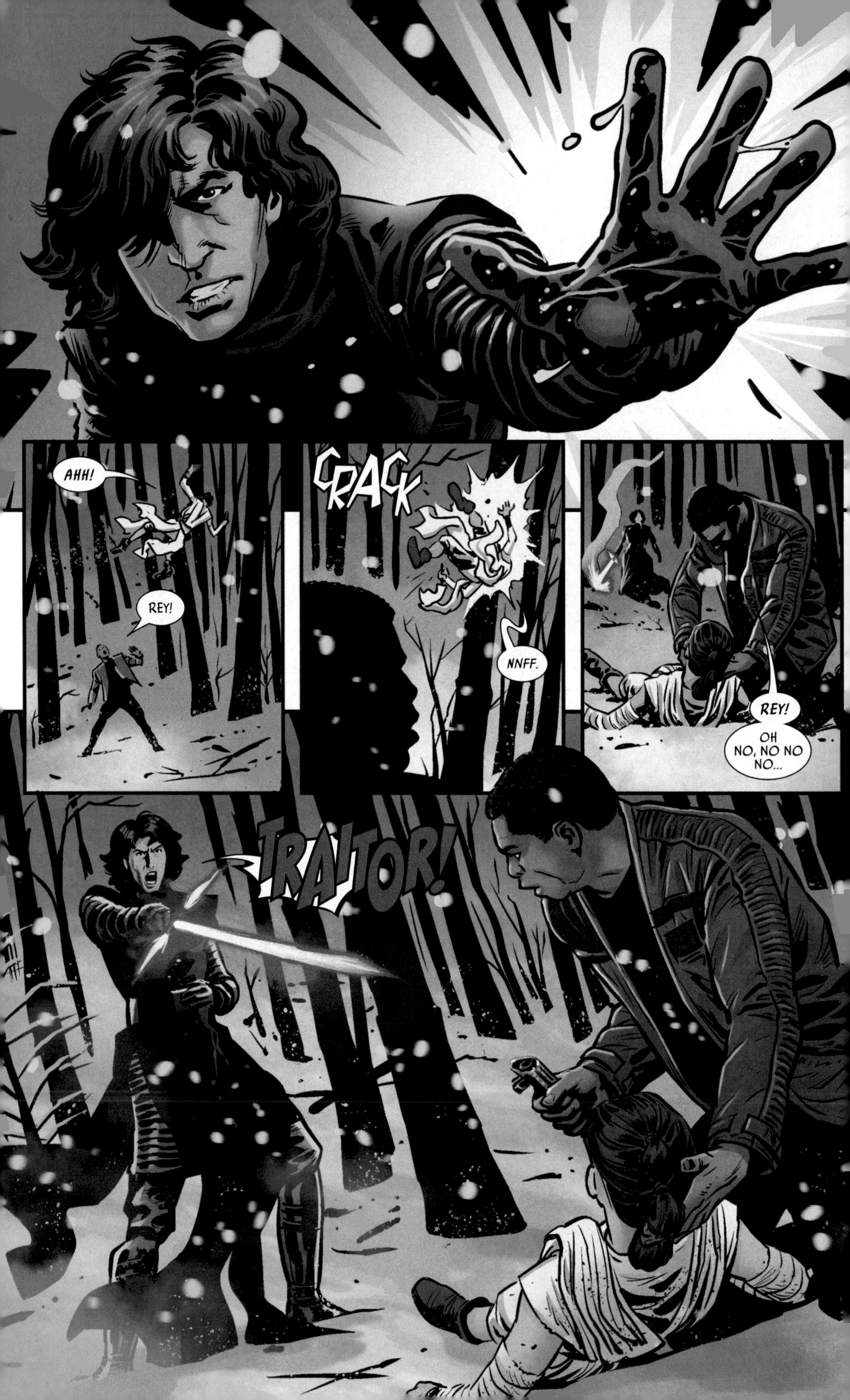
AHH!
REY!
CRACK
NNFF.
REY!
OH NO, NO NO NO...
TRAITOR!

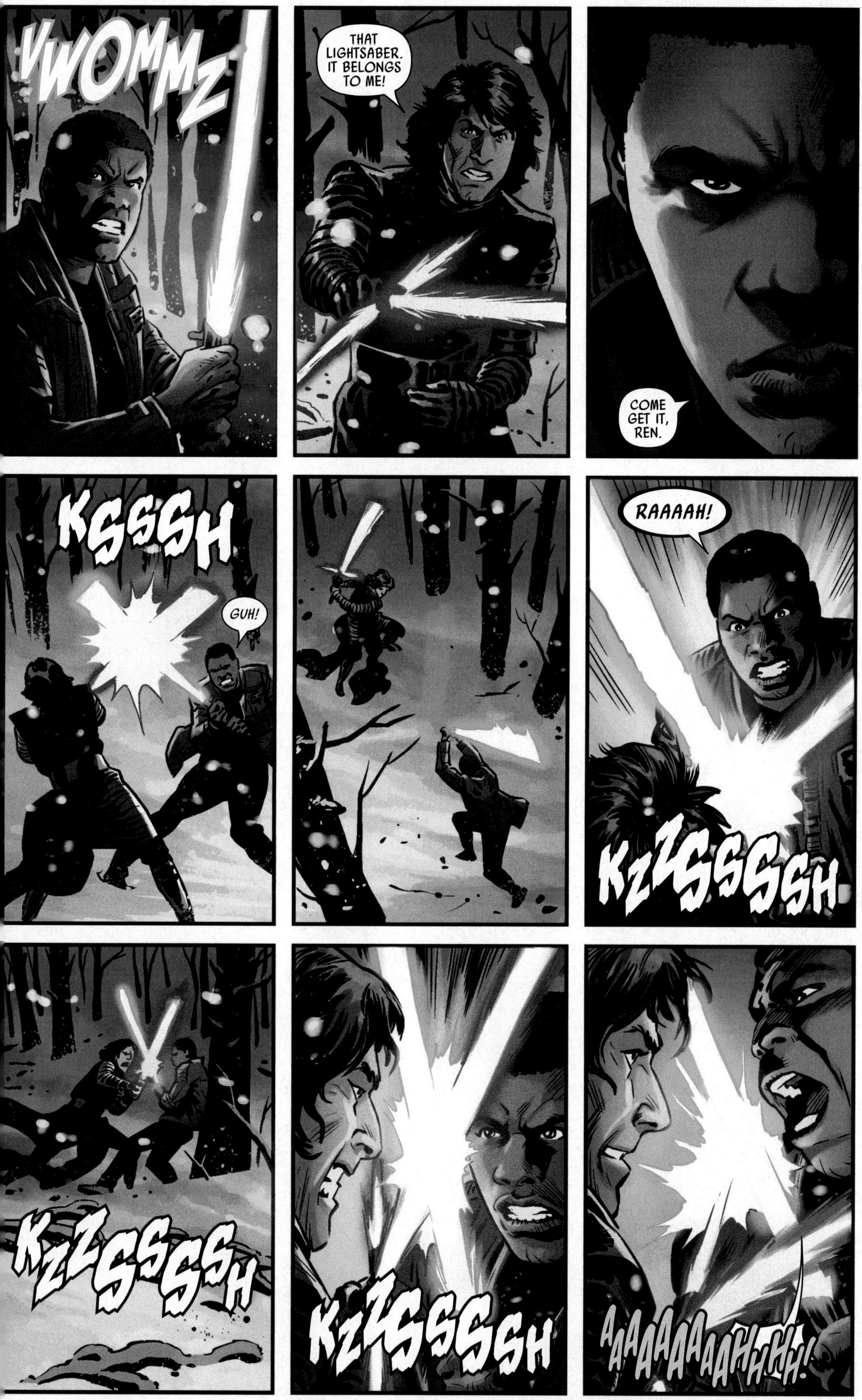
VWOMMZ
THAT LIGHTSABER. IT BELONGS TO ME!
COME GET IT, REN.
KSSSH
GUH!
RAAAAH!
KZZSSSSSH
KZZSSSSSH
KZZSSSSSH
AAAAAAAAAHHHHH!

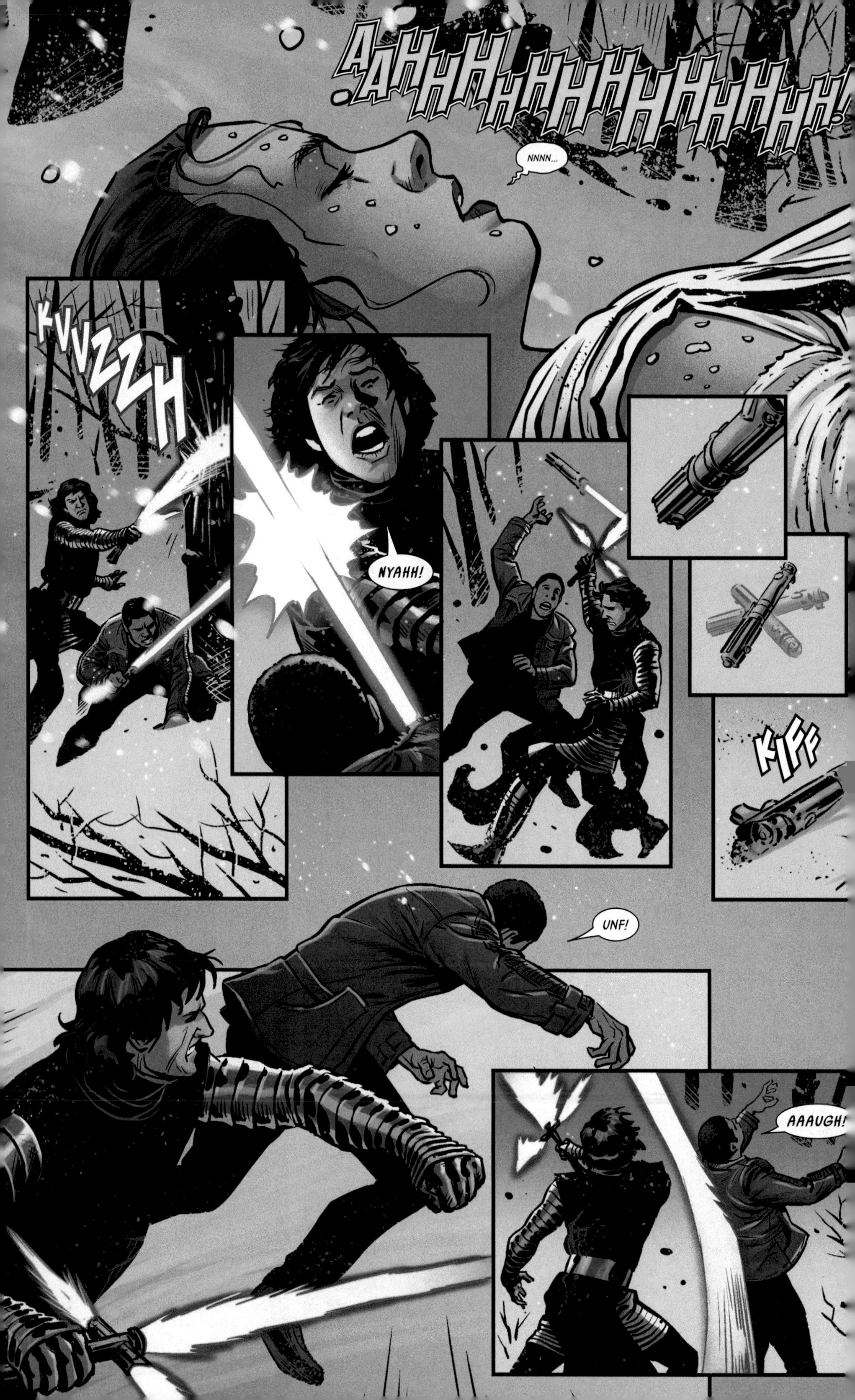
AAHHHHHHHHHHHHHHH!
NNNN...
KVVZZZH
NYAHH!
KIFF
UNF!
AAAUGH!

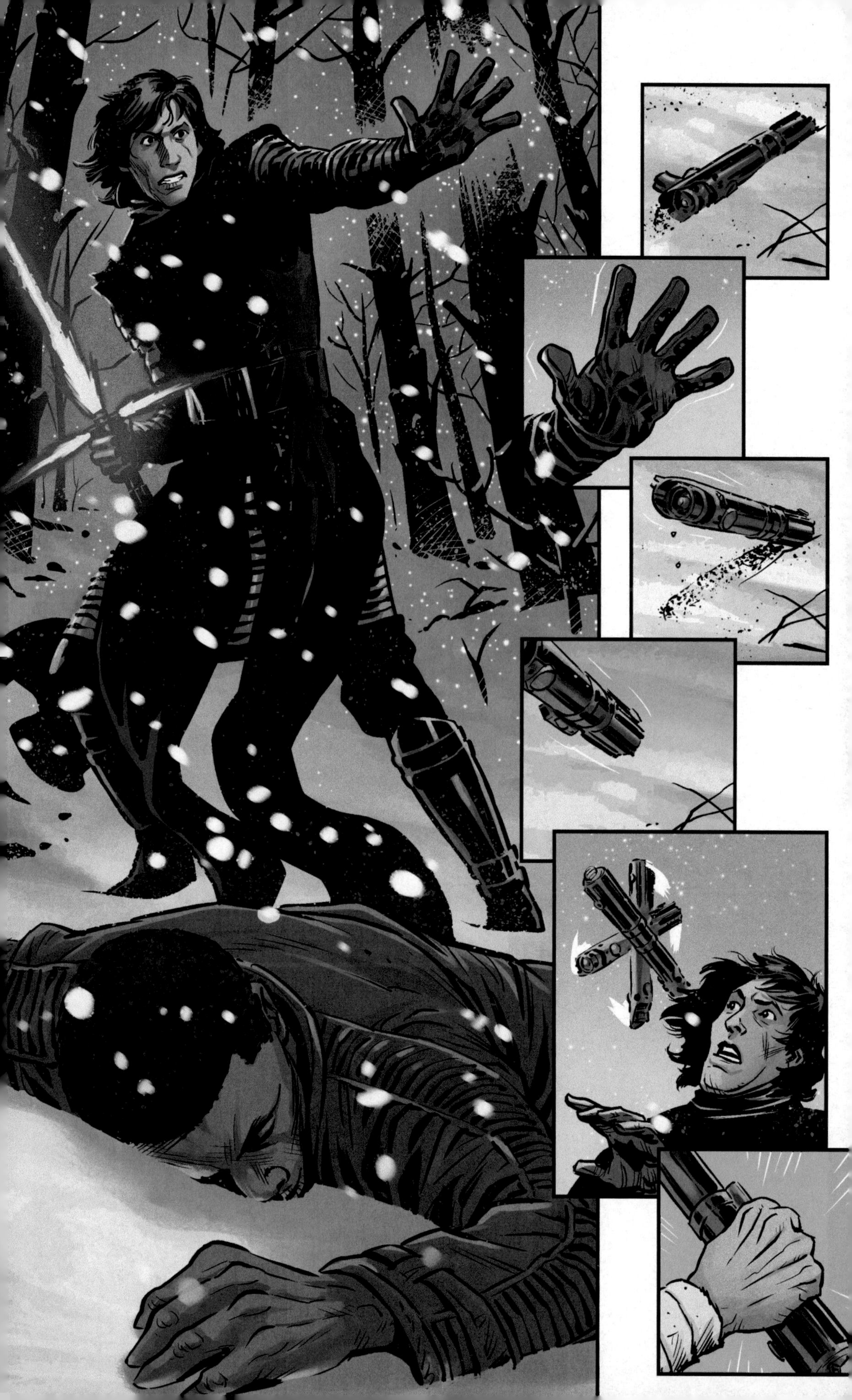

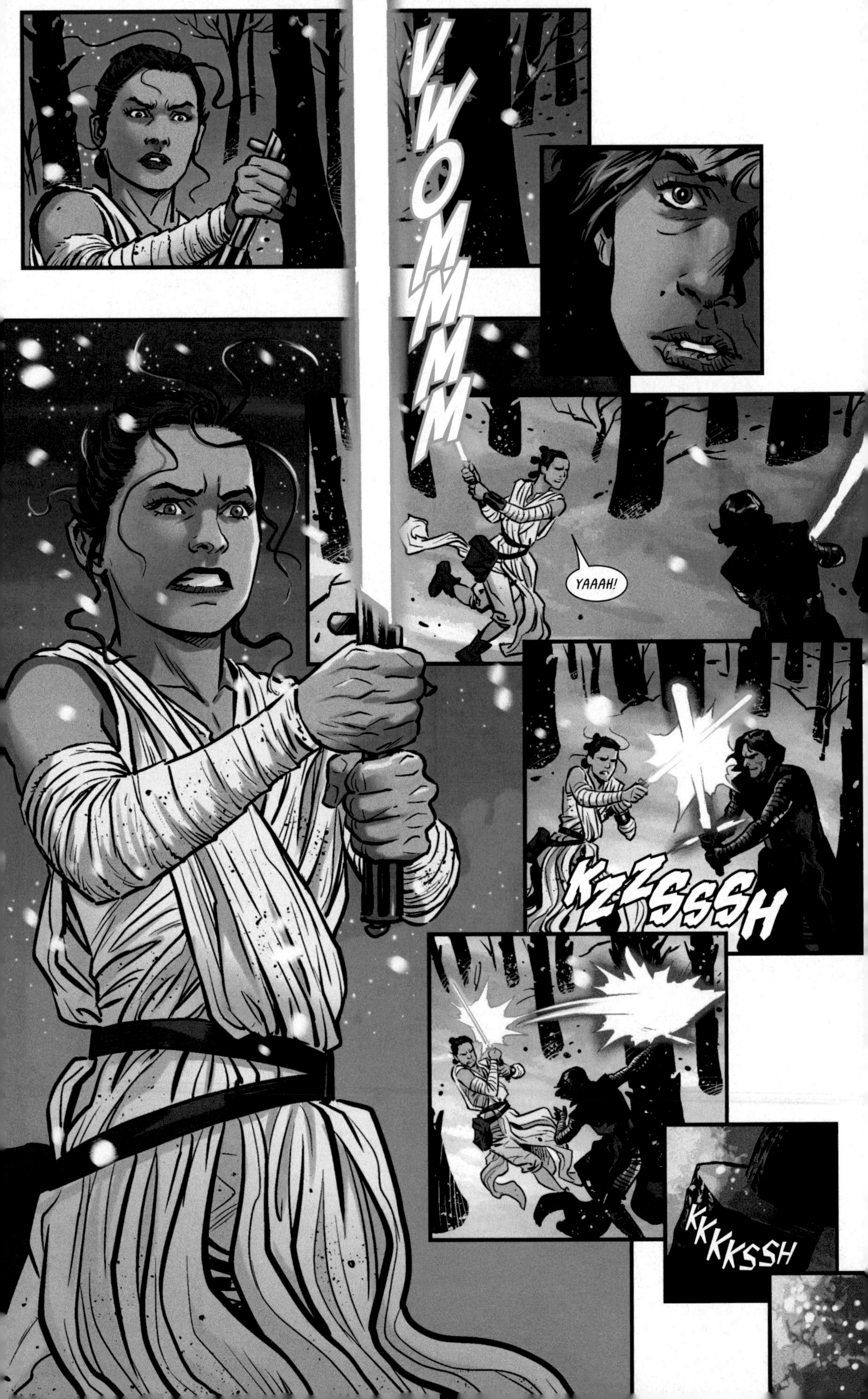

VWOMMMMM
YAAAH!
KZZSSSSH
KKKKSSH

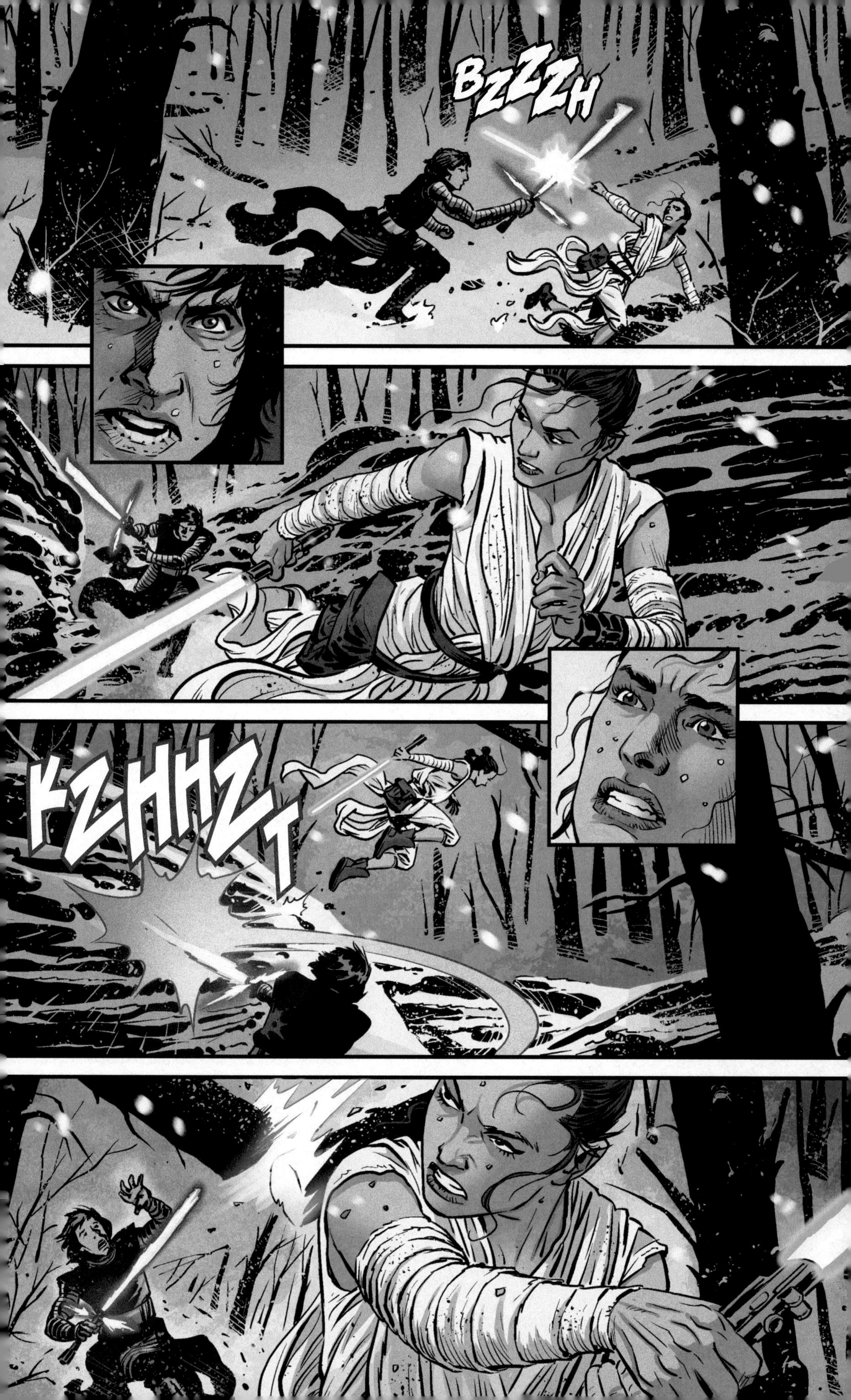
BZZZH
KZHHZT

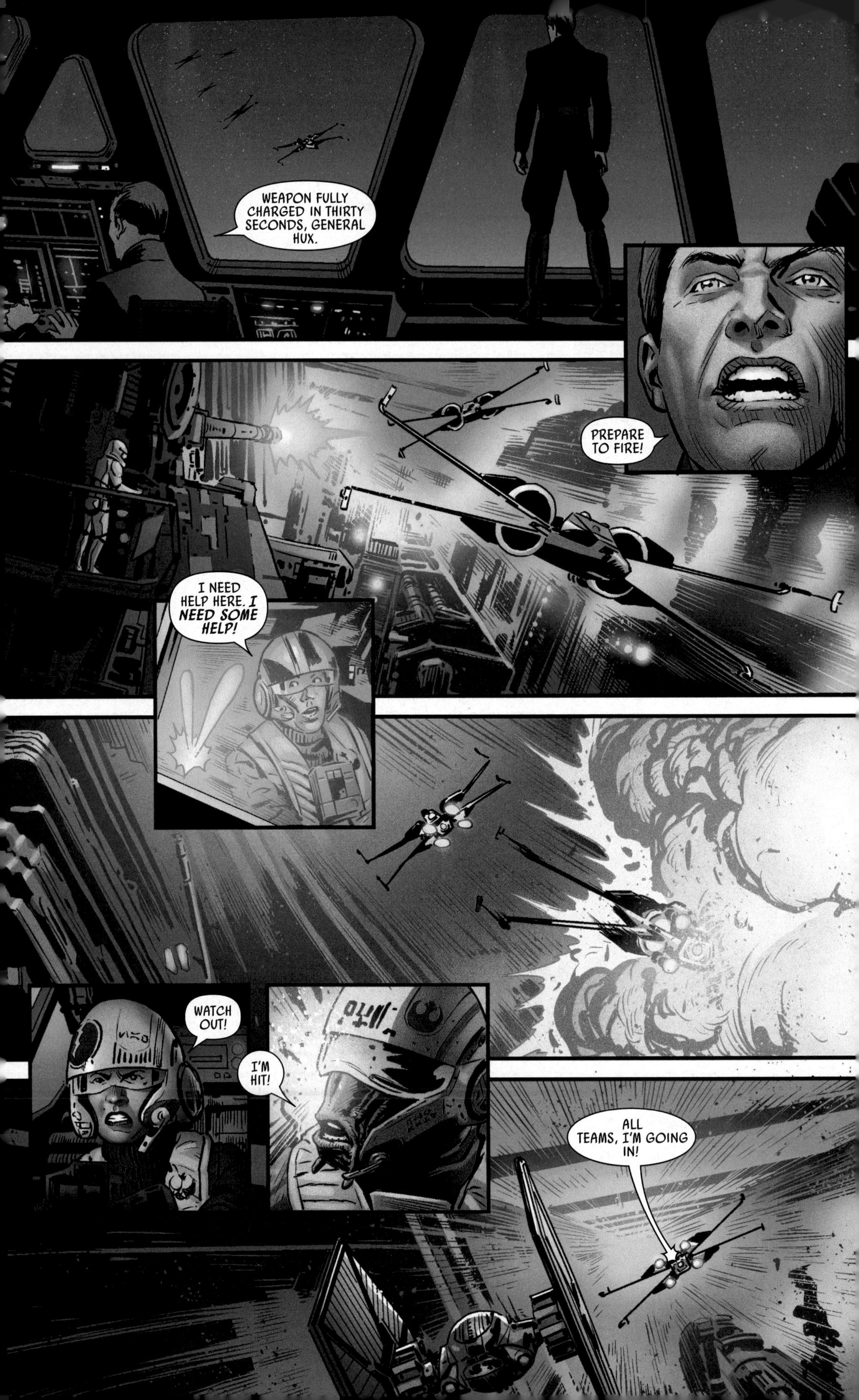
WEAPON FULLY CHARGED IN THIRTY SECONDS, GENERAL HUX.
PREPARE TO FIRE!
I NEED HELP HERE. I NEED SOME HELP!
WATCH OUT!
I'M HIT!
ALL TEAMS, I'M GOING IN!

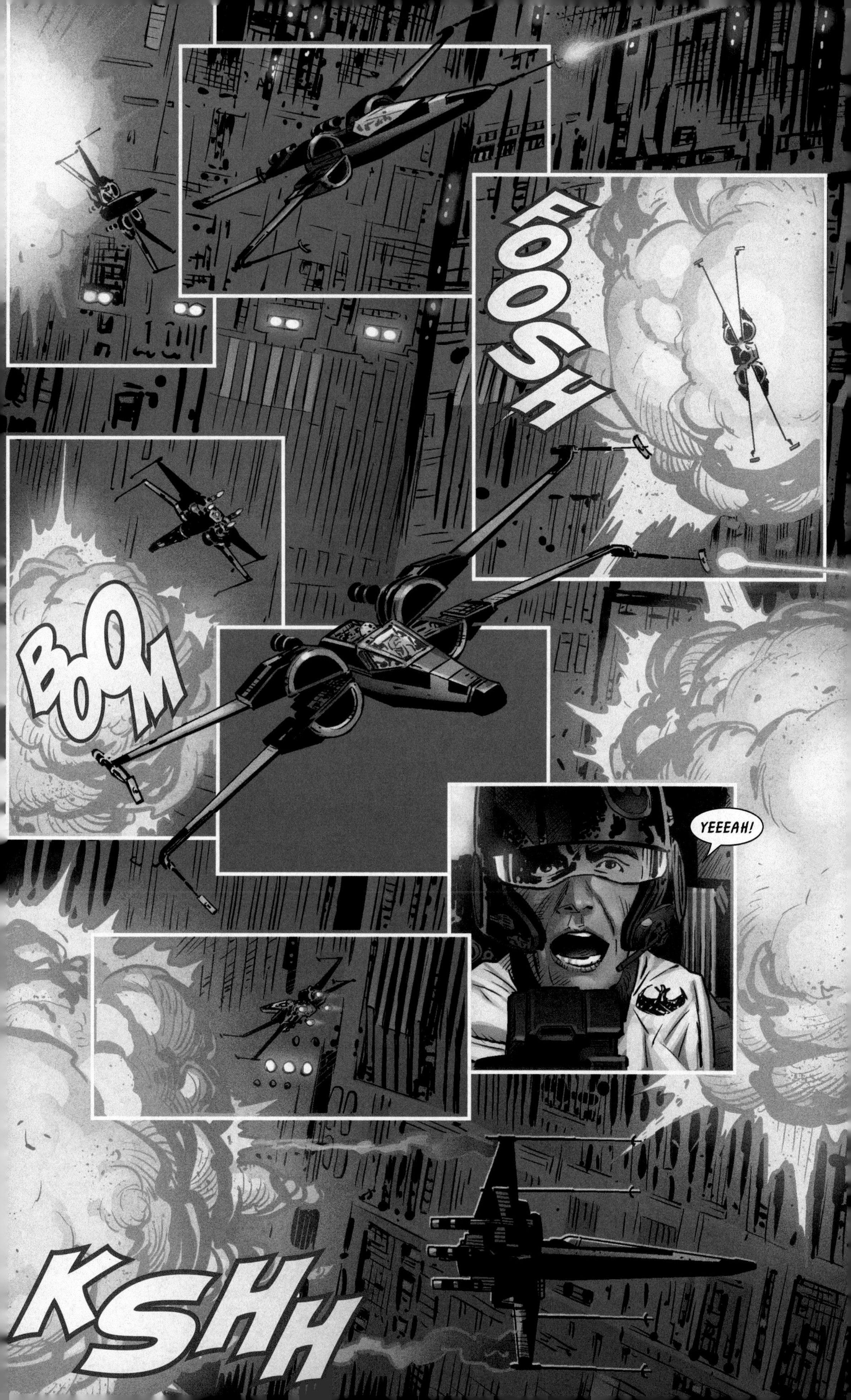
FOOSH
BOOM
YEEEAH!
KSHH

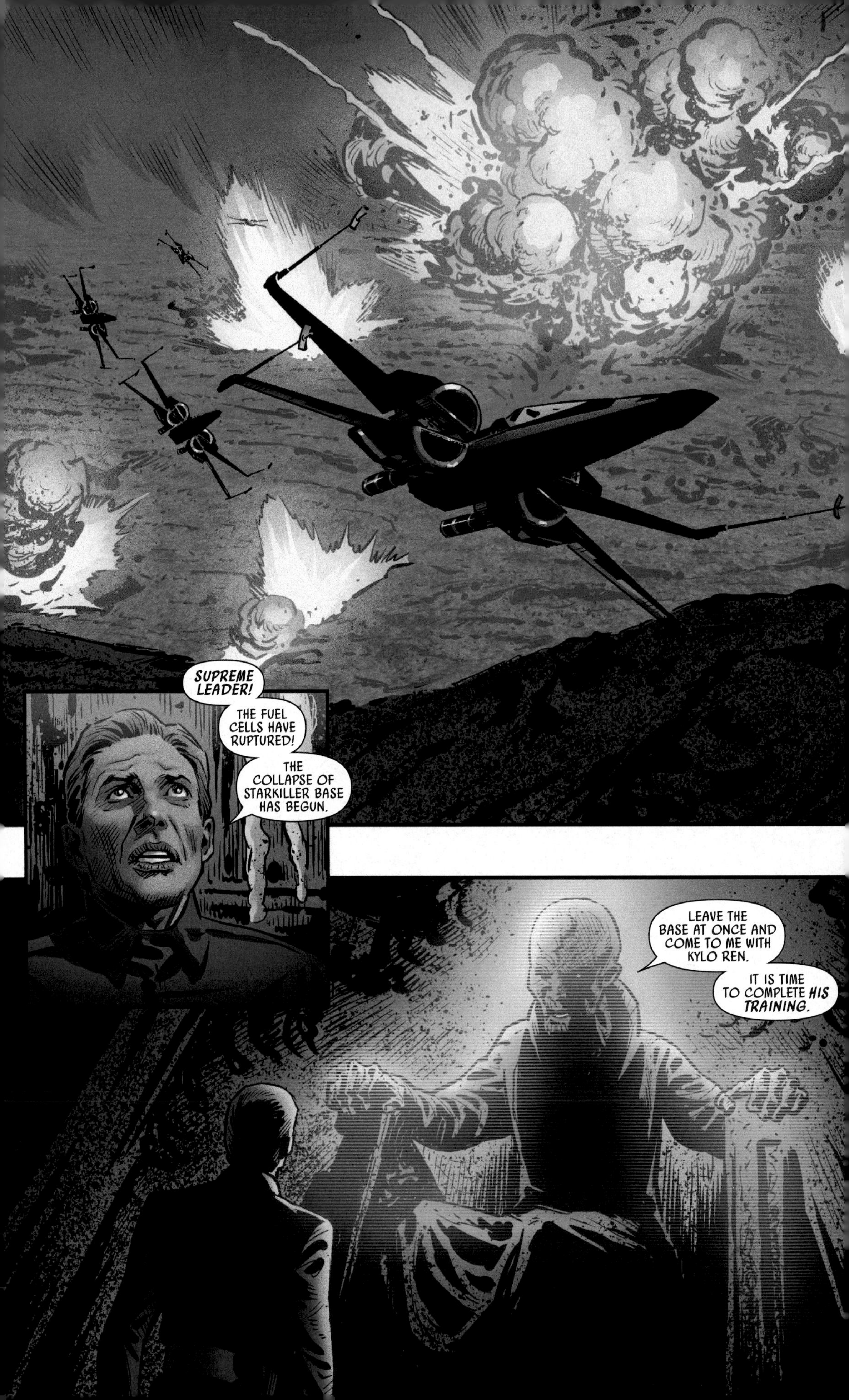
SUPREME LEADER!
THE FUEL CELLS HAVE RUPTURED!
THE COLLAPSE OF STARKILLER BASE HAS BEGUN.
LEAVE THE BASE AT ONCE AND COME TO ME WITH KYLO REN.
IT IS TIME TO COMPLETE HIS TRAINING.

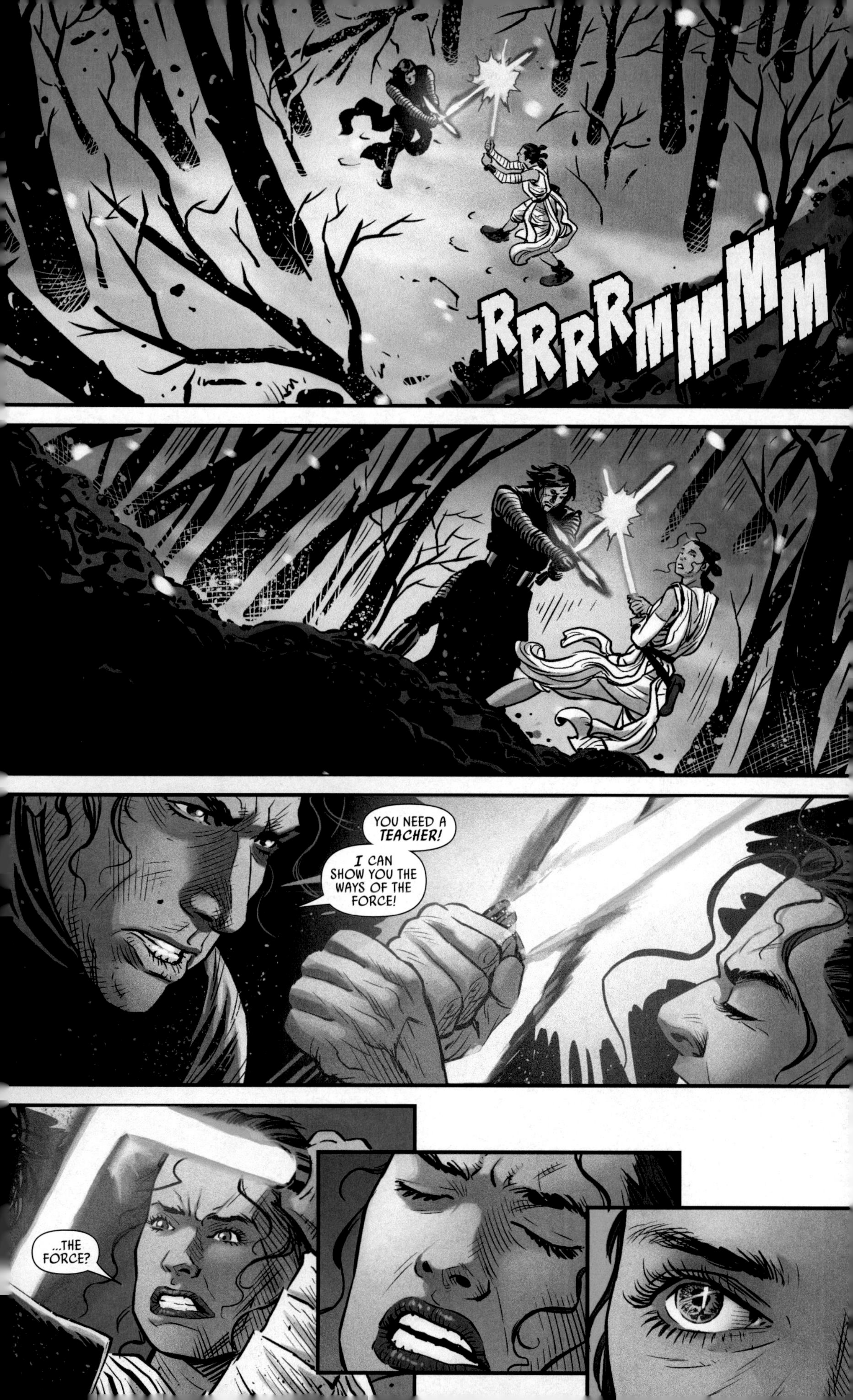

RRRRMMMMM
YOU NEED A *TEACHER!*
I CAN SHOW YOU THE WAYS OF THE FORCE!
...THE FORCE?

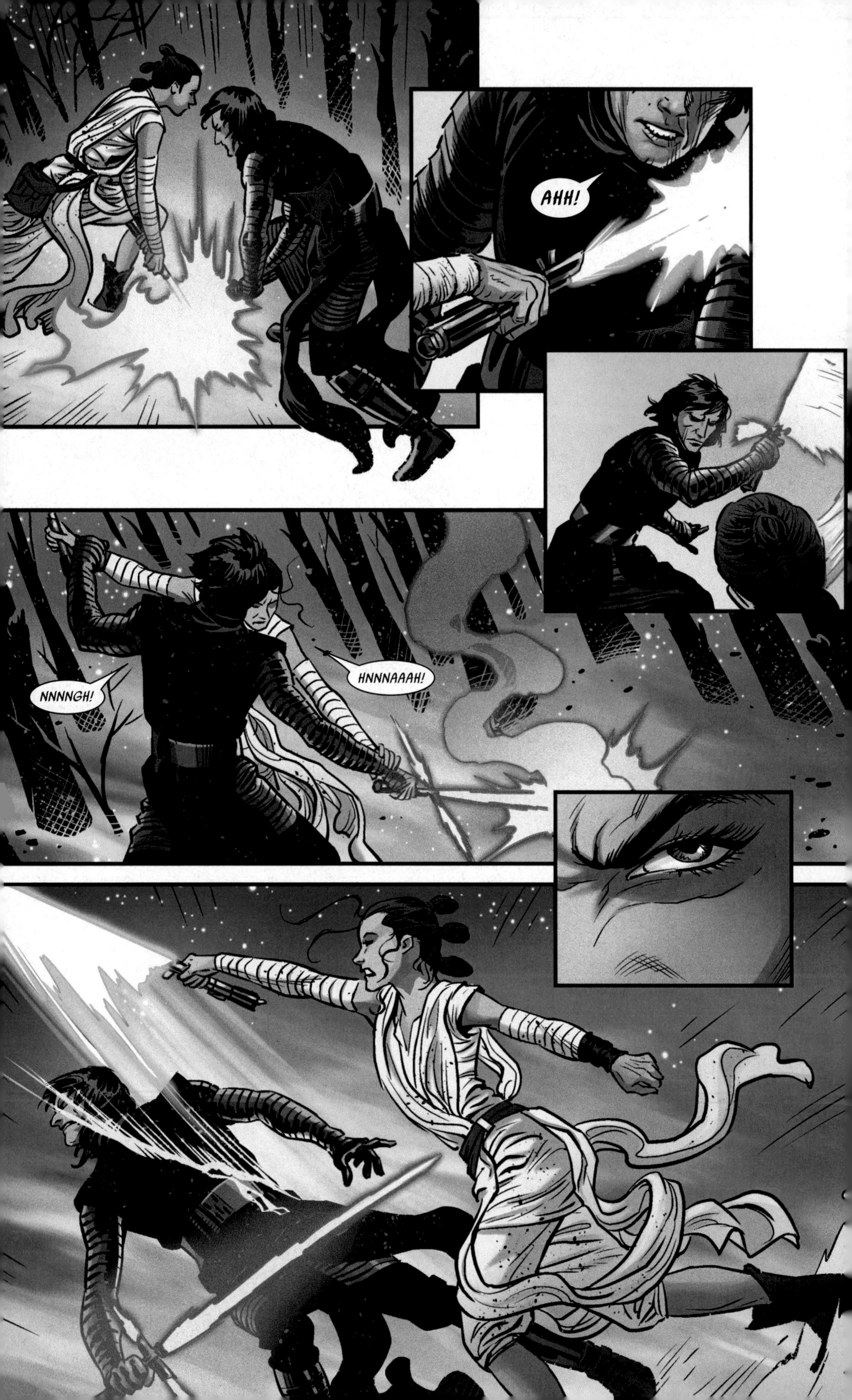
AHH!
NNNNGH!
HNNNAAAH!

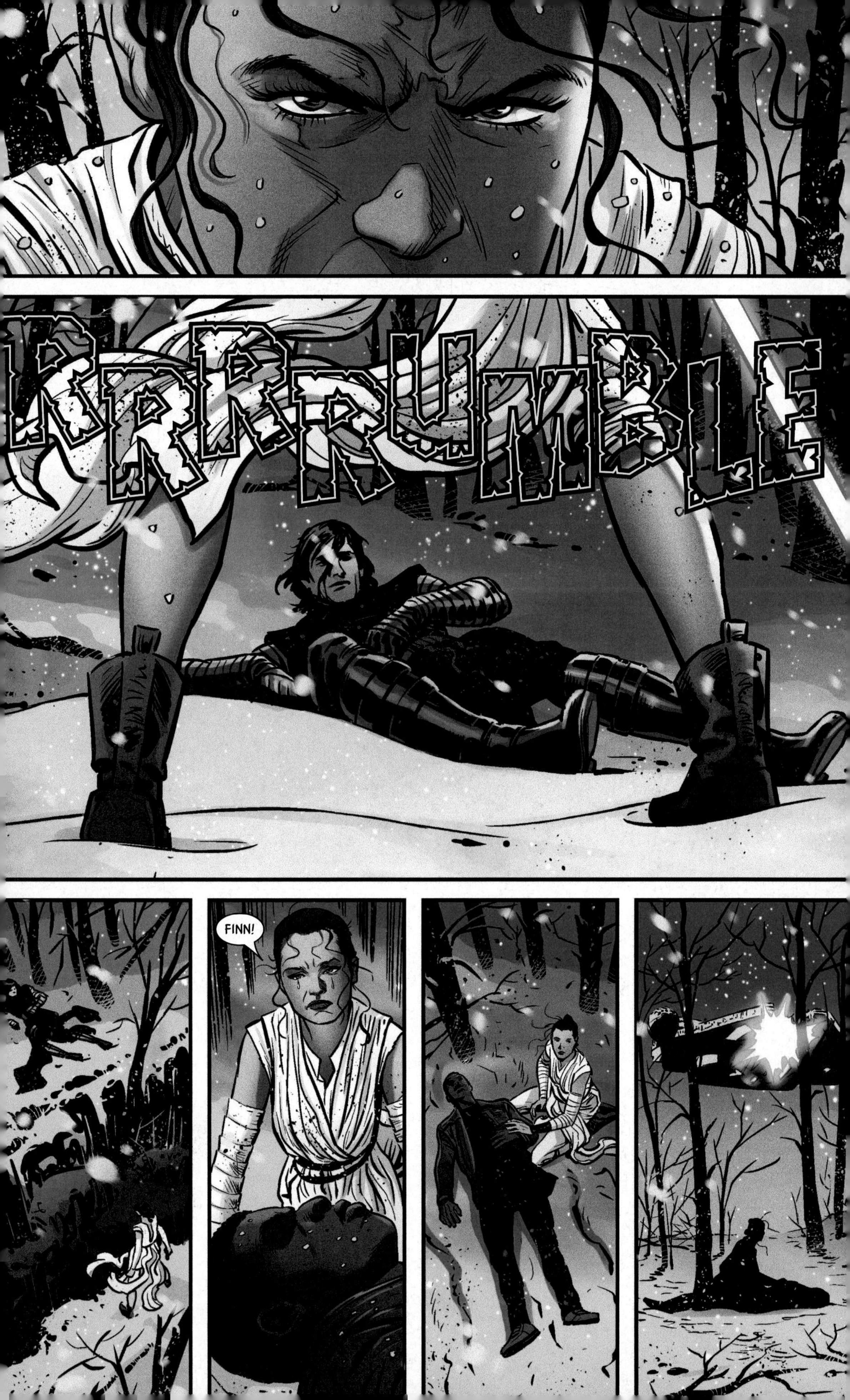
KRRRUMBLE
FINN!

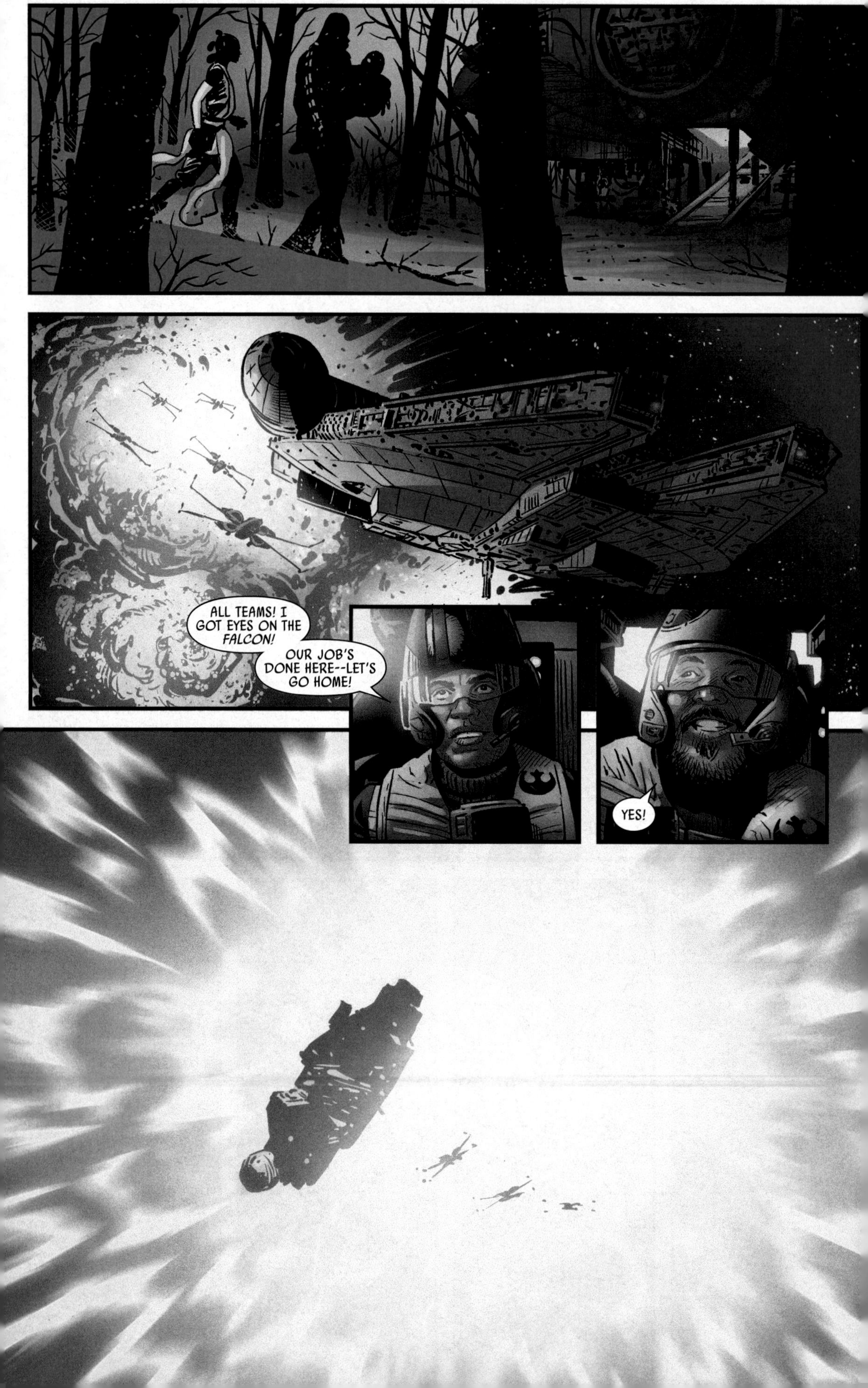
ALL TEAMS! I GOT EYES ON THE FALCON!
OUR JOB'S DONE HERE--LET'S GO HOME!
YES!

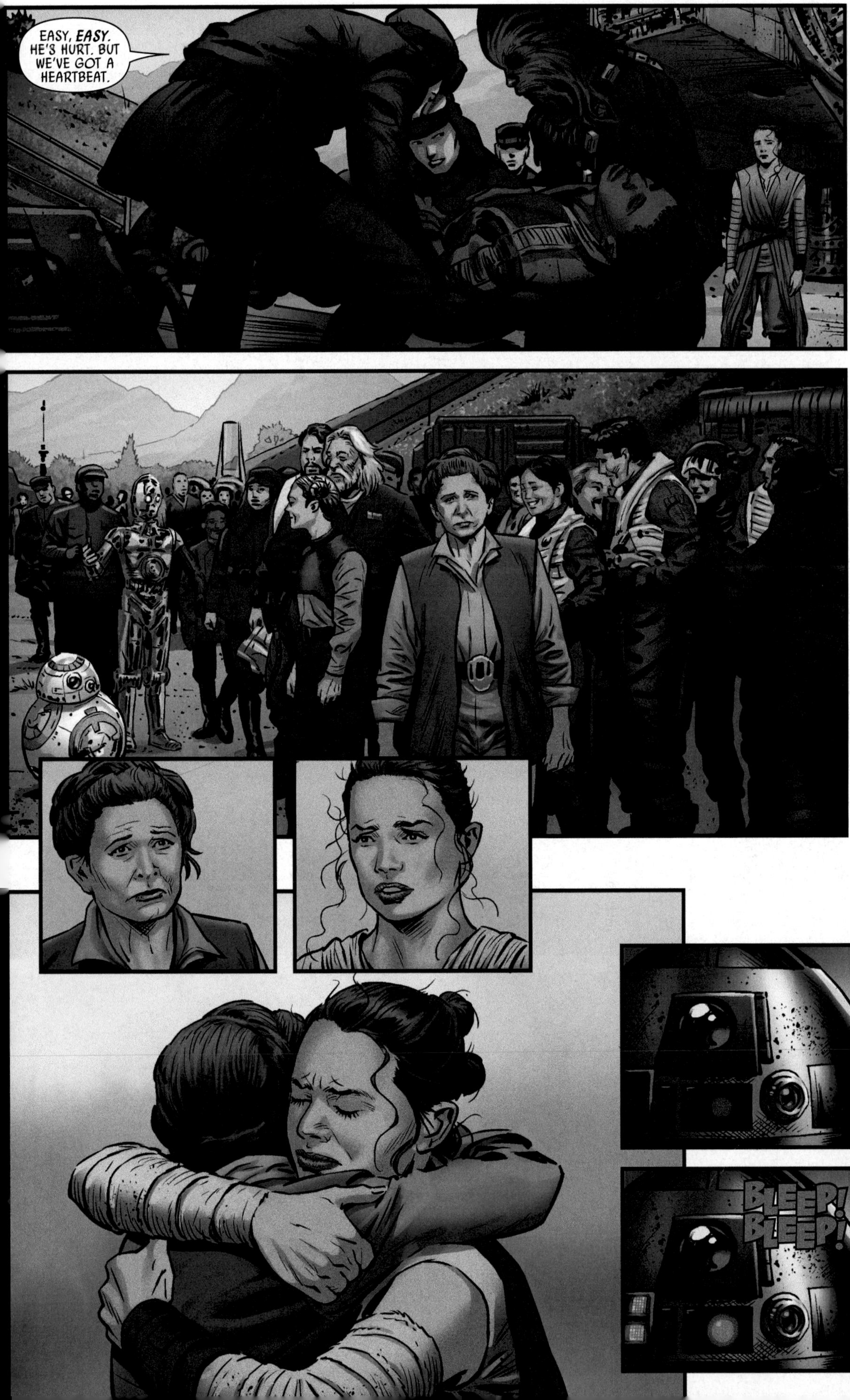
EASY, EASY. HE'S HURT. BUT WE'VE GOT A HEARTBEAT.
BLEEP! BLEEP!

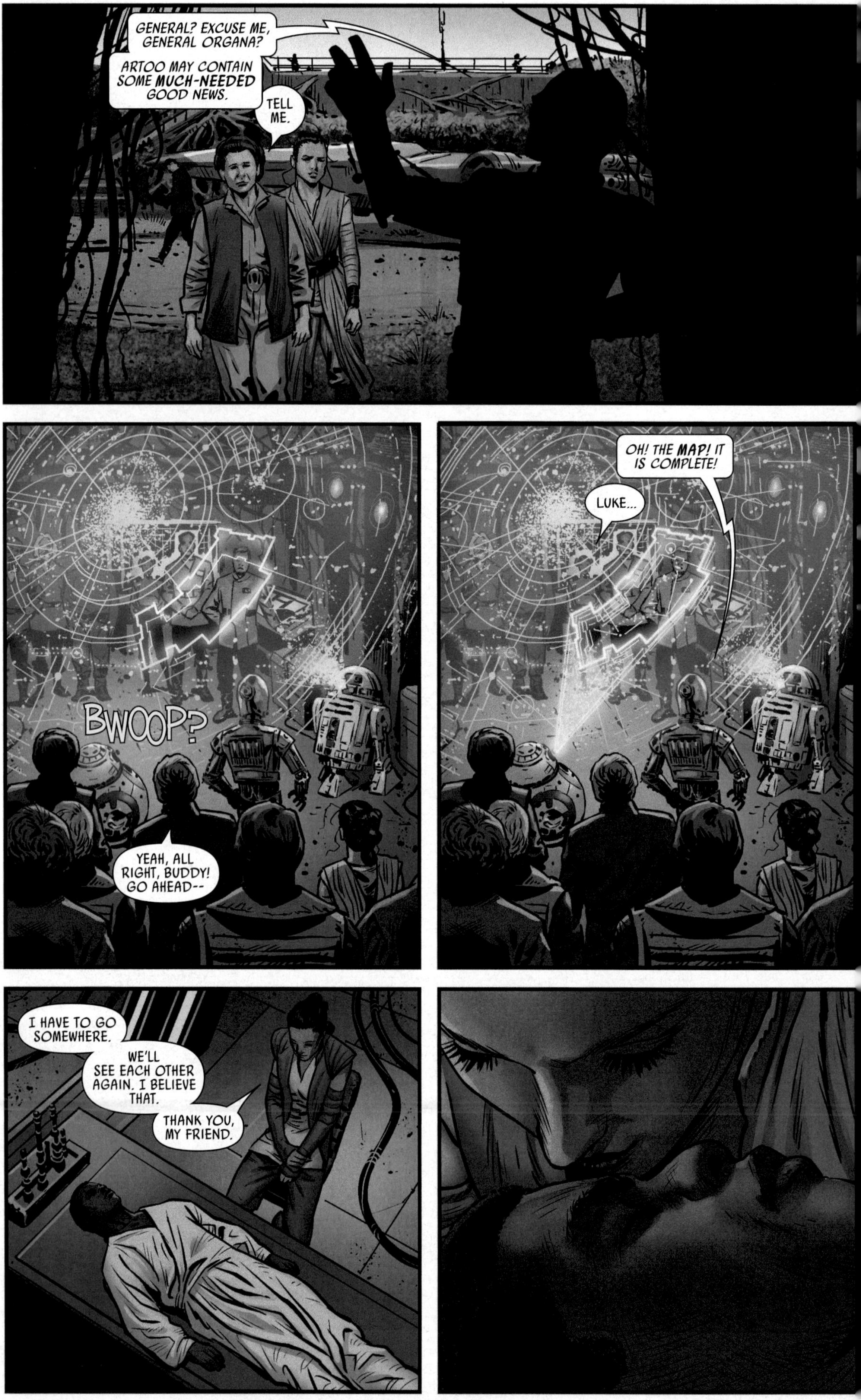
GENERAL? EXCUSE ME, GENERAL ORGANA?
ARTOO MAY CONTAIN SOME MUCH-NEEDED GOOD NEWS.
TELL ME.
BWOOP?
YEAH, ALL RIGHT, BUDDY! GO AHEAD--
OH! THE MAP! IT IS COMPLETE!
LUKE...
I HAVE TO GO SOMEWHERE.
WE'LL SEE EACH OTHER AGAIN. I BELIEVE THAT.
THANK YOU, MY FRIEND.

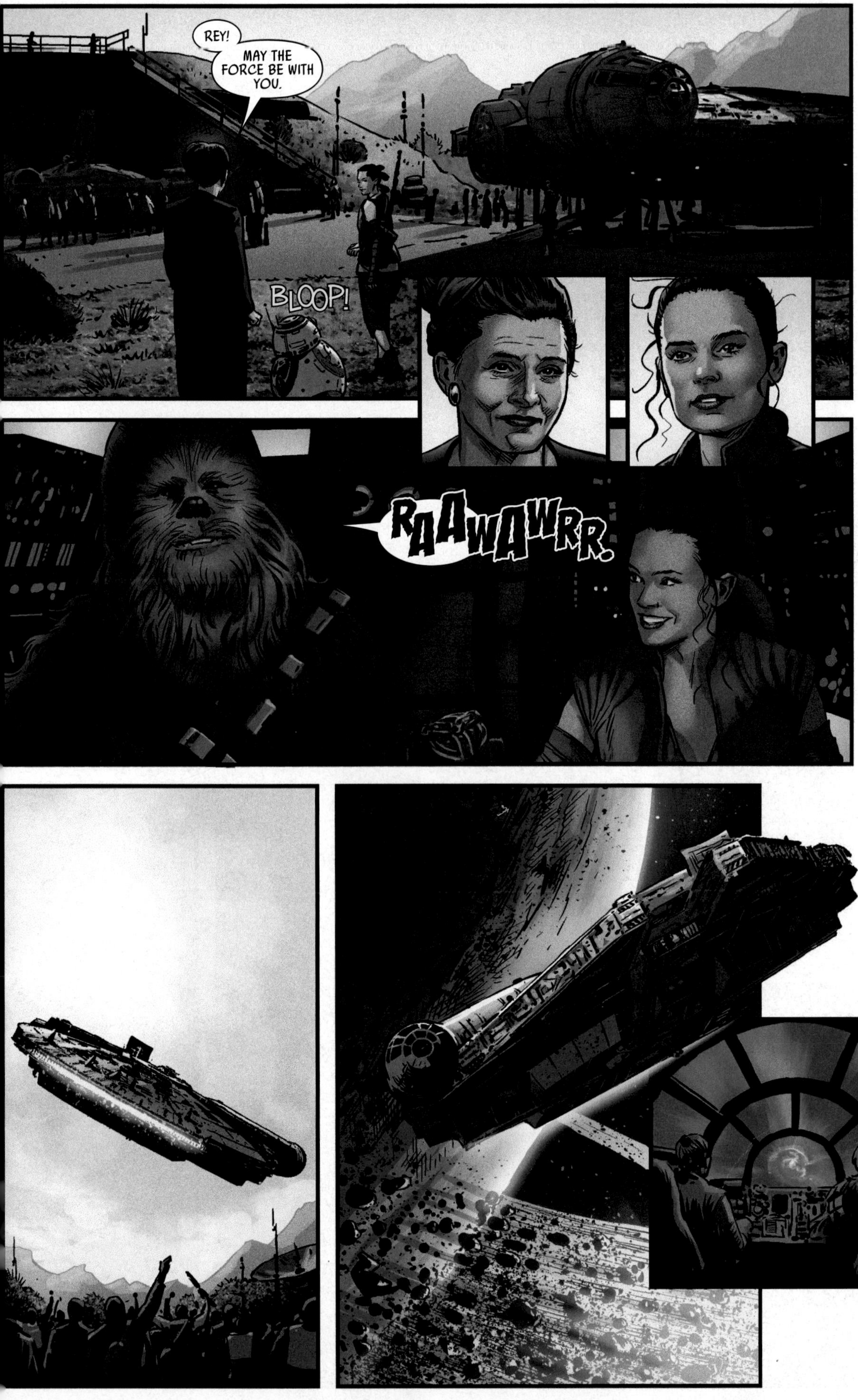
REY!
MAY THE FORCE BE WITH YOU.
BLOOP!
RAAWAAWRR.

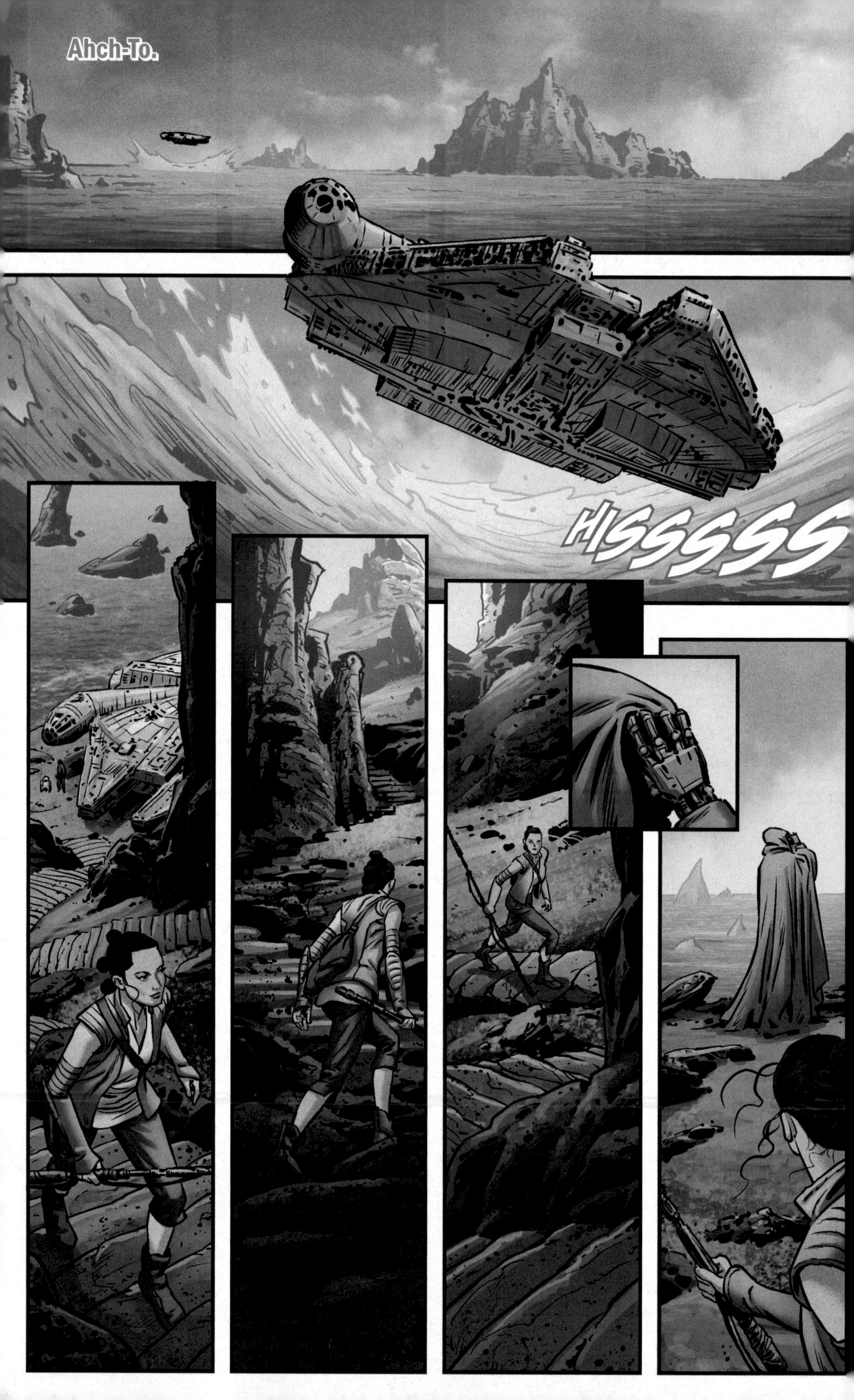

Ahch-To.
HISSSSS

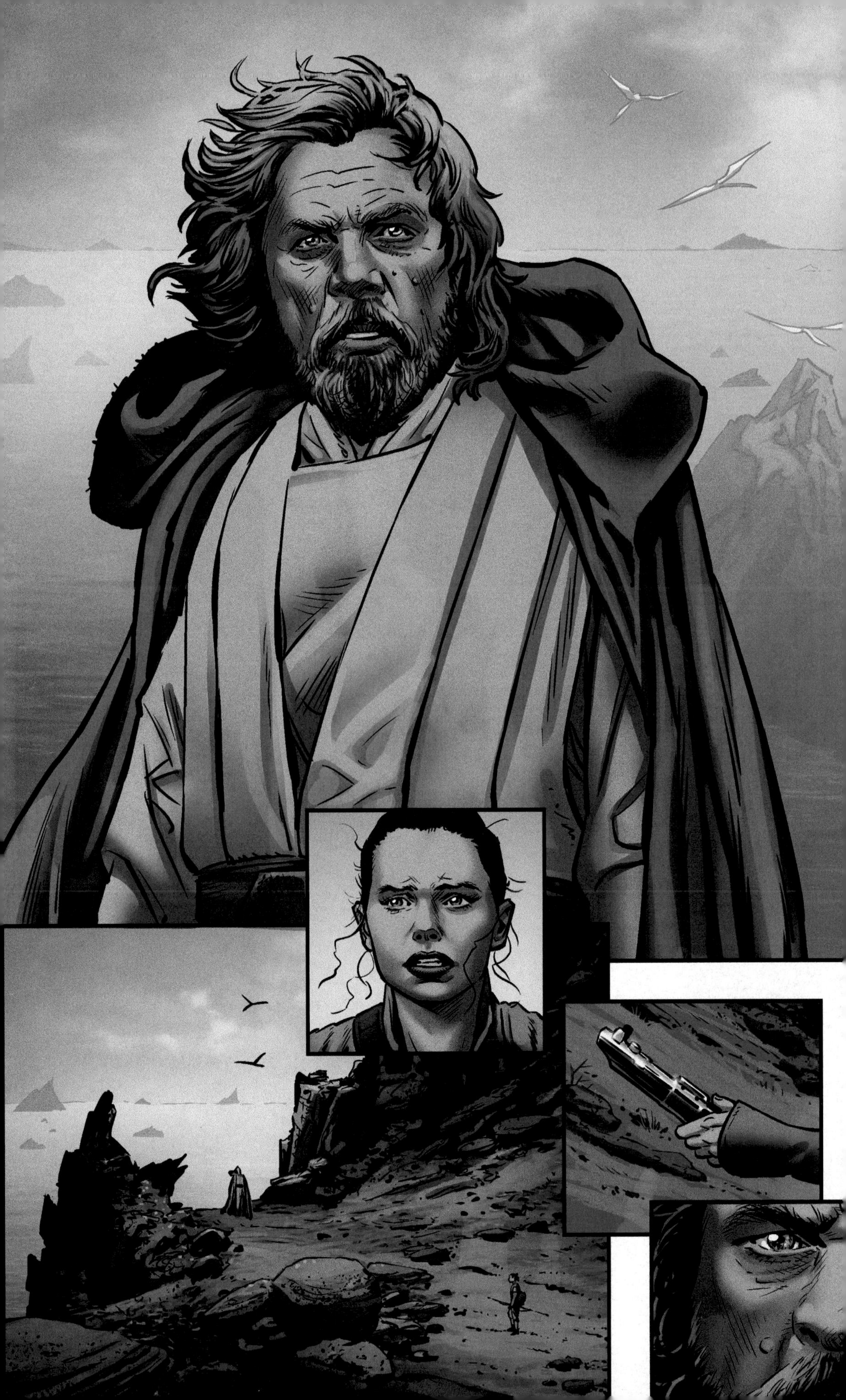

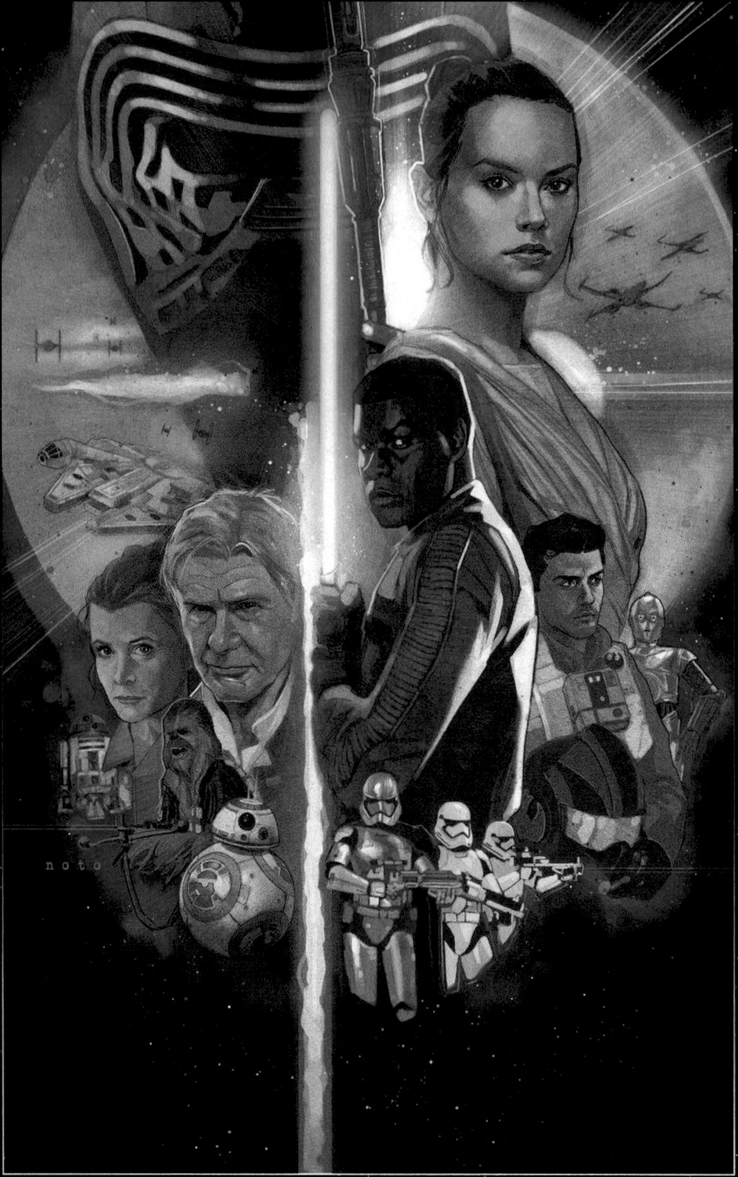

Issue #1 variant by Phil Noto

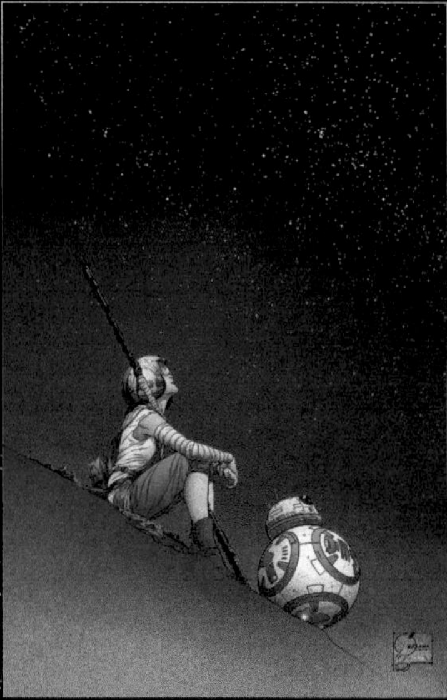

Issue #1 variant by
Joe Quesada & Richard Isanove

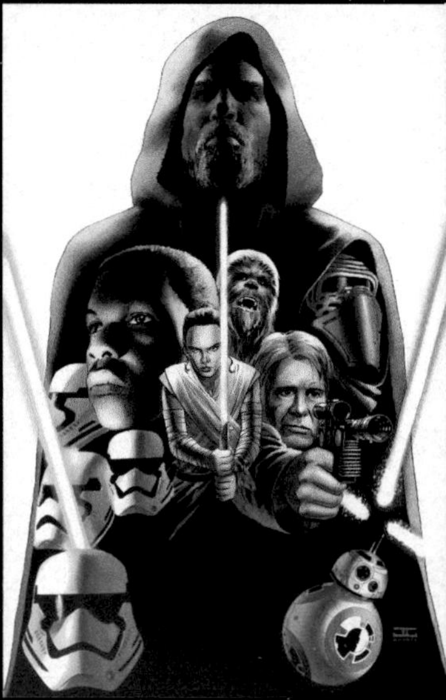

Issue #1 variant by
John Cassaday & Paul Mounts

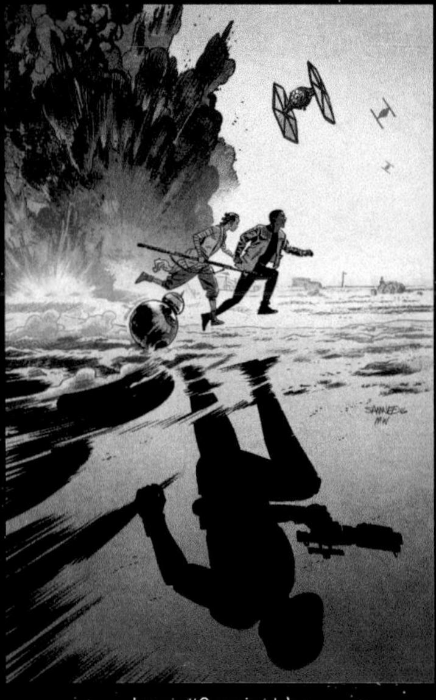

Issue #2 variant by
Chris Samnee & Matt Wilson

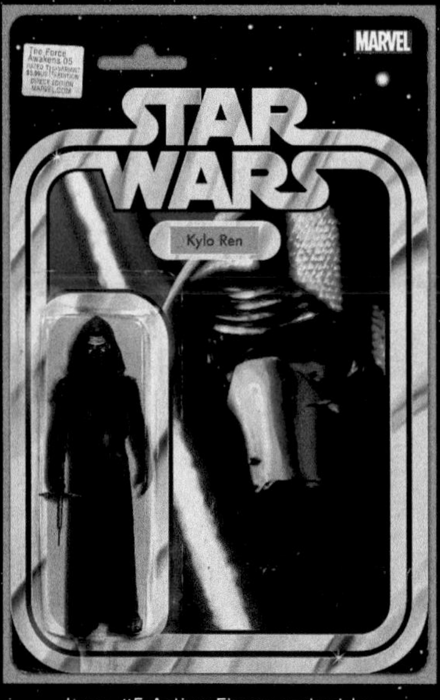
MARVEL
STAR
WARS
Kylo Ren

Issue #5 Action Figure variant by
John Tyler Christopher

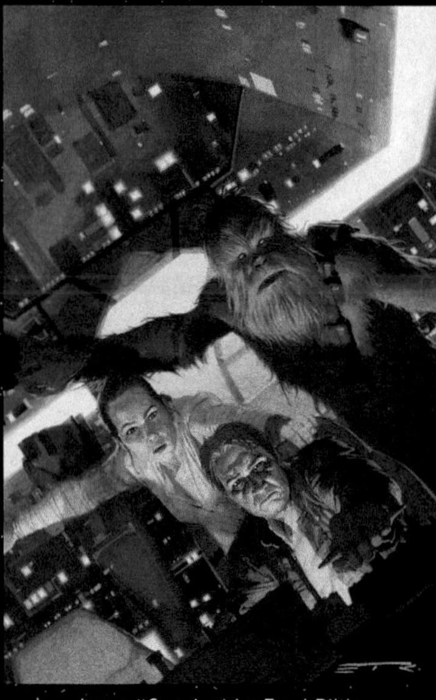

Issue #6 variant by Esad Ribic

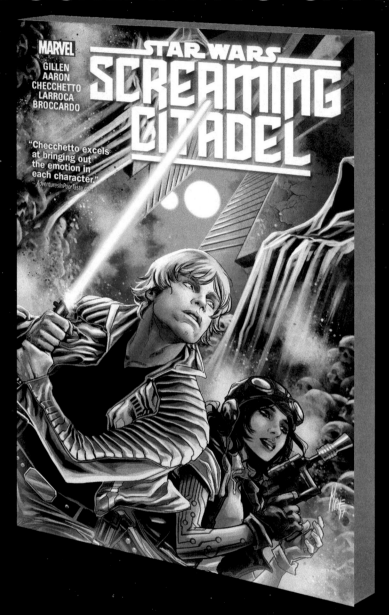

THE DARK LORD OF THE SITH'S FIRST DEADLY MISSION

**STAR WARS: DARTH VADER: DARK LORD OF THE SITH
VOL. 1: IMPERIAL MACHINE TPB
978-1302907440**

ON SALE NOVEMBER 2017
WHEREVER BOOKS ARE SOLD

TO FIND A COMIC SHOP NEAR YOU, VISIT COMICSHOPLOCATOR.COM

OR THE FULL STORY, READ

STAR WARS: DARTH MAUL
978-0785195894

ON SALE NOW
WHEREVER BOOKS ARE SOLD

TO FIND A COMIC SHOP NEAR YOU, VISIT COMICSHOPLOCATOR.COM

WHAT IS A PRINCESS WITHOUT A WORLD?

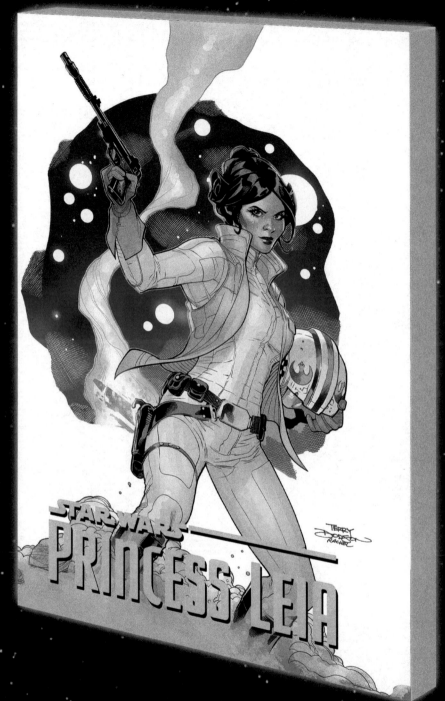

STAR WARS: PRINCESS LEIA TPB

978-0-7851-9317-3

ON SALE NOW!

RETURN TO A GAL

THE CLASSIC MARVEL ADAPTATIONS
NOW WITH REMA

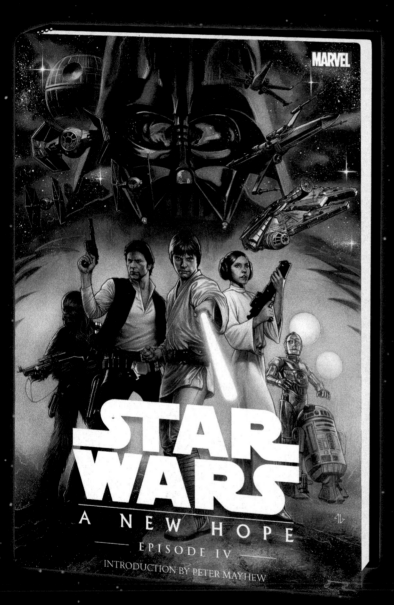

STAR WARS: EPISODE IV – A NEW HOPE HC
978-0-7851-9348-7

STAR WARS: EPISODE V
978-0-7851-9367-8

BETRAYED BY HIS MASTER AND CRAVING VENGEANCE, MAUL STRIKES BACK!

STAR WARS: DARTH MAUL - SON OF DATHOMIR
978-1302908461

ON SALE NOVEMBER 2017
WHEREVER BOOKS ARE SOLD

TO FIND A COMIC SHOP NEAR YOU, VISIT COMICSHOPLOCATOR.COM

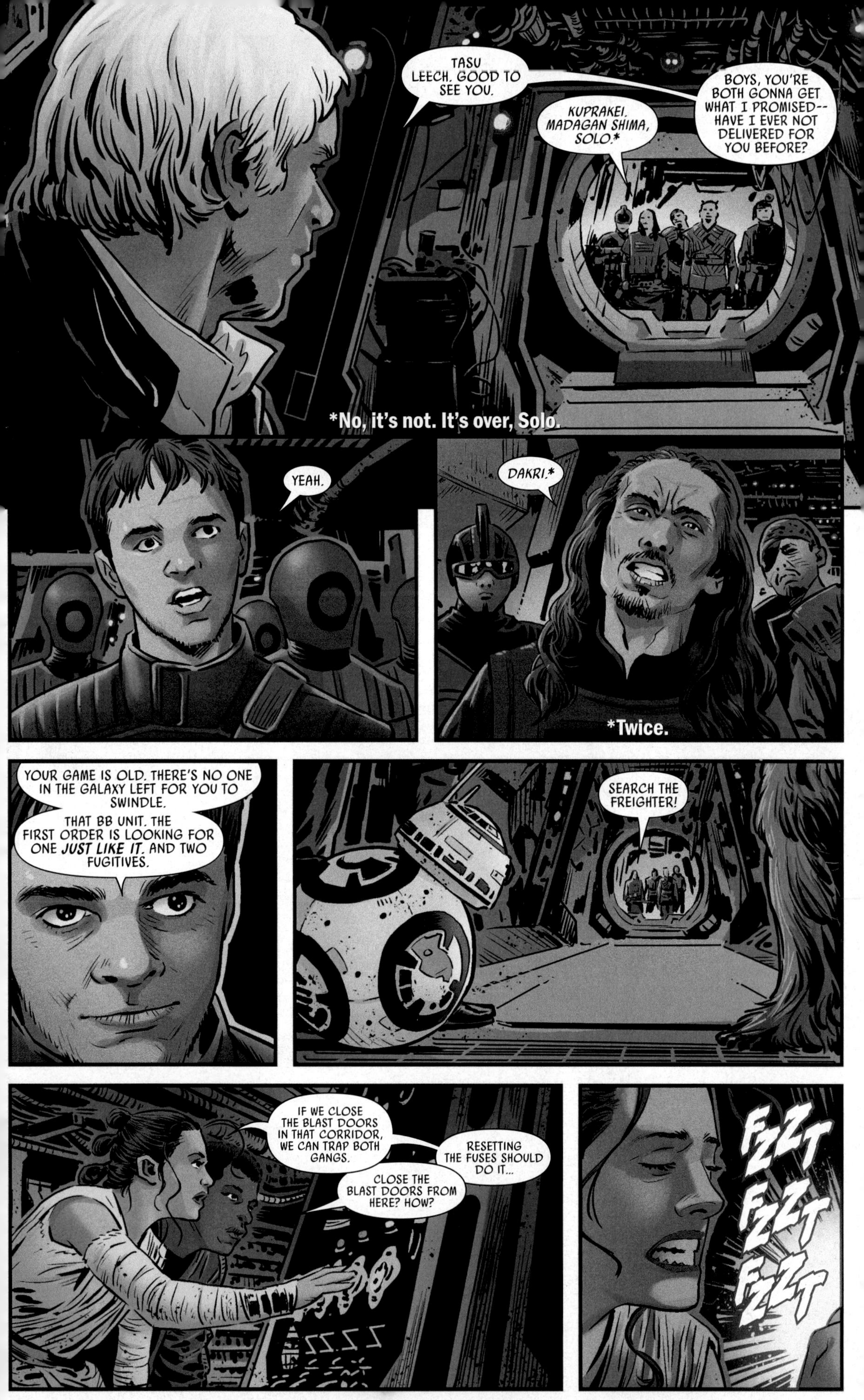
TASU LEECH. GOOD TO SEE YOU.
KUPRAKEI. MADAGAN SHIMA, SOLO.*
BOYS, YOU'RE BOTH GONNA GET WHAT I PROMISED-- HAVE I EVER NOT DELIVERED FOR YOU BEFORE?
*No, it's not. It's over, Solo.
YEAH.
DAKRI.*
*Twice.
YOUR GAME IS OLD. THERE'S NO ONE IN THE GALAXY LEFT FOR YOU TO SWINDLE.
THAT BB UNIT. THE FIRST ORDER IS LOOKING FOR ONE JUST LIKE IT. AND TWO FUGITIVES.
SEARCH THE FREIGHTER!
IF WE CLOSE THE BLAST DOORS IN THAT CORRIDOR, WE CAN TRAP BOTH GANGS.
CLOSE THE BLAST DOORS FROM HERE? HOW?
RESETTING THE FUSES SHOULD DO IT...
FZZT
FZZT
FZZT

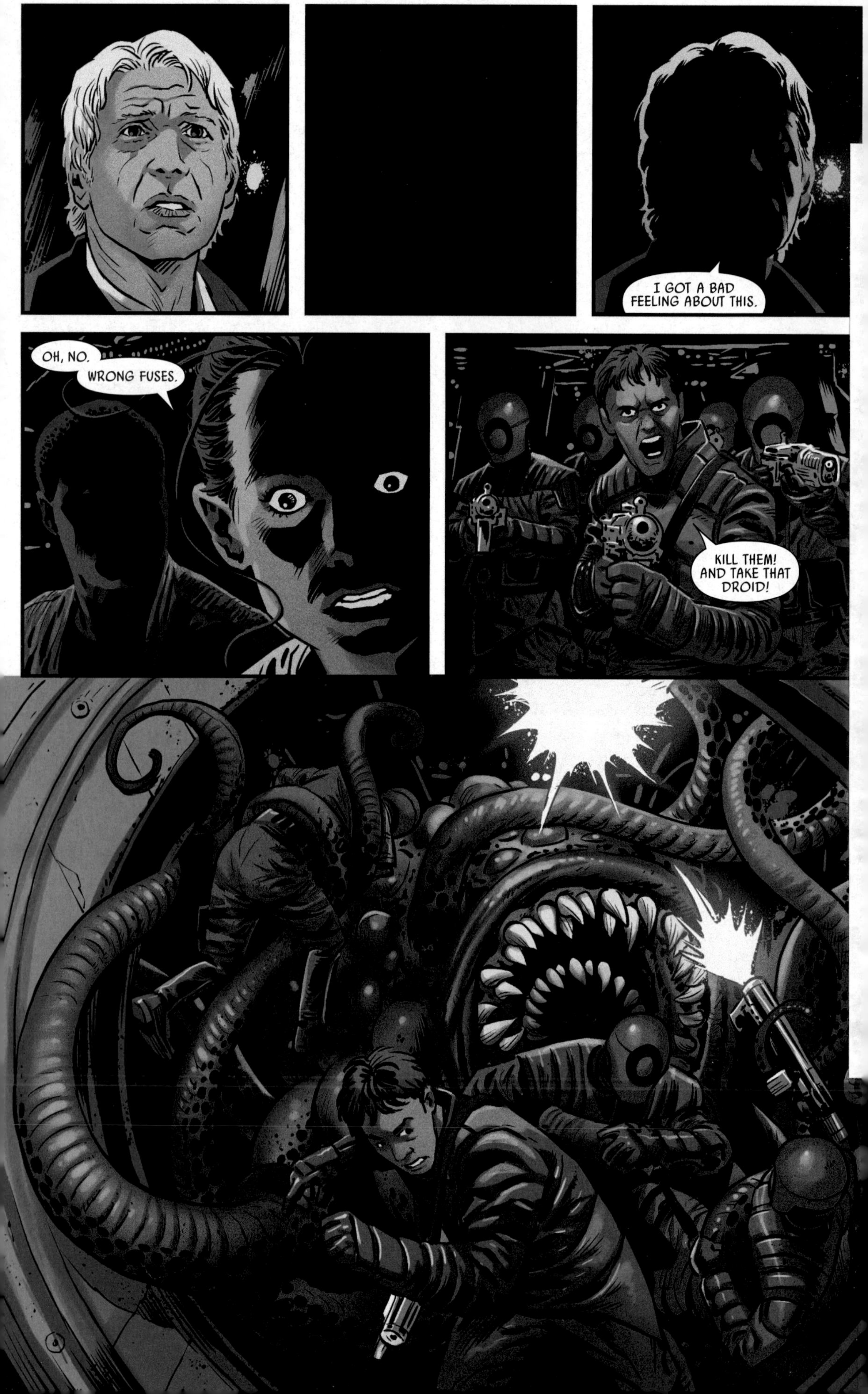

I GOT A BAD FEELING ABOUT THIS.
OH, NO.
WRONG FUSES.
KILL THEM! AND TAKE THAT DROID!

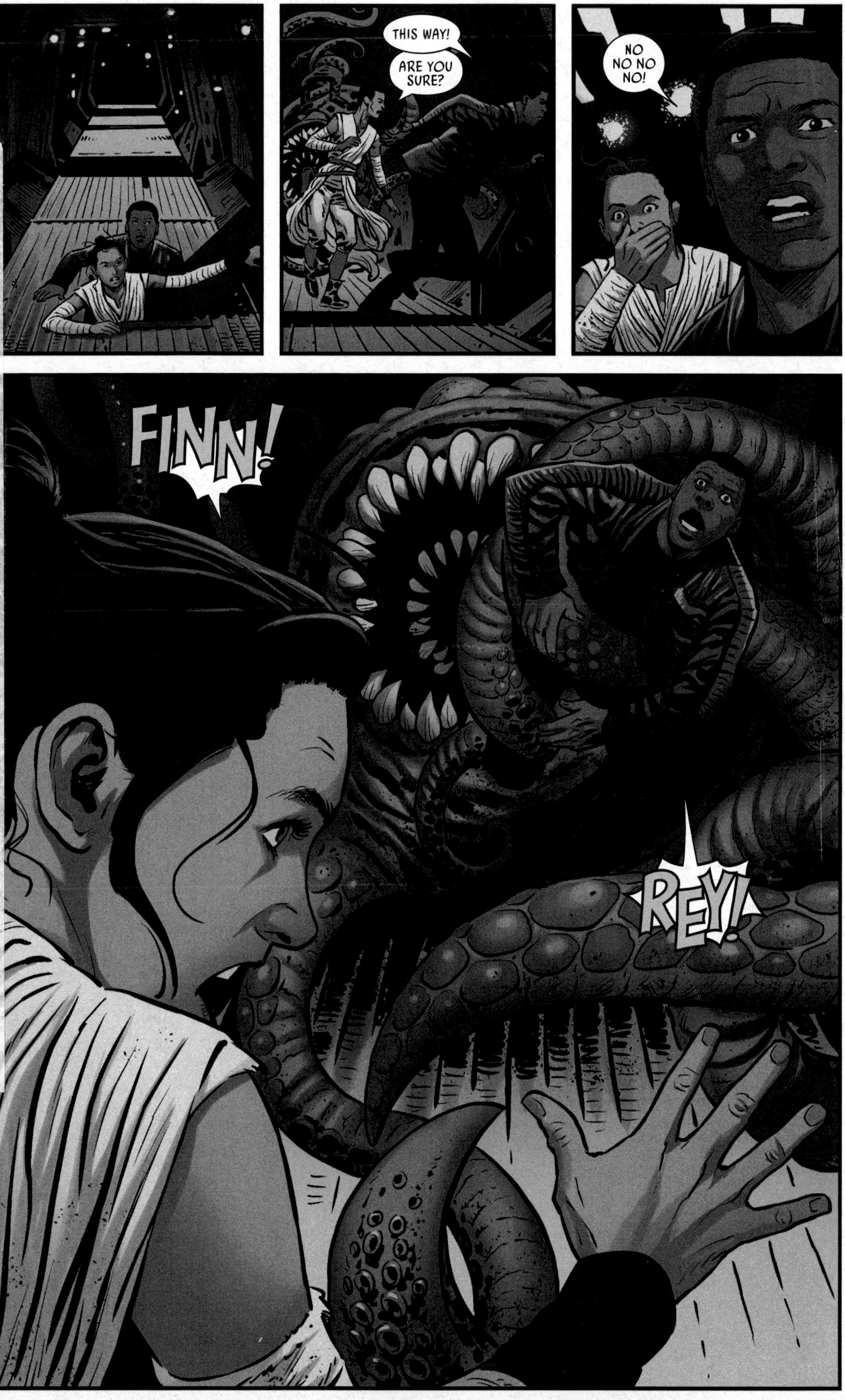
THIS WAY!
ARE YOU SURE?
NO NO NO NO!
FINN!
REY!

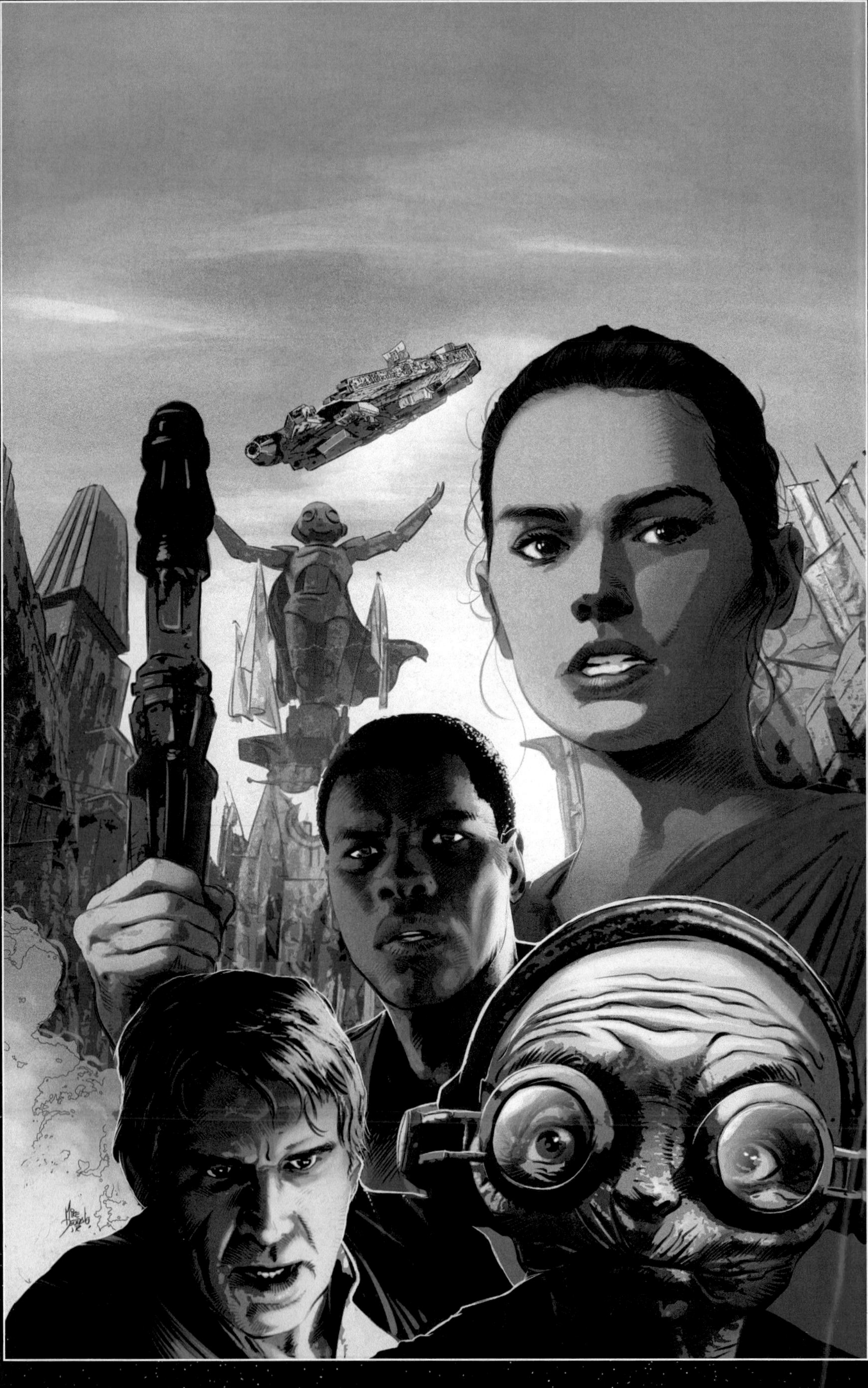

THE FORCE AWAKENS #3